Ponywise

Ponywise

Susan McBane

KENILWORTH PRESS

*This book is dedicated to all ponies
everywhere. May they have kind,
knowledgeable owners who treat them
as friends, not servants.*

First published in Great Britain by
The Kenilworth Press Ltd
Addington
Buckingham
MK18 2JR
1988

Enlarged edition 1992

British Library Cataloguing in Publication Data
McBane, Susan
    Ponywise.
    1. Livestock: Ponies. Care – Manuals –
For children
    I. Title
    636.1'6
    ISBN 1-872082-24-6

Phototypeset by Falcon Graphic Art Ltd
Wallington, Surrey and Textype, Cambridge
Printed in Great Britain by The Bath Press,
Bath, Avon

Contents

Acknowledgements

Books always involve a lot more 'messing about' than people realise. I should like to thank everyone who helped in any way with *Ponywise*, but particularly the following: Dougie and Marjorie Reid for their initial encouragement with the original version of *Ponywise*; and, for their help with photographs, Jack Hicklin, Carolyn, Karen, Joanne, clients, horses and ponies of West End Liveries, Denton, Manchester; Hydrophane Laboratories Limited, Diceabed International Limited, *Pony* magazine, Ray Saunders and John Birt. I am also grateful to Dianne Breeze for her excellent line drawings and to Carole Vincer for her cover illustrations.

1. Buying a pony

Every year riding seems to grow in popularity and more and more children and teenagers try to persuade their parents to buy them a pony of their own. Very often the parents know even less about looking after ponies than their children do, with the result that pony, child and family are put in danger.

Riding and caring for a pony, especially if it is your own, is a wonderful hobby and, like other hobbies, the more you know about it the more you get out of it. But it *can* be dangerous if you don't know what you're doing. I hope this book will save some family the expense, worry and possible disaster of buying an unsuitable pony or of looking after one in the wrong way and, equally important, that it will save some pony somewhere from a home which, perhaps, is not right or ready for him.

Ponies are living creatures, flesh and blood, capable of being healthy or ill, happy or sad, comfortable or in pain. They require a good deal more time and attention than the family dog. If he is to thrive a pony needs specialised, knowledgeable care *every day*, sometimes several times a day depending on how you keep him.

Who is going to look after the pony? Is the family going to share the work, or is it all going to be down to you? Although you may be keen, even desperate, for a pony of your own, you may find that once you are an owner the relentless responsibilities of visits once, twice or maybe three times a day are just too much for you, no matter how loath you will be to admit it. If your family won't or can't help in these circumstances (or when you are ill) the pony is going to suffer unless you can make other arrangements.

It is both a responsibility and a privilege to own a living creature, whether it's a goldfish or a pony. Animals are not toys to be stored away, out of sight and mind, when the owner does not feel like bothering with them, is too busy because of homework or is ill. You'll have to consider all these points carefully and decide how the work is going to get done before you actually buy a pony.

How good a rider are you?

You may already have an idea of the sort of pony you want but before finally deciding be honest with yourself and assess how good a rider you really are. Have you ever ridden a pony you couldn't control – one you just couldn't stop, who bucked you off or played up to get its own way? If so, you'll know how frightening it is to be 'overhorsed', in other words, mounted on an animal who is too much for you. Not only is it dangerous, but also it could put you off riding for life.

If you come from a 'horsy' family, you could well learn pony care at home and learn to ride on your very own pony. For most people, though, it is preferable to have ridden at a good riding school for at least a year, even if only once a week, learning to ride *and* look after ponies. Riding schools have to be licensed by your local council but unfortunately this is no guarantee that they will teach you well. A far better guide is to go to a school approved by the British Horse Society and Pony Club or the Association of British Riding Schools. Many are approved by both.

You can locate the approved riding schools in your area by writing to both organisations and asking for a list of these in your area. The addresses of the BHS and ABRS are given in the Appendix.

To be able to own and look after your own pony you should already be able to ride and control a well-mannered pony on your own, and have a good knowledge of the Highway Code so you know how to behave on the roads. In the stable you should be capable of simple tasks like mucking out, bedding down and grooming, know how to tack up, untack and clean and check tack for safety and fit, and also know how to feed your pony even if someone else works out the diet for you. Finally you need to understand and comply with the basic safety rules and methods of handling when rugging up, leading a pony in and out of a stable or field, tying up and asking him to move around his stable. With this kind of knowledge pony owning should not present any real problems.

Ask your instructor

If you *have* been going to a riding school, your regular instructor will be able to tell you how you are shaping up. If not, consider making an appointment for one of the staff to 'examine' you, as it were, to find out just how good a rider you are, what sort of pony you can manage, how much you know and what you can actually do in the way of stable management. Once you have an expert opinion you can go ahead and consider what else is involved in owning your own pony.

If your instructor says you need more experience, keep riding under good

instruction as often as you can afford it, read all you can about riding and pony care, and help to look after the ponies at your riding school or those belonging to friends to obtain that much-needed experience. Then ask for another assessment in six months' time.

This course of action could save not only money but also heartache and danger when things go wrong with an unsuitable pony.

On the other hand, if you are quite competent, it's not much fun to underhorse yourself if you want a bit of excitement. If you want to jump, hunter trial and compete at all seriously, you'll have to have a pony who can perform. If your riding is up to these things you are unlikely to be satisfied with a pony who won't or can't join in simply because he isn't athletic enough.

Pony types

The 'wild' ponies of Britain are known as natives. They have bred, developed and run more or less freely in their various districts for many years and have become hardy, sensible and sure-footed. They make the most of what food they can get and grow thick coats to protect themselves against bitter winter weather.

The different breeds of native pony, often known as mountain and moorland ponies because of the nature of the land on which they live, are named after different areas of Britain. There are Shetlands and Highlands from Scotland, Fells and Dales from the north of England, New Forest, Dartmoors and Exmoors from the south of England, four Welsh types from Wales, and finally the Connemara from Ireland.

Most ponies, however, are 'mongrels'. This word is not used to describe ponies as a general rule but it gives exactly the right impression. It means that the pony concerned is a mixture of several breeds – maybe a real 'Heinz 57', and often none the worse for it. Registered ponies with pedigrees and official papers are normally much more expensive than those of mixed breeding. On the other hand, many ponies whose breeding is quite unknown are so good at their jobs that they fetch high prices despite their lack of pedigree.

Both registered and unregistered ponies are often cross-bred with small Arab and Thoroughbred horses. In other words, one parent will be an Arab or Thoroughbred (normally the father, or sire) and the other will be a pony. The result is a more refined, breedy-looking pony combining the qualities of both parents; perhaps not so steady and hardy as most native ponies but less thin-skinned, sensitive and highly strung than most Thoroughbreds or Arabs. These make good 'in-between' ponies and most of Britain's show ponies are bred this way.

For a first-time, fairly novice owner, a pony who is practically all native type is probably the safest and most satisfactory kind. These come in all sizes from the tiny Shetland types, through the middle range of Fells, Welsh Section A and B, Dartmoors and Exmoors, to the larger breeds such as Highlands, Dales, New Forest, Welsh Section C and D and Connemaras, which are suitable for teenagers. A native pony will probably have a steadier nature than a more highly bred pony and will be easier to look after, though they can by no means be neglected. Such a pony is often quite happy living outdoors all year round, provided the field is suitable.

If you are more experienced and fairly competent, you can aim for a more highly bred pony, with perhaps a quarter or half Arab or Thoroughbred blood.

It is quite possible to find a sensible cross-bred pony – not all Arabs and Thoroughbreds and their crosses are scatty idiots – and they will give the better rider scope for more athletic work and competition.

Ponies bred this way, however, do need more care and will almost certainly have to be stabled sometimes, even if only at night in winter. But for any pony a stable should be available if needed for times of accident or illness, so this should not present too much extra difficulty.

Where will you keep him?

Most people would like to be able to keep their pony at home as part of the family. Unfortunately, ponies need such specialised care that, unless you or your family really know what you are doing, it is often not a good idea. Apart from the fact that most families do not have stables and grazing at home, it is very unfair to risk the pony's well-being by making him live among people who cannot look after him properly.

It can be worrying for the family if things start to go wrong and they don't know how to cope, and mistakes in handling, feeding or tack can put both you and the pony in danger.

If your family is knowledgeable and you have facilities for grazing with adequate shelter then you will be able to keep him at home, which is certainly the cheapest option. Otherwise, you'll have to look around for somewhere else. Consider the distance you will have to travel from your home and how you are going to get there. Is it within reasonable biking distance? If not, can you afford the time and money to travel by bus, or will you have to depend on your parents to take you there in the car?

What will he need?

Most ponies are happier living out for most of the time than being kept year round in a stable. They also tend to stay healthier, provided they have adequate feed and shelter, and because they are exercising themselves regularly, they aren't over-fresh when ridden. They are usually calmer in temperament, too.

Even though wild ponies are creatures of wide open spaces, they are free to find their own shelter from bad weather. They find woods, shrubbery, or the lee of hills, to protect themselves from the worst of the wind.

Ponies in a field cannot do this as they are confined to a fenced area which is very small by comparison. An open, windswept field with no trees or hedges is *not* suitable for a pony living out most of the time unless it has a field shelter, where the pony can stand out of the weather when he feels the need. The field also needs a clean water supply.

A stable is a great advantage when the pony is sick or injured so it will be necessary to make sure one is available for an emergency, even if you don't use it often.

Ponies shelter naturally with their bottoms to the wind and rain. If your pony is to live out most of the time, make sure his field offers some form of shelter, either natural or purpose-built.

Ponies can be kept on their own but this is not normally very satisfactory. They are herd animals and need the company of their own kind if they are to feel happy and safe. Ponies forced to live alone can be very difficult to handle, out of sheer excitement, when they find themselves with other ponies at a show or out on a hack. So it is best to find somewhere where there are other horses and ponies.

Some people provide cattle or donkeys for company, and although these are better than nothing, other ponies are best.

You'll obviously need a saddle and bridle and a basic grooming kit. You may or may not need rugs, depending on how the pony is kept and on his breeding. If he is a thin-skinned, sensitive type, a rug at night in winter will be needed, otherwise you may well be able to manage without one. You'll also need a headcollar and rope. It's not practical to lead him about in a bridle and this would also put unnecessary wear and tear on it.

You will have to provide regular supplies of feed and bedding for the pony, except possibly if he is out in summer. Even in winter, a pony living out will need extra food and bedding for the field shelter.

Preventive veterinary medicine – in other words, examinations, treatments and vaccinations – will all be needed if your pony is to remain healthy, and since ponies will be ponies, he is almost bound to be hurt at some point. With experience, expert help and a good veterinary book, you will be able to deal with slight injuries yourself, but you must be prepared to call in the vet for anything more serious.

If you want to compete or hunt with your pony, you'll need transport. If you don't own a trailer or horsebox, you can hire transport or hitch a lift with a friend. Otherwise, your shows or meets, rallies and other events will have to be within hacking distance of where the pony is kept, which could cut down your opportunities.

So there is quite a lot to bear in mind, and you and your family must be clear about all these points before you take the plunge and buy a pony.

The cost of it all

If you *do* decide to take that plunge, there's one last consideration: how much is it all going to cost?

This is where parents start to look even more anxious than they have done up to now! It's no help to tell you that prices of ponies, accommodation and equipment vary tremendously according to what sort of pony you want, where you live and how he is kept – but they do.

First of all, no one should imagine that they can keep a pony on the cheap. Many people think that 'A little pony can't cost very much, can it?. . .We can keep it in Farmer Bloggs' field down the road and it'll live on grass. . . .He won't charge us much because

we're neighbours and it'll be nice to be able to ride free instead of paying to ride at the local riding school.' But it isn't like that at all, as you may have guessed already.

At the time of writing (1992), a pony can cost anything from £150 for a tiny one suitable for small children to £850 for a larger one suitable for teenagers and able to compete locally with a fair chance of success.

A saddle and bridle can be obtained reasonably, for about £300 if you buy good quality secondhand items. New ones may cost up to £600.

A rug could cost about £30 secondhand for a small pony and up to £75 or more for a new one to fit a larger animal. Then allow another £100 for grooming kit, haynets, buckets and extras like first-aid kit and mucking-out tools.

Rented grazing could be roughly £10 to £30 per week depending on the area of the country, the quality of the land and the size of the field. A stable might cost about the same to rent again, depending on the area and whether or not it includes somewhere to keep your tack and other equipment.

Especially in winter when the grass has no feed value, a pony could eat his way through about £5 to £12 worth of food per week depending on his size, the weather and how he is kept. Bedding will cost another £5 or more per week. Straw is the cheapest bedding and shredded paper probably the most expensive. Paper is excellent for ponies with breathing problems and so are vacuum-cleaned straw and shavings. They create healthy surroundings for any pony, being practically dust-free, but do cost a bit more.

If you decide to buy a stable (assuming you have somewhere to put it) you could pay about £750 for a basic loose box, and you will then have maintenance costs for wear and tear, but these should be slight for a well-behaved pony. Buying your own field (which takes you into the landowner category) might give you a marvellous feeling but could set your parents back £1,000 to £5,000 or more, depending on the area of the country.

It may not be possible to erect stabling on your field because of local building regulations, but in most areas no one can stop you putting up a field shelter as it is classed as a temporary building and has no door. You can check on this with your local council's planning department. A field and shelter are all most ponies really need, and you can rig up slip-rails (bars) to fit across the shelter's entrance when it is necessary to keep the pony in.

Be warned, however, that keeping ponies in fields or stabling (whether your own or someone else's) away from your home and with no one keeping an eye on them is a risky undertaking, in view of the popularity of horse-stealing these days. If the field you buy does not adjoin your house, perhaps it's not worth the worry and expense, even though it *is* nice to be independent.

Veterinary expenses should be few with a well-managed pony: apart from regular worm medicines and vaccinations and the odd illness or injury, they should not be great.

Farriery will probably cost you more. If your pony is shod and does a fair amount of roadwork, as most ponies do, he will need new shoes about every six weeks, and at present (1992) a new set of four costs between £15 and £30 depending on where you live in the country, for rates do vary. This could be less if the feet simply need trimming and the old shoes are still thick enough to put back on (this process is called a 'remove').

Your starting-off costs will be by far your greatest expense. After that you need to be able to spare, say, £30 a week for running costs and to be able to put something aside for emergency veterinary treatment, tack repairs, an unexpected lost shoe and so on, before you can say you can afford to keep a pony.

It's not all doom and gloom, though. Your whole family will get pleasure from your pony if they are animal-lovers, your parents will enjoy seeing *you* happy (even if they don't admit it!) and you just might win a little money back at shows, although don't count on it.

Many hobbies cost a great deal more than pony-owning. Perhaps you have other pursuits that you would be prepared to give up to have a pony? How much do your parents pay for you to ride at a riding school (including the cost of getting there)?

There are all sorts of ways to help pay for a pony's keep, so don't let the cost alone put you off.

Getting expert help

In such an important venture as buying a pony it is sensible to seek expert advice, even if you have to pay for it. This will involve yet more expense, but by avoiding an unsuitable pony you could be saved hundreds of pounds in vet's fees (if after the sale you discover there is something seriously wrong) or in damages paid out as the result of the pony's lunatic behaviour. You could also be saved from buying a pony who is either too much of a handful for you or who simply cannot or will not do what you expect.

There are four experts you might need, and two of them are, I believe, essential.

Horse consultant

This is a person who normally earns his or her living with horses and who can help find and inspect a suitable pony for you. A good guide to choosing such a consultant is the qualifications he or she has; generally, those with the more senior qualifications of the British Horse Society or Association of British Riding Schools will have the right knowledge and experience to help you. Look for the letters BHSII (British Horse Society Intermediate Instructor) or the more senior

BHSI (British Horse Society Instructor) or the BHS's top qualification FBHS (Fellow of the British Horse Society). Also, the following qualifications awarded by the Association of British Riding Schools will mean that their holders can help you: RSPD (Riding School Principals' Diploma), RMD (Riding Master's Diploma) and FABRS (Fellow of the Association of British Riding Schools).

A sensible adviser will not only recommend a suitable pony but will also make sure you like it too, for no matter how super a pony is, it's a waste of money if you don't.

Veterinary surgeon

Most people regard it as essential to have a pony 'vetted' before buying. This involves thorough inspection of the animal, and the veterinary profession can be proud of its reputation in medically examining horses and ponies and in advising for or against buying an animal for whatever purpose the client has in mind.

This last point is most important. You must tell the vet what you want to do with the pony so that he or she can assess whether or not the pony will be sound (healthy) enough for the job. It's no good saying you want to potter gently along lanes and bridlepaths if what you really want to do is become a top-flight showjumper or win your Pony Club hunter trials.

Be honest with your horse consultant and your vet so they can be as sure as is reasonably possible that the pony they are checking for you will fit the bill.

A good way to find a suitable vet is to write to the British Equine Veterinary Association (the address is given in the Appendix) and ask for a list of practising members in the area where the pony lives. The pony's existing vet will be unable to act for you because he or she already works for the seller and would find it difficult to advise against a client's animal, but another vet in the same area would be able to do it for you, and using someone local will cut down on the travelling fees you will have to pay.

Never buy a pony whose owner refuses to let you have it vetted. He or she may say something like: 'Take my word for it, there's nothing wrong with him. Why spend money on a vet?', but no matter how convincing this may sound, always have a proper veterinary examination so you can be as sure as possible that everything is in order.

Vetting is one expense you really must not skimp on.

Solicitor

Many people buy ponies without consulting a solicitor and rely simply on the certificate and report given by the inspecting veterinary surgeon. However, if you insist that the pony you buy is, say, guaranteed safe in all traffic, easy to catch, good to shoe, or whatever, you will probably need a legally binding document called a warranty.

The solicitor will explain to you and your parents what a warranty is and will deal with the seller (or the seller's solicitor) on this matter. The subject of warranties is something you should talk to your horse consultant about, too. Many people do not bother with them, but it could just be that if a seller refuses to give a warranty, there is something wrong with the pony as regards its behaviour.

Insurance broker

Insurance is quite optional and many people don't bother with it, perhaps because they had a bad experience with an insurance company in the past. On top of all your other expenses, you may feel that the cost of the premium (fee) is simply not worth it, especially as, in the event of a claim, you may not receive all the compensation you hope for.

There are various sorts of insurance. You can insure the pony against death (should he die, be killed or have to be put to sleep) and against loss of use (when the pony is unable to do his job for a variety of reasons – for example, a showjumper might be insured against becoming unable to jump due, say, to arthritis). These two sorts of insurance are the most expensive and the ones whose claims present the most problems, particularly in the case of expensive animals. The more valuable the pony the higher the premium.

Another type of insurance is against vets' fees. If your pony were to have a serious accident or fall gravely ill, the veterinary bills could run into hundreds of pounds. Many people feel it is worth the comparatively low premium (about £2 per week at present) to insure against this possibility, which is a very real one.

The final type of insurance, which I feel *is* essential, is called 'third party insurance'. This means that if your pony causes damage to persons or property and someone claims against your family for the cost of that damage, the insurance company will foot the bill. As the pony's owners, you are responsible in law for his behaviour. If, for example, he kicks another pony and breaks its leg and that pony has to be put down, you may be required by law to pay his owner a sum equivalent to his value. However, if you have third party insurance, your insurance company should pay.

Third party insurance is not normally very expensive, but if you are a member of the Pony Club or the British Horse Society you receive automatic third party insurance *free*. The membership fee costs less than the premium so it's rather silly not to join, apart from all the other benefits you enjoy from membership.

Insurance companies advertise regularly in horsy magazines so you could send off for a few brochures. If your parents have an insurance broker already, perhaps for household and car insurance, you could ask him or her to sort something out for you. Be warned, however, that the small print on insurance policies can be just as difficult to understand as that on warranties – an insurance policy is, after all, another legal document – so ask the broker to explain it properly and confirm in writing (not just in a conversation) that the policy *will* cover you for what you want.

Of these four experts, the insurance broker is the only one you won't have to pay. He receives money (commission) from the insurance company for introducing you as a customer. However, his commission *is* paid by you indirectly because it is included in the cost of the premium.

It might cost slightly less to deal with the company direct, but you have no one to help you understand all the hidden meanings in the policy. (A solicitor should be able to help you here, too.) The insurance company won't point out any drawbacks because they are trying to sell you the policy.

Keeping a pony at home

If you really feel that you and your family could manage a pony at home there are certain points to look into first.

Some councils are against having horses in residential areas, so it might be wise to contact your local BHS and Pony Club representatives for advice *before* you get in touch with your local authority. This way you won't set the council against you before you've even started.

If you live in a conservation area it might be very difficult to obtain permission to erect the type of buildings (stables, field shelters) you want as they will have to blend with the local environment. However, in other areas you do not need permission to erect a stable provided it fulfils certain conditions. Your parents will be able to check the full requirements, but basically if the stabling you plan is no larger than one tenth of the cubic content of the original dwelling house, or 50 cubic metres, subject to a maximum of 115 cubic metres, you can erect stabling adjoining your house as it will be classed as an enlargement of your domestic accommodation. If the stable does not actually adjoin the house things may be different, for instance if you want it at the bottom of the garden.

You'll also have to obey certain rules under the Public Health and Safety regulations. Here, the council will be concerned about general safety (e.g. can the pony escape and cause a nuisance to your neighbours or cause an accident on the road?) and also about health problems which can be caused if you do not keep your stable scrupulously clean. If the stable or your surrounding ground becomes littered with droppings, foul-smelling and a lure for flies, you will probably receive complaints and may be forced to keep the pony elsewhere if things don't improve.

Some local authorities are more fussy than others about drainage. It is true that many ponies live quite satisfactorily in stables which have no drainage at all, i.e. the floors have not been built with a slope towards an outlet for the urine and there are no drains outside or even near the boxes.

The reason for this is usually that the floors are self-draining, which means that the urine can seep away into the earth below (a system which is quite common in Ireland but rarer in Great Britain). Floors like this are often made of bricks laid with a small space between them (about 1 cm/⅜ in.) on top of fine gravel which, in turn, has been laid over coarse rubble. Another similar type of floor has loose-weave (coarse) asphalt laid on fine rubble over coarse rubble. It is important that the asphalt is simply rolled lightly to smooth it and *not* rammed down hard, which will clog it all together so the urine cannot drain through.

Any floor, self-draining or otherwise, can be kept in an acceptable condition if the owner is scrupulous about mucking out and does not allow wet and smells to build up.

You can use ordinary earth floors, just laying straw on top of bare earth, with absolutely no problems (except that some ponies might paw the ground and dig big holes) but if your council will not permit this, you will have to place your stable near an existing drain and have the stable floor sloping slightly towards it with an outlet nearby in the wall (a hole just a few centimetres/inches square will do) so the urine can run towards the drain. Actually, you will find that hardly any urine *will* drain out because most of it will be soaked up by the bedding, but you have to keep the local authorities happy.

The authority may also insist on certain areas being concreted, such as walkways, especially immediately outside the stable, but this is something your parents will have to discuss with them.

You may think it a good idea to put a drain actually inside the stable, as was often done in years gone by. Such drains, usually in the centre of the box with the floor shaped and sloped slightly on each side to fall towards them, caused a great deal of trouble. For a start, bedding always got down them and blocked them, despite having a grid on top, and ponies often managed to dislodge the grid and get a leg down, causing awful injuries and frightening themselves as well.

Nowadays most old stables with central drains have them blocked off for those reasons.

All stable drains should be flushed out frequently (say once a month, with soda or bleach) to keep them free of smells and clear of accumulated slime and dirt. They should be properly cleaned out once a year.

Your muck heap can be your biggest problem in a residential area and it is a good idea to muck out direct into plastic bags, such as those your bedding might come in or old fertilizer sacks. These can be sealed tightly and sold to neighbours or nurseries as manure. If necessary, tell all your neighbours that they can have manure free if they come and collect it and ask them to spread the word to their gardening friends.

If you live in the country, of course, your problems may be less, particularly if your house is not near others.

Fire regulations also have to be complied with, so ask your Fire Service about requirements; hay and straw are very flammable.

If you do not have a paddock at home you will have to fence off either part of the garden area for the pony to use as a leg-stretching plot or arrange grazing near by. Some people do keep ponies stabled all the time without ever turning them out, but this isn't good for privately-owned ponies because they usually receive far less exercise than they really need. Two hours' exercise a day may sound a lot, and you may have a job to fit in this much in winter, but it is really nothing to an active, strong pony. Freedom to walk around, roll and kick up his heels, even in a small patch at home, is far better than being cooped up in a stable most of the time.

If you have room for only one pony at home, you'll still have to think about company for him. It may be possible to arrange daytime grazing with other ponies, and bring him home at night. If you have more than one stable, you could offer accommodation to other people's ponies in return for help with the chores.

You could charge money for accommodation, of course, but if you do your parents will be required to pay tax on the income, and if the stables are in a residential area and are classed as a business, the local council might like to close them down, although this may not be the case elsewhere.

Don't imagine that you can keep your pony in the garage and not provide a special stable or shelter. Ponies must be kept safely and in proper housing; stables are specially designed for the job, as you'll see in the next chapter. The garage could be used for storing hay and bedding, though – fire regulations (and parents) permitting.

Keeping a pony at livery

If you have limited experience of pony-keeping and no really knowledgeable person at hand to advise you, for the pony's sake and your own safety keep him at a riding centre approved by the BHS or ABRS. If there is no suitable school in your area, look for a livery stable recommended by your horse consultant. This is a stable which takes in and looks after other people's animals. You need one where the ponies look happy, well fed and cared for. At present, there is no approval scheme for livery stables so all you have to guide you is personal recommendation.

There are two main types of livery: full livery, and part or half livery. With full livery your pony is cared for entirely by the staff at the stable and you should not need to do any work at all, unless you wish. The cost includes a stable which is mucked out and bedded down, all feed, tack cleaning, exercising and grooming. You might have to pay extra for grazing; however, if your pony is out a good deal of the time and much of his food is grass, an allowance should be made so you don't pay so much for other feed.

You will have to pay for shoeing, schooling (training the pony) if required, veterinary expenses and your own tack, rugs and grooming kit. Mucking-out tools are the stable's own.

Some places offer grass livery, whereby the pony is kept out at grass all the time. Although this costs less, it can, as mentioned earlier, be very inconvenient not to have the use of a stable.

For full livery you can expect to pay between £20 (for a small pony) and £45 (for a larger one) per week depending, as ever, on the area and the facilities offered. Your consultant will advise as to whether the charge seems fair.

If you need something cheaper and can do some of the work yourself, ask about part livery but be very sure exactly what you are expected to do and that you can carry out your own jobs regularly.

Some riding schools offer cheaper livery if you allow them to use the pony for clients. This is not usually a good arrangement, however tempting it may sound. They tend to need the pony most at times when you yourself wish to ride, such as evenings and weekends, which could cause ill-feeling between you. Also, it is not good for a pony to have too many riders, however good, as everyone gives aids (signals) to the pony in a slightly different way and the pony may become confused. This is why riding school ponies are not usually as responsive and sensitive as privately-owned ponies.

Some places, known as do-it-yourself livery yards, rent stabling and/or grazing and leave the owners to look after their animals entirely themselves. For novice owners, this is certainly not recommended. If you are experienced and really know what you are doing it can be satisfactory, particularly if the yard has a manager or owner who sees that reasonably high standards are kept and who will supervise the more novice owners and help with advice when needed.

You may be able to keep your pony at a friend's home provided you are certain he will be treated as part of the family and not like a second-class citizen, simply there to bring in a bit of extra cash.

It may sound like an ideal arrangement to keep a pony on a farm, particularly if it is one which rents grazing and stabling to bring in extra money, but you must be very careful about this sort of arrangement.

At first, you might think that your pony will have lots of fields to run and graze in, that you'll be able to buy food and bedding cheaply from the farmer, that you'll be able to ride all over the farm, and that the farmer will give advice and help when you are stuck.

In practice, it will probably not be like this at all. For a start, the farm land will probably not be available for riding on as it will be growing crops (including grass, for grass is a crop when properly farmed). You may be allowed to ride on certain areas (and will probably be asked to keep to the edges) but you certainly will not be able to go wherever you want.

And those same fields will not all be available for your pony to graze in. If it is a dairy farm, the grass will not be suitable for ponies as it will be far too rich and probably cause serious digestive problems (such as colic – a bad tummy-ache which can even kill ponies) and a very painful foot disorder called laminitis, which cannot always be put right.

If you do buy food and bedding from the farmer it may not be suitable for your pony. Ponies need specialised *horse* feeds; calf nuts and cattle meal can poison ponies in certain cases. Hay and straw may be available, but I am afraid that some farmers will sell only their worst stocks to pony owners, keeping the best for their own animals. Poor hay and straw can cause various illnesses in ponies, which we'll discuss in Chapter 10, so you don't gain there either.

Lastly, most modern farmers don't know the first thing about horses and ponies. They simply have not been brought up with them and, because so few farms have horses these days, they have no knowledge or experience of them. They tend to treat them like cattle both in management and handling, and think the same sort of housing and grazing will do for both types of animals. Nothing could be further from the truth. The horse's digestive system is quite different from the cow's and extremely sensitive to wrong feeding methods and poor quality food. Also, horses do not behave or think like cattle and cannot be handled in the same way.

You may be lucky and find a farmer who genuinely does know about horses and ponies. If so, you are lucky as they are few and far between.

Wherever you finally decide to keep your pony, you are strongly advised to keep him at a place where there will be knowledgeable people to help and advise you. For newcomers to pony owning, I feel it is best to keep your pony, at least for the first year, at full livery at an approved riding centre or some other place recommended by your horse consultant. You can learn a great deal just by being around a yard like this, you can be sure your pony will be properly cared for, you will probably be able to have expert instruction, and after a year or so you can decide whether you want or are able to keep him in some other way.

What to look for

When you visit what you hope will be your pony's new home, the main thing to guide you is the condition of the horses and ponies there. You may not have an expert eye but everyone can tell a thin, scrawny animal from a properly fed one, whether it is a horse or a gerbil.

If you can see the ponies' ribs and backbones, if their hips stick out and if they have a down-trodden, miserable air about them, you can be sure this is not a fit place. It doesn't really matter if the paintwork is peeling a little, if the yard isn't spotless or the muck heap is a shapeless mound rather than a carefully shaped 'brick'. It's the condition of the animals which matters.

Do the stables look light and airy or are they dark, poky and smelly? Are the beds thick and clean, or dirty and skimpy? Are the animals reasonably clean, or thick with grease and dandruff in their coats? And are their rugs and blankets clean or caked with droppings?

And most importantly, do the horses and ponies come and greet you with ears pricked and an interested, calm look on their faces, or are they fed up, ears back, nasty tempered or just not interested?

Be sure to ask where people ride. Is there only one small, muddy enclosure for you all to share? Is there a proper outdoor manège (school), an indoor school, fields, bridlepaths, quiet lanes or busy roads? Most people like to go out hacking, but in safety away from the busiest roads. Also, if you do want to hack, but there is nowhere suitable to do it, you will not be happy if you have to ride round and round a school or field all the time.

Many yards close off their fields to their clients in winter, which often means that the ponies cannot be turned out (essential if you are at school all day and no one else is going to exercise the pony) and you have nowhere at all to ride, either.

You must make sure that any facilities offered are open to you all year round, or find somewhere else.

That all-important person, your consultant, will help greatly, but at least you now have some idea of what to look for.

Finding your pony

Once you have considered everything we've talked about so far and are sure you can afford the time and money for a pony, you can embark on the exciting task of finding the pony himself.

If you have been attending a riding centre and have a favourite pony there, it may be that the owners will sell him to you. This has many advantages because you already know the pony and you will be saved much time, travelling expenses and indecision. If you intend to keep the pony at livery at the centre, you'll simply carry on his stable routine as before but visit him more often.

The staff may exercise him, if you are paying for this, but it is generally not a good idea to make the pony available for use by school clients because the school will probably need him most at the very times you do. Also, most ponies improve considerably once they are ridden by only a few people instead of all and sundry, provided their riders are fairly competent.

If there is no such pony, however, you'll have to start looking elsewhere, and a very good place to start is at a reputable dealer's yard. Again, personal recommendation is the best route because there is no approval scheme for dealers. Your consultant or the local Pony Club District Commissioner or BHS Riding Club official should know the good from the bad within a reasonable distance from you.

If you tell these people and your other horsy contacts that you are looking for a *good* pony, word may get round and people might ring you up offering ponies. You can look through the advertisements in horsy magazines or even place an advert yourself.

I don't recommend that you buy a pony at a sale or auction, especially not for your first time, unless you go to a high-class one with a good name and the pony is sold 'subject to veterinary examination', or with some arrangement whereby you can return it within a set period (usually twenty-four to forty-eight hours) if it turns out to be wrong for you or unsound (lame or ill). If you can't resist going to sales, which are usually very sad places, *you must take along your consultant.* Let him, or her do the bidding (buying) and don't wave at a friend across the ring or you could find that you have bought a Shire stallion – not quite what you want at this stage!

If you insist on a pony of a certain breed, contact the breed society, who may have a

register of ponies for sale. However, most breed societies can only help in finding young stock, which are *not* what you want.

Some people do not mind what sex their pony is, that is, whether it is male or female. Others usually feel that geldings (males who have been doctored so that they cannot sire or produce a foal) have a calmer and more easy-going nature than females (mares) although this is certainly not always the case. However, it is not a good idea to buy a stallion (an undoctored male who *is* capable of siring foals) unless you are a very expert rider and your family also have a good deal of knowledge and can help you. Stallions are usually more difficult to handle, more excitable and can, in inexperienced hands, become dangerous when near mares.

In horses, the process of doctoring males is called 'gelding' and a male horse which has been doctored is, therefore, also called a gelding. Mares are not usually doctored except for health reasons; even then they are still called mares.

You'll be best off with a pony at least six years old who is well schooled and reliable, safe in traffic, and who can do the work you want. Old ponies need not be scorned and, like humans, some age quicker than others. Many a good pony in its teens and even twenties is still working as the family pony and giving very satisfactory service. Such ponies often 'nanny' their young riders and look after them, although there are a few who have become crafty with age, but your consultant will be able to spot them. One advantage with an older pony is that they are usually cheaper than younger ones.

There are agencies advertising in horse magazines who can find ponies for you to look at. They keep your details and contact sellers with suitable sounding ponies; they also tell sellers what you are looking for, marry you together, as it were, and you take it from there.

If you find you can afford to keep a pony

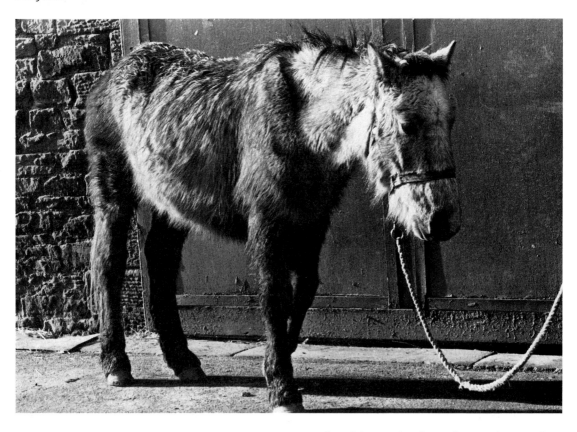

If your pony is to thrive he must have specialised care, every day. Too many unfortunate animals end up like the one above, the result of ignorance and neglect.

fairly easily but haven't the money to actually buy one, why not contact one of the horse and pony charities (again, they often advertise in magazines, or your consultant will know where they are)? They usually want to 'home' their ponies with suitable people and may be glad to see you, although some have a waiting list.

Their ponies have usually been rescued from bad homes, been restored to good health and are ready to find a loving family who can look after them properly. To ensure they never again fall into bad hands, the ponies remain the property of the charity, who will 'vet' you to make sure you either have the knowledge yourself to care for the pony, and the premises, or are going to keep it at a suitable place. They will also make regular visits to check on the condition of the pony.

This arrangement works well for many people and could help considerably with the money side of things.

Finally, you may have a friend who has a pony but is finding the cost of keeping it a bit too much. You might be able to work out a pony-sharing arrangement, or even borrow the pony or lease it (this means you 'rent' it by paying an agreed sum per week, month or year). This can work out well, but you are advised to enter into the deal very carefully indeed and to iron out everything concerning the pony's care, the work it will do, whether anyone else is to ride it, where it is to live, veterinary aspects such as regular checks, worming and vaccinations, and so on.

Many people have come to grief, literally, over pony-loaning, so get everything straight from the outset, have a solicitor draw up a proper legally binding agreement and take

out as reputable an insurance policy on the pony as you can find (to be agreed with the owner).

Trying him out

Once you have found a pony to look at, make an appointment to see it and try it out. It is not essential to look at scores of ponies and if you do you'll probably become thoroughly disheartened in the process. Some people advise you to look at several but you may come across your ideal pony very quickly, and if so there's no point in continuing the search. By the time you go back to him he may well be sold.

Never make an appointment to see a pony and then not turn up. If you can't make it, ring as soon as you know, partly for the sake of good manners and partly because if you get a name as a time-waster people with decent ponies will not bother with you.

It is hard to believe that this is the same animal, happily restored to health. Some horse charities will loan out rescued ponies to knowledgeable, caring homes. This pony is owned by the Horses and Ponies Protection Association.

Obviously, take your consultant with you and leave a good deal of the inspection to him or her. It's going to be *your* pony though, so here's how things will probably go, and what you should look for yourself.

Note whether the pony seems friendly or frightened and bad-tempered, and, if he is in a field, whether he is hard to catch. You should know almost at once whether or not you like his personality and this, too, is important.

Firstly, the pony will probably be standing in the yard for you and your family and adviser to look at. Your adviser will check his conformation and then ask for the pony to be walked away and trotted up, preferably on a loose rope, as restricting his head can disguise faulty action. The pony should move straight, free and sound.

Next he should be saddled and bridled and the pony's normal rider should mount. Note how the pony responds to being tacked up and mounted. A pony who flinches when saddled up may have been roughly treated at some time, or he may have back trouble. 'He's a bit cold-backed' a seller may tell you, but most animals who cower or sink down from a saddle have painful backs and this is something to mention to the vet, if you decide to have the pony vetted.

If the pony pokes his nose in the air when bridled he might have been hurt at some time, or he could have trouble with his teeth or ears and you could spend ages trying to get ready for a ride.

Watch the pony being ridden, first in the paddock and then on the road so you can see him going and how he behaves in traffic. Then ride him yourself and see how he reacts to a stranger.

If you are happy so far, take him back into his paddock for a canter and perhaps a jump. Ride him both to left and right. Most ponies have a better side on which they go more easily, but if he is completely awkward on

The correct way to trot up a pony to examine him for lameness. Be at his shoulder and leave the lead-rope quite loose so that it does not restrict the pony's head movement. Hold the spare end of the rope in your free hand.

one side he could need a lot of expert training before he becomes good to ride.

You should walk, trot and canter on both reins and jump, if you can. If there are no jumps around, ask for a small obstacle to be erected. It's no good buying a pony to jump if you can't try him.

Some sellers are willing to allow a week's trial at your home, particularly dealers, but others are not. A trial is an advantage because you get to know whether you suit each other, whether the pony is safe in traffic and cooperative with a stranger and whether he will jump and go well away from what he considers to be home. He must like you as well as you him, remember, or he will never do his best for you.

You can also see how he behaves in the stable and whether you feel comfortable handling him.

Ask about a trial if you really like the pony. If one is possible, you will have to insure the pony at your expense for the trial period.

Before this, though, a vet will have to examine the pony for you. Tell the vet you've found a pony you like and ask him to make an appointment with the seller. He or she will send you a report and a certificate stating the pony's state of health and giving general information plus a detailed description. If the vet 'passes' the pony for what you want to do, arrange your trial, or, if you aren't having a trial, for him to be delivered to your home, livery yard or wherever you're going to keep him.

When looking for a pony, it is as well to remember that no animal is perfect. They all have something about them you don't quite like – maybe the neck is a little short, or the back slightly long or perhaps one leg is carried slightly crookedly in action. A pony could have some behavioural fault; he can be super in every way but, for example, won't go through water or is terrified of pigs (many ponies are). Your adviser should discuss everything with you and ask the seller if the pony has any 'quirks' like this. Everyone knows there is no such thing as the perfect pony – you just have to decide whether or not you can live with his particular 'black marks'.

Settling in a new pony

As soon as your pony arrives at his new home you are bound to want to tack up and go for a ride or take him to show a friend straight-away. At the risk of sounding like a spoilsport I am going to suggest that you do not do this just yet.

Think about the pony for a minute. He has perhaps just had a long and tiring journey from his other home and has arrived at this strange place, where both the surroundings, the smells, the people and the other animals, horses, ponies, dogs and cats, are completely unknown to him – no familiar stable or field, no friends and no humans whom he has grown to trust and respect.

How lonely, uncertain and perhaps even a little frightened he must feel. It would not make a good impression on him if, after all this, some strange human suddenly slapped a saddle on his back and expected him to start work at once without a chance to settle in properly. This bad impression might stay with him for quite some time, affecting his attitude towards you and his new home in general.

How much better it would be if he were made to feel welcome and allowed to get to know you a little, and his new home.

When he first arrives, take him into the stable yard and let him stand for a minute to have a look round. Lead him around a little, and don't be surprised if, during this leg-stretch, he whinnies a lot calling for his friends.

If it is evening, he should be stabled for his first night as it is dangerous to turn a pony out into a strange field, either alone or with companions, when darkness is falling. He will not know the field's boundaries and

could get injured on the fencing. The other ponies might attack him if they are not properly introduced, so keep him in for his first night.

The stable should be made ready before his arrival, thickly bedded down and with clean water and good hay waiting. You should buy a couple of bales of his usual hay from his former owner so that he doesn't have a sudden change of diet which could seriously upset his digestion. His new hay should be gradually mixed with it, and eventually take over, by which time he will be accustomed to it.

Speak gently to the pony and do not rush about him, however excited you are. Ponies always, however, appreciate firm, sympathetic handling. A strange pony, particularly, needs leadership as well as understanding.

If he is used to feed other than hay, mix him a feed as well. You should have asked his former owner exactly how much of what foods he is used to so you can carry on with his normal diet. If any changes are felt necessary in your ownership, you can gradually make them after he has settled in.

Let the pony eat in peace, if he will, but if he feels too upset to eat, do not worry.

If the pony arrives in the morning, however, and is to live out, he could go straight to his paddock, but do not, under any circumstances, turn him out with a bunch of ponies he does not know. Ponies have quite well-defined social structures, in other words there are boss ponies, middle ones and underlings. In the wild, new ponies trying to break into an established herd are often given a hard time, being bitten, kicked and made to feel miserable, and this behaviour carries over into domestication.

Meeting his new friends

It is important that he should be introduced to his new friends properly otherwise fights

Dos and don'ts

DON'T take on a pony that is too much for you. A glamorous, flighty pony that is hard to control could badly frighten you and put you off riding for life.

DON'T think you can keep a pony in a shed at the bottom of the garden or in any field that is handy. Like people and other animals, ponies need reasonable living conditions.

DON'T be afraid or too proud to ask for advice from experts. It could save a lot of heartache and money.

DON'T buy a pony you don't like. No matter how super he is, he has to be your friend, and how can you be friends with someone you don't like?

DO consider keeping your pony at a good livery yard or riding centre for at least a year. You'll learn a great deal from the general goings-on in the yard, and there will be someone expert on hand to help with problems.

DO be sure to have your intended pony vetted before giving a decision. You can't be too careful about this.

DO be prepared to give up some other hobbies or interests if you have a pony – he will take up a lot of time.

DO be sure to be covered by third-party insurance in case your pony causes injury or damage. If you join the Pony Club, this insurance will be free – and there are lots of other benefits from membership.

DO introduce your pony to his new friends properly. It will make a big difference as to whether he settles in or not, and, therefore, to his happiness in his new home.

and injuries could result.

Some stables insist on keeping horses in isolation (away from others) when they first arrive. Many other stables do not bother and haven't the facilities in any case. If all the animals have had their injections and the newcomer has passed his veterinary examination, there is little chance of any disease developing, but you'll have to obey your stable's rules on this.

If there is just one other pony with yours, introductions are easy. The two will probably be stabled near by and will be able to see one another from their stables. They should ideally be taken on a ride together before being turned out, when there will probably be little trouble.

If the new pony has to be introduced into a herd of ponies he should certainly not be put straight in with all of them. The others, particularly the leader of the herd, are almost certain to treat him as an intruder as they would in the wild. Your pony should be allocated a companion from the herd, one who is sweet-natured with other ponies and will accept yours. These two should be led around together and then turned into a field on their own. Then, over a period of a few days, they can be joined by others until your pony feels part of the herd.

This may sound like a lot of trouble, but it is important and any responsible stable owner will know this.

Gradually, your pony will find his place in the herd and, like all ponies, have his own friends and enemies, just as you may do at school. This is life – sadly, we can't all be liked by everybody!

After your pony has settled in for a day or two, with nothing but good experiences and impressions, start riding him and enjoying your new friendship. Even if he is at full livery, look after him as much as you can yourself. He has to learn that he is *your* pony, not the staff's or one particular groom's.

Whenever you arrive at the stables, go

straight to him with a piece of apple, carrot or some mints. Stroke him (most ponies prefer being stroked rather than patted or thumped) and talk to him, always in a friendly tone of voice. He'll soon recognise this special person and whinny excitedly or run to the gate when he sees you, and that will give you a marvellous feeling.

Some people say giving titbits causes ponies to bite and become spiteful when the titbits run out. I have found that if you keep titbits for certain times, such as when you first meet in the day, you will have no trouble as the pony will not expect them at other times.

Once your pony has settled in, think about joining your local branch of the Pony Club or junior section of a riding club. There you will meet many horsy friends and can attend events, competitions and social gatherings. You will be able to obtain good instruction very reasonably, in riding and pony care, and there is usually an expert only too glad to help with everyday problems, or to help put right something you did not even realise was wrong.

2. How to keep your pony

How nature meant ponies to live

To understand what is involved in the different ways of keeping ponies and how they will affect the ponies, it is necessary to understand how they live in nature.

Most wild ponies live in a herd, a very close community, surrounded by family and friends and led by either a senior mare or a stallion. The leader decides where the ponies will graze, drink and rest. Stallions also fight off intruders and keep the herd together. The only ponies who may live alone are young males who are old enough to mate and have become a threat to the stallion because they might steal his mares. These are usually driven off to make their own way in life, although sometimes they group together in 'bachelor bands'.

In nature, horses are prey animals, and other wild animals – for example wolves, wild dogs and members of the cat family such as lions and cheetahs – prey on them, hunting them down and killing them for food. Horses soon discovered that there was safety in numbers and learned to live in herds. A hunting animal wants only one kill and if you are in a group there's less chance of that one being you.

Ponies, therefore, feel safer and happier in company. Even though today's ponies have never been preyed on, this natural instinct remains and rules much of their behaviour.

Because of this also, ponies cannot risk sleeping for long periods. They doze for about half an hour then wake and start grazing or take their turn on watch. They eat for about eighteen hours out of twenty-four in natural conditions, sleep for a total of about three or four hours and spend the rest walking about, associating with other herd members or resting.

Therefore, ponies are wandering, grazing animals. They live on open plains, on hills or mountains, and sometimes in forests. They do not live in caves or dens (although wild horses have been known to use caves for shelter). They spend a lot of time walking slowly about eating, which means, obviously, that they need a lot of gentle exercise and some food passing through their digestive systems nearly all the time.

Depending on where in the world wild horses and ponies live, they may have water freely available or they may have to make special treks to watering places.

Our mountain and moorland ponies usually have plenty of streams and lakes to drink from, but in hotter climates like Africa, zebras (closely related to ponies) have to walk to water night and morning to drink. In periods of drought, zebras have been known to go for four days without water or even trying to find it, then their herd leader suddenly gives a signal to the herd and they all set off, usually in single file, on a long trek to the nearest water hole to drink.

Incidentally, this way of going in single file is common to all the horse family. Ponies on

26

Dartmoor and Exmoor, when moving from one grazing area to another, are often seen to do it. They normally gallop in a bunched-up herd only when they are being chased by men or dogs, which to them represent predators.

Domesticated ponies are not like zebras, of course, and it would be very wrong to think that we can leave them without water for days on end. It is safer and more satisfactory for them to have water constantly available, either in a trough or other container in their field, or from a clean stream, or in buckets or automatic waterers in their stables.

In nature, they are free to find their own shelter in woods, behind shrubbery or hills, and in hollows and canyons. Domesticated ponies in an open field surrounded by post and rails or wire fencing are in a very unnatural environment. They cannot find shelter and may suffer if we do not provide it. Fields with hedges and trees offer some protection, but ideally ponies need some form of overhead shelter, preferably in the form of a shed.

Wild ponies are, of course, never groomed by man nor shod. Their skin naturally produces grease and dandruff to help protect against wet and they grow long, thick coats in winter to help keep them warm. Even in domestication, grass-kept ponies are not groomed as much as stabled ones because they need this protection. Stabled ponies, though, can develop dirty, diseased skin if we do not groom them, because they are not exposed to the rain which washes some of this grease and scurf away.

As for shoeing, wild ponies' feet are unlikely to wear down to the extent that they become footsore. However, putting shoes on prevents any wear at all, so a farrier has to trim our ponies' feet to keep them in correct shape. Wild ponies' feet wear down just enough naturally.

Nature does not attend very well to teeth.

A pony chews his food in a grinding motion. His top jaw is slightly wider than his bottom one, so as he chews the teeth wear down unevenly; the outside edges of his top back teeth and the inside edges of his lower back teeth become very sharp from wear, and some ponies also develop large hooks in later life on their very back teeth in their lower jaws and on the front of their upper back teeth.

A veterinary surgeon will file or rasp your pony's teeth smooth and remove the hooks but wild ponies don't have this attention.

Dental problems are one of the commonest causes of death in wild horses and ponies. Their teeth either become sharp and develop such large hooks that they cannot eat properly, or the teeth wear right down in old age with, again, the result that the pony cannot eat. He either starves to death or becomes so weak from lack of food that he is easily caught by a predator.

Problems of worms and disease do not affect wild ponies so much as our domesticated ones. Domesticated ponies usually live in very over-crowded conditions compared to wild ones. The latter move on when pasture becomes over-grazed or wormy and other animals move in to eat what they have left. The ponies' worm larvae (immature forms of worms) are eaten by these other animals but since the larvae can only live in ponies, they are killed.

Although wild ponies can catch diseases, infections are not spread because herds are not in contact with others of their kind. But in domesticated conditions, germs can easily be passed from pony to pony (in yards and at shows etc) till large numbers are affected. This is why we vaccinate ponies against influenza, for example.

By now, you might be thinking that the closer to nature we keep our ponies, the healthier and happier they must be, and you are right. This doesn't mean, though, that they can't be stabled, kept in paddocks or worked. It just means we have to adapt our methods of looking after them and our ideas of what they need as closely as possible to nature and I hope this book will help you to do that.

Stable and field – how to tell good from bad

If you want to keep your pony as naturally as possible and with the most convenience to yourself, in terms of time and money, aim to keep him in a field with good shelter rather than mostly stabled, but with a stable available in times of sickness or injury. A stable somewhere *is* necessary occasionally and it's also convenient to have somewhere under cover to prepare your pony for a special event such as a show. It's difficult to get him reasonably clean if he lives out entirely. If you have no stable of your own, try to pay a stable owner a small amount per week, say a pound or two, to reserve the use of a stable for you when you want one. Another animal could use it in the meantime and the owner will receive rent; then when you want to use it more regularly, perhaps by stabling your pony at night in winter, you could pay the normal rent.

Loose boxes

A loose box is by far the best type of stable for your pony. This is like a 'room of his own' usually with at least one window, and a door to the outside, split into a bottom half and a top half. The top half should always be kept fastened back to let in air, and so he can see out because ponies don't like to be shut away. The bottom half of the door should be just a bit higher than his withers so he doesn't have to crane his neck to look out and he won't feel he can easily jump out.

The box should measure about 2m (about 6 ft 6 ins) square for a tiny pony of under 12 hh and up to 3m (about 10 ft) square for a 14.2 hh pony. If it's too small the pony won't

be able to move around comfortably or lie down and get up easily. He needs to be able to lie flat out on the floor to sleep properly so must have room to do this. Ponies also doze, either standing up or lying on their bellies with their legs tucked under them.

Small stables are often the cause of ponies getting cast – i.e. the pony has lain down near a wall with his legs against it and tucked under in such a way that he cannot get up of his own accord. Ponies often panic and injure themselves by thrashing around when cast.

The window should be protected inside with a strong mesh or barred grille and should be left open, like the door. Neither should be shut unless a very strong, cold wind is blowing directly into the box.

It's a good plan to have the box lined half way up with strong boarding known as kicking boards, to protect against damage if the pony does kick.

The inside of the stable should be as smooth as possible so the pony cannot hurt himself on protruding nails or screws, broken or splintered wood or low beams. The pony should have at *least* 1 m (3 ft 3 ins) of space above his head, preferably more. The doorway should be not less than 2 m (6 ft 6 ins) high for a small pony, higher for a larger one. In width, it should be 1.25 m (about 4 ft 3 ins) so the pony is less likely to bang his hips when he goes through.

Most stable floors these days are of concrete, which is cheap and fairly hard-wearing. It is not, however, the best flooring as it is cold, hard and absorbs the pony's urine, but if you keep plenty of clean bedding down it can be acceptable. Other good stable floors are asphalt, bricks (if level) and compacted shale or earth.

Some local councils insist on drainage to agree with local health laws, although in practice the bedding will soak up nearly all the urine. On concrete floors, drainage can be provided by V-shaped grooves meeting at

The bottom half of this stable door has two bolts, to add extra strength and for the pony's own safety. Note the interested expression on the pony's face.

a central grooved channel which runs away to an outside drain through a small hole in the bottom of the wall. The flooring should have a slight slope to afford drainage of urine – about 1 cm in 1 m ($\frac{1}{2}$ in. in 1 yd).

The stable floor should, in any case, be above ground level by a few centimetres (inches) to prevent rainwater or other water (such as emptied buckets or hosepipe water) running into the stable and waterlogging it.

Stable floors should also be fairly even rather than rough and lumpy, and non-slip. Even if there is bedding down all the time, some ponies scrape it around and if the floor beneath is slippery the pony can fall and seriously hurt himself. Wood, for instance, is quite unsuitable for a stable floor as not only does it wear quickly and absorb urine, but also it is slippery when wet.

A stable should be sturdily built as ponies are amazingly strong when they kick, push or pull (if tied up) and can easily bring down a weak building. Converted garden sheds and hen houses are not suitable for this reason. Brick is the best material; concrete blocks (not breeze blocks) or strong timber, preferably double-lined, are other good alternatives. Any box is improved by being lined half way up with kicking boards, as previously described.

There should not be a gap under the door as this will create floor draughts. Also, the door should open outwards, otherwise if the pony is lying down behind it you won't be able to enter except by climbing over the door which could frighten him and be dangerous.

The bottom half of the door should have two bolts, one at the top and one at the bottom, never a single bolt half way up. This gives extra strength and avoids the possibility of the pony being able to force open the bottom corner when lying down and managing to put a leg through, which could cause a nasty injury. If he were to kick against a 'free' corner and push a foot through in this way, the result could be the same.

The roof should be of a substance which does not cause the stable to become like an oven in summer or a fridge in winter, so avoid metal and asbestos. Opt instead for wood, preferably a double layer, covered with insulated roofing felt or, ideally, proper slates or tiles.

Sometimes you will find loose boxes built inside a large building, often simply taking the form of individual pens and being completely enclosed with partitions, except for a door over which the pony can look out. In America and some other countries, this is the most usual form of stabling as it gives protection against the extremes of weather found in those countries. The advantage is, to the humans, that they can work without being exposed to the climate. In Britain, this type of stabling is becoming more common than in the past, and provided the building is light and airy, it is a good method. There are usually boxes down one or sometimes two sides of the building, which open into wide passageways along which horses, people and equipment come and go.

Stable fittings are objects fixed inside the stable for convenience, for example mangers, hayracks and tie-rings. A tie-ring is very useful not only for tying up the pony but also for fixing up haynets; the other fittings you can manage without.

If you want a manger, choose the type which fits across a corner so the pony doesn't bump himself on it, and the same with a hayrack. The manger should have its top about level with the point of the pony's shoulder or *slightly* higher. It has to be a comfortable height for him to eat from without the risk of him getting a foot in it. It should have a rounded lower edge to prevent injury to his knees if he stamps while eating. Ideally it should be boxed in underneath for this reason – you can use the space inside for a cupboard to hold the grooming kit and a headcollar.

The hayrack should be fixed at about the height of the pony's head. If it is too low he could knock himself on it or catch a foot in it; if too high it will be uncomfortable for him to eat from and bits could fall down into his eyes.

Rather than spend money on these fittings, you could give feed in a big, strong plastic bucket and hay can be fed loose on a clean corner of the floor or in a haynet hung from the tie-ring. Don't hang the net swinging from a beam as the pony needs to push it against the wall to bite the hay. The net should be hung at the height of his head.

Water can be given in buckets rather than

There are several points to consider in this cut-out loose box. The good points are (1) the kicking boards which are sloped slightly from bottom to top, making it less likely for the pony to become cast, the straw bedding being banked up round the sides also helping in this; (2) the corner manger which is smoothly boarded in, so preventing the pony banging himself on it, knocking his knees on it during feeding or getting his head or legs under it; and (3) the haynet securely tied at pony's head height. The not-so-good points are: (1) the window guard which (to allow for the inward-opening window) protrudes inside the box and is easy for the pony to knock his head on; (2) the two buckets of water which, though good in themselves, should be in different corners, because if a pony does a dropping in one of these it will almost certainly fall in both, leaving no clean water; (3) the bedding scraped away from the door (it should be left in place partly to help prevent ground draughts and partly for the pony to stand on during long hours spent looking out); and the tie-ring on the right of the manger, which is much too low enabling a tied-up pony easily to get a leg over his rope with possibly disastrous results.

specially plumbed-in automatic waterers, although the latter save work. Use two buckets and stand them in different corners, but always use the same two corners so the pony knows where to find them in the dark. If you stand them together and he does a dropping in one (which ponies do with annoying regularity), some dirt will be bound to fall into each bucket and the pony will then quite rightly refuse to drink either of them, but by putting them in different corners he'll always have clean water available. One bucket is not enough to last the pony through the night.

If automatic watering is used, you must check daily that the device is neither overfilling and flooding the box nor jammed or blocked, leaving the pony without water. The best type have a plug at the bottom (fitted flush with the bottom so the pony can't pull it out) so you can clean the container regularly.

Stalls

Another form of stabling is stalls. Here the ponies are tied up in compartments each about 2 m (6 ft 6 ins) wide with their feed containers fixed at the front. They can lie down and get up but can't turn round, roll or look about them without turning their necks right round. In most stall arrangements the ponies face a blank wall.

This is *not* a good way to keep a privately owned pony who doesn't get the work of, say, a riding-school pony. It is very restrictive and causes a great deal of boredom. If you are absolutely stuck you could use it until you find somewhere else, but the pony should be turned out most of the time and only stalled when strictly necessary.

Stalls open into a wide passageway and, as the ponies' tails are always towards the passageway, mucking out is much easier as the dung is always in the same area. Stalls may be convenient for humans but not for

ponies, except in an emergency. Many ponies, anyway, pull back when tied up and fight the halter rope, which can cause injury and a lot of inconvenience.

Fields

It's surprising how much trouble a pony can get into in a field. If there is a weak spot in the fence, he'll get through; if there's a broken bottle, he'll tread or roll on it; and if there's a tree he'll bump into it. Well, maybe things aren't quite that bad, but ponies do seem to be more accident-prone than horses; maybe that's because they are so inquisitive and determined. Ponies can wriggle their way through gaps in fences which horses would ignore and are usually the ones to start off a galloping/bucking spree when bored. Stabled ponies, being even more confined

than grass-kept ones, can get into just as much trouble, it seems, from persistently trying to demolish their stables when they feel they have been indoors too long.

What sort of things should you look for in a suitable pony field? For a start, the land should be as well drained as possible. Even in summer, you can tell normally wet land by the tufts of round, spiky marsh grasses growing on it. This land will be under water in all but the driest weather and is useless for keeping ponies. The field should ideally slope slightly towards some outlet for the rainwater, such as a ditch or stream, otherwise it will be easily poached (trampled and muddy) in wet weather.

There should be some natural shelter if possible. Hedges which are thick all the way to the ground, and the height of the ponies' heads, are ideal. Thin, straggly ones provide little in the way of shelter or even a windbreak. Clumps of bushes are welcome for the ponies to stand behind, and thickets

This is a basic field shelter, quite adequate for two animals. If it is kept bedded down (and the droppings removed frequently) and has tie-rings fixed inside for haynets, the horses or ponies will welcome it during extreme weather at all times of year, but particularly summer and winter.

or spinneys of trees provide overhead shade and shelter.

The prevailing wind in a district gives you an idea of where the natural shelter should be. Notice which direction the trees are bending. If they are all bending over to the left, obviously the wind is blowing from the right. Is there anywhere the ponies can shelter? A beautiful, thick hedge is no use at all if the wind is blowing towards it and the ponies cannot stand behind it.

If there is little or no natural shelter, a field shelter must be provided. People often say ponies don't use field shelters but that is not so in my experience. Some ponies do use them more in summer to escape from sun and flies than in winter to shelter from rain and wind, but nearly all ponies *will* use a shelter provided they aren't frightened of it.

A useful type is an open-fronted shed with the roof sloping to the back. Any handyman or do-it-yourself enthusiast can make one out of used timber. It should be sited on the driest part of the field so the inside doesn't become soggy with draining rainwater, and have its back to the prevailing wind. The roof, preferably of wood, should have a covering of roofing felt for protection. You don't need windows or fittings, although a few rings for tying haynets in winter are an advantage.

The open front ensures enough space for more than one pony to enter at once – for two ponies a shed 3.5 m (about 12 ft) by 3 m (about 9-10 ft) is big enough and in height, as with a stable, there should be at least 1 m (3 ft 3 ins) space above the ponies' heads at the lowest level of the roof (the back). The four corner posts should be sunk into the ground for about one third of their length and the sides fixed to them. There is no need to provide flooring – straw bedding can be put straight down on to the grass or earth and the droppings removed daily – nor is it necessary to supply drainage.,

It is important to let the ponies know it's safe by having a high, wide entrance so they can see in properly and it doesn't look like a dark cavern. They will soon associate it with comfort (no flies, no wind) and with hay in winter, and you'll notice an improvement in their conditions, too, because when ponies are comfortable and content they put on weight and stay healthier.

Fences

The hedging recommended for shelter also serves as a really good field boundary. The thicker and pricklier the hedge the better.

The best man-made fencing is wooden

Barbed wire fencing of any sort should be avoided for ponies, but it is especially dangerous when it is loose and flimsy like this.

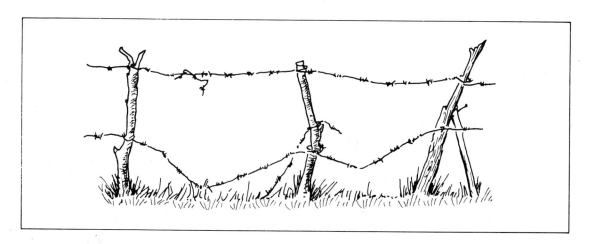

posts and rails, but this is expensive. Wooden posts and thick, smooth wire is a cheaper, good second choice but the wire must be kept really taut; if it is loose the ponies could catch their legs in it. If they were to paw it, they could snag the wire between shoe and hoof and tear off the shoe, seriously injuring the foot, or if they were to get caught they could break the fence or pull it down.

Fence posts should be sunk into the ground for one third of their length and should be well treated with preservative, preferably not creosote, which can be poisonous. Most suppliers sell ready-treated wood. The top rail or wire should be at least the height of the ponies' backs and the bottom one the height of their knees. Two rails are quite adequate but if you want a third, place it mid-way between the others.

Types of fencing *not* suitable for ponies and horses are barbed wire (which can cause really serious injuries and lifetime scars); garden sectional fencing (too weak); palings (too weak); metal railings with spiked tops

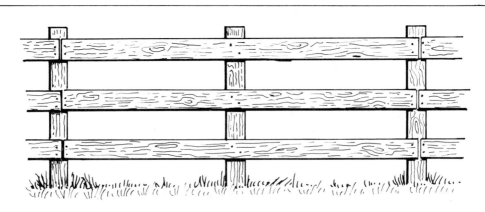

Wooden post and rail fencing is the safest for ponies. Here, the rails are on the inside, so presenting a smooth surface should galloping ponies rub against it. The top rail, however, should be a little higher, level with the tops of the posts, so the corners don't cause a serious injury to any pony trying to jump out.

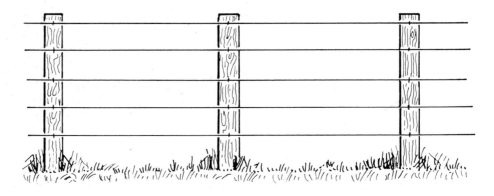

Smooth or plain wire fencing is a good, cheap alternative to the more expensive post and rail fencing. The wire must, like any wire, be kept really taut. With wire fencing of all types, it is advisable to keep handy a pair of wire clippers, in case of accidents.

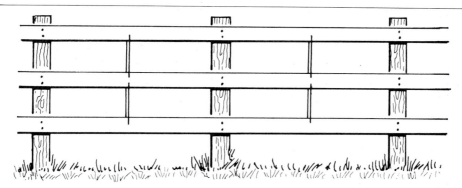

Flexible rail fencing, like this, is made of wire-reinforced PVC rails which come on a roll and are nailed to wooden posts. The wires between the rails simply help keep them in position. This fencing is safe and has the advantage that it can be easily removed and taken to another field – especially useful if you rent grazing for short periods.

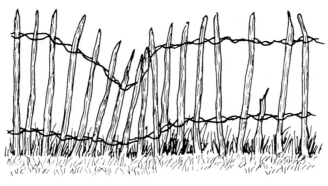

Chestnut palings are far too weak to keep ponies where they belong.

Metal railings, especially the spiked type like this, are extremely dangerous and can inflict horrible injuries on ponies who try to jump out. Ponies can also get their hooves caught between the uprights.

Natural hedges are the best fence if they are thick, dense and at least as high as the ponies' backs (like any fencing). The pricklier they are the better. Watch out for poisonous plants growing in them, though. They also provide a windbreak but are not adequate shelter on their own.

(can kill ponies if they try to jump out and become impaled); sheep-netting (ponies can get their hooves through with dire results); ordinary wire netting (much too flimsy); and plastic garden fencing (again, too weak).

Fencing of any type can be expensive. If it is your own land or you have the use of it for several years, it is worth having it properly refenced. Otherwise, it will have to be repaired as necessary.

For people who have to move fields a lot, portable fencing can be a good option. This can either be electric fencing or wire-reinforced flexible plastic rail, sold in rolls.

Electric fencing can be powered by battery or from a mains supply. For horses and ponies, use thick (heavy gauge) wire and tie strips of coloured plastic to it (cut up fertiliser bags will do) so they can see it properly.

Lead the pony up to the fence and press his nose to it. He'll receive just enough of a shock to warn him away in future, but he won't actually be hurt. The wire can be erected on its own metal posts about a metre (yard) inside other fencing or run along the tops of existing posts.

Flexible fencing can be cut into strips and used instead of rails or wire on existing posts. To find a supplier, watch for manufacturers' advertisements in horse and pony magazines.

Both these sorts of fencing can be taken down easily when you move and re-erected at your new field.

Gates and slip-rails

If possible, try not to have a gate opening on to a roadway as traffic can cause problems when you are coming and going and it makes it easier for thieves to lead ponies out and away. In any case, keep gates padlocked at both ends and fix them so they cannot be lifted off their hinges.

Wooden gates are good, as are tubular steel ones (aluminium is not strong enough). The bottom half of the gate should be filled in with strong mesh to stop ponies putting a leg through.

The fastening should either be a simple chain fixed by a bolt or staple and attaching by means of a hook or spring-clip to another staple on the gate-post, or a strong bolt. Don't buy the sort of fastening often called a hunting latch, which has a metal rod sticking up which you pull back when riding to pass through without dismounting. The rod gets caught in headcollars and can poke ponies in the eye if they are milling about round the gate waiting for feed to arrive.

Slip-rails, strong wooden or metal bars which fit into slots on gate-posts, are an alternative to gates but ponies can learn to put their necks under them and jiggle them about till they fall down – then they are away. If they have to be used, fit strong, giant-sized bolts through the post and slip-rails to prevent this.

Freeze-marking

Because horse stealing is so common now, it is advisable for every pony to be freeze-marked with his individual code number, usually on his back where his saddle goes, so it can't be seen when he is tacked up. This deters thieves because it is difficult to sell the animals without their identity papers; also the company who does the marking will usually offer a large reward to anyone, including auctioneers, coming across a stolen freeze-marked pony.

You can obtain details about the scheme, which is approved by the Pony Club and the police, direct from the marking company, or from the Pony Club (see Appendix for addresses). There are several companies who run freeze-marking schemes, and they usually advertise in pony magazines.

As well as freeze-marking, take clear colour snapshots of your pony from front, back and both sides. Take pictures of the four chestnuts on his legs, which can be used to identify him (like our fingerprints) and of

Points to remember

● The more naturally you keep your pony the less problems you are likely to have. It is not good for a horse or pony to be kept stabled most of the time without enough exercise. Two hours a day is probably the least amount of exercise a healthy pony should have. Nature meant him to be on the move most of the time, so try to ensure he is turned out for at least an hour a day in addition to his ridden work.

● Many a field can be made acceptable if you invest in your own set of portable fencing. Flexible-rail fencing and electric fencing are probably the two most practical types, and can quickly convert into a suitable field one which you would otherwise have turned down because of unsuitable or broken-down fencing.

● Have your pony freeze-marked. It's the best way of preventing him being stolen, or of getting him back if he is.

A slip gate, showing how it slots into special holders on the posts and is simply lifted down and moved to one side, rather than unfastened and swung to one side like a proper gate. Some ponies learn to put their necks under the top rail and lift off slip-gates and slip-rails.

any special marks or scars he may have. Have as many copies as you can afford printed so you have enough to distribute to all animal sales in your region, to the police and to the Horses and Ponies Protection Association (see Appendix for address), who run a lost and found register and can help in your search for your stolen pony. They will give you general information on how to safeguard your pony if you send them a stamped, addressed envelope.

Field water supplies

Your pony obviously needs a supply of clean water. Most fields have water piped from the mains to a trough, which should be checked daily to see it is neither overflowing nor blocked. Ice must be broken twice a day in winter, as ponies don't seem able to do this for themselves, and debris – like dead birds, leaves and rubbish – fished out whenever you visit the field. If you leave a (clean) plastic football floating on the water, its slight movement in the breeze and when the ponies drink helps prevent ice forming except in a fairly severe frost. When you do have to break the ice, take it out of the trough as otherwise the water will re-freeze very quickly, and pile it up out of harm's way. Don't leave it on the ground near the trough or, indeed, anywhere inside the field as if the ponies tread on it they can cut their feet and legs. During a hard spell, it will not melt and can form a dangerous heap.

tractor or lorry tyre and tied to the fence post. Fill them up once or twice a day by hosepipe. In freezing weather, store the hosepipe indoors – if the water freezes inside it you'll have no way of supplying water to your pony.

If you have a clean, stony stream, the ponies might be able to drink from it if the approach is not steep. If it is muddy, has a sandy bottom or looks anything but clear, it is best fenced off as the ponies could become ill or get colic from the sand if they suck it up. Your vet can have the water checked for pollution, if you wish.

Ponds are usually too dirty to drink from

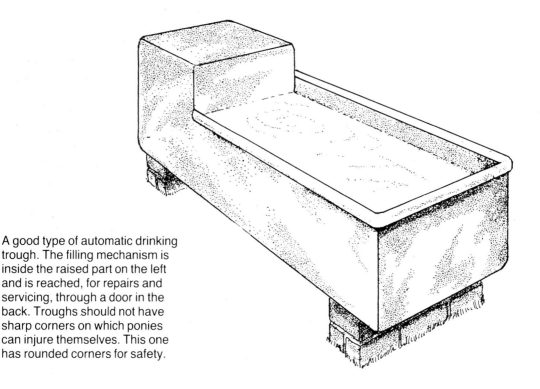

A good type of automatic drinking trough. The filling mechanism is inside the raised part on the left and is reached, for repairs and servicing, through a door in the back. Troughs should not have sharp corners on which ponies can injure themselves. This one has rounded corners for safety.

The filling mechanism, whether automatic or a hand-operated tap, must be inside a cover to stop the ponies fiddling with it or knocking themselves on it.

Water can be supplied in large plastic containers like dustbins, jammed into an old

and often have dangerous approaches. In winter they can freeze and if the ponies wander on to them the ice will break and the ponies could either drown or die of cold and exhaustion struggling to get out again. Ponds and deep dykes are better fenced off.

Field hazards

Always keep an eye out for any rubbish which might appear in the field and clear it away. If there is any farm machinery or equipment left in the field, have it taken out or fence it off, otherwise it could cause serious injury. Watch particularly for chain harrows left in the grass. Ponies cannot see these and can gallop right on to them, puncturing their hooves on the spikes.

If you have a choice of fields, try to avoid those by roadsides, beside gardens or with rights of way going through them. People often try to befriend ponies and feed them, not understanding that it makes ponies peevish and troublesome. Also, public access makes it easier for ponies to be stolen, harassed by pet dogs or chivvied by vandals or joy-riders.

Garden shrubs and plants are often poisonous to ponies. The ponies either eat them over the garden fences (annoying the householders) or people dump their garden rubbish in your field, often as a supposed treat for the ponies. The result is one or more very sick ponies. Even grass mowings can cause serious illness because ponies gulp them down without chewing them properly and this can cause colic. Colic is even more likely if the cuttings are not absolutely fresh but have begun to rot.

If you have to use a field adjoining dwellings, it is worth asking the householders not to throw garden rubbish over the fence and explain why. However, there is nothing you can do to stop the ponies putting their heads over the fences, except putting up an extra line of fencing, say electric fencing, to keep the ponies away from the gardens.

The stabled pony

Keeping a pony stabled is a real test of your character and ability – character because of the willpower and selflessness needed to always put the pony before whatever else you want to do, and ability because of the knowledge needed to care for a pony in a completely unnatural state, dependent on you for everything. It is certainly not a suitable way for a novice.

The pony will need ridden exercise for a good two hours a day to keep him healthy. Even then he may find the confinement of his stable difficult to bear because of the boredom and being forced to stand more or less still for twenty-two hours out of twenty-four. This would never happen in the wild, of course, and many ponies become irritable, kick their boxes, mangle their beds or develop stable vices such as crib-biting, wind-sucking or rug-tearing. Crib-biters grasp the tops of doors or kicking boards with their teeth, arch their necks and suck air into their stomachs; wind-suckers draw in air without biting anything. Some ponies become box-walkers – they walk round and round their boxes, the way some zoo animals pace their cages; others start to weave, swaying from foreleg to foreleg, nodding their heads up and down and from side to side.

These strange behaviours result as much from the distress the animals feel at being cooped up as from the boredom involved. Vices can affect your pony's health and once established are difficult to stop. Rather than seeking a way of forcing the pony out of a bad habit it is better to stop him *wanting* to resort to his vice. The best thing is to keep him in such a way that he doesn't start these antics in the first place. Highly-strung, well-bred ponies seem particularly prone to stable vices, although others can acquire them too – and don't assume that because a pony has none it means he enjoys being in a stable for twenty-two hours a day.

The stabled pony can eat and drink only when you give him food and water and cannot graze on his natural food, grass. He may have to wear clothing which might irritate him, particularly if it isn't straightened and adjusted frequently, and he cannot enjoy natural contact with his friends.

In more natural conditions, ponies avoid their own droppings, which they find objectionable. In a stable, a pony may have no choice but to live with and stand in his droppings, and also lie on them sometimes, unless someone is there to skip out the box every time a dropping appears, which is very unlikely. To be fair to the pony, his bedding will need attention at least twice a day, and preferably more often, if his surroundings are to be kept reasonably hygienic.

So from your point of view, you will have to attend to him (at the very least) twice a day and probably three times, even when you are at school, unless you can get someone else to do it. You will have to feed him, water him, groom him, muck him out, exercise him and clean his tack and clothing. And this has to be done all year round, no matter what the weather, how busy you are or how tired you feel.

Believe it or not, there *are* some advantages in keeping a pony stabled. It is easier to keep him clean and smart-looking, the pony is always there when you want him and, if he is a well-bred pony, it is easier to keep him warm with rugs and blankets, especially if he is clipped (see Chapter 6). It is also easier to get a pony really fit when he is stabled.

Many ponies, despite what I have said, do love their stables, especially during the day in summer when they want to come in away from flies and sun, and at night in winter, when they can lie down and rest on a good bed and have a nice feed and ration of hay. It is only when they are kept in too long that trouble starts. Riding-school ponies, who work harder than privately owned ponies, often do well mainly stabled, but for privately owned ones it can be very stressful for pony and owner.

Keeping the pony at grass

Provided the pony has reasonable facilities, that is, enough grass in his field, safe fencing, clean water, shelter and company, he will probably do very well out at grass. He can eat, drink and exercise when he wants, enjoy the company of a friend or friends and dine on his natural food, grass.

The set-backs are that in summer he can suffer a great deal from heat and, particularly, flies if he has no shelter. Many people say flies are just something ponies have to put up with and ignore the fact that they can cause inflamed, ulcerated eyes, and jarred legs from the ponies stamping in irritation or galloping away from them in desperation. Manes, forelocks and tails do not give anything like enough protection and the flies come straight back when they are flicked off anyway.

Ask your vet to recommend a really good fly repellent, something like Absorbine SuperShield or a farm-type, long-lasting one, called a 'residual' repellent, and ask the vet to show you how to use it.

In winter, the pony's problems can be wind, wet and cold, and maybe lack of food and water. British winters are normally cold and wet rather than bitterly cold with snow and ice, although there are exceptions. There is practically no food value in winter grass, so you will have to take hay to the ponies at least once a day, probably twice. They might need concentrate foods, too (see Chapter 3). You'll also have to break the ice on their water. You'll be spared exercising, if you don't want to, and most of your grooming. Although you won't have to muck out a stable, you will have to remove droppings from the shelter and, ideally, from the land, too. This is explained in Chapter 3.

You'll have to keep a watch for exposure ailments like mud-fever, rain rash and rotten feet, in wet conditions, although native-type ponies are less likely to succumb to these than are horses or well-bred ponies. Lice can become a problem with grass-kept ponies, as well.

In summer, you can easily clean the pony and tidy him up for local shows and events, but in winter it's more difficult because of his long coat and the mud, unless you can keep him in the night before a special occasion. You can fence him in his shelter if you rig up slip-rails, but if there are other ponies, as there should be, you'll have to keep them all in or yours could try to jump the rails to get to his friends. Also, they might want to use the shelter, as normal.

Ponies kept on rich spring grass can develop laminitis and colic (see Chapter 10) or they may simply get so fat that they can't work properly or be made fit. In winter, unless you can arrange storage nearby, you'll have to cart feed, hay and bedding to the field, which can be a real chore, and sometimes it will be pitch black when you go to the field, so you'll have to carry a lantern or torch.

Combined system

Under this system the pony spends part of his day stabled and part out at grass. In summer he can be brought in during the heat of the day – especially useful if you are having to restrict his grass intake or if he has no shelter from flies or sun – and turned out at night. In winter, he can be out during the day and stabled at night.

The combined system is particularly ideal during term-time as you don't have to exercise the pony on weekdays, yet at weekends you can mostly stable him if you wish and can tidy him up on Friday night.

Yarding

This is a good system which is little used in Britain but popular in other countries. The ponies are kept in fenced areas with

---

The six essentials for a happy, healthy pony

Food A pony needs the right amount (not too much and not too little) of the right sort of food for him, for the work he does and the way he is kept. Always ask for advice if you are unsure what, or how much to feed.

Water Fresh, clean water is vital. A pony can drink up to 45 litres (8 gallons) a day in hot weather or if working hard, so always make sure he has enough and that it is clean, with no dirt, droppings or stale food in the container. Check automatic waterers and troughs, and, if your pony has a bucket, leave **two** overnight.

Shelter Although most ponies love being out in the open air, they do need shelter from weather and flies. If your paddock has little natural shelter such as trees, especially in high summer and mid-winter, do provide a shed for ponies who are out a lot.

Company Ponies are herd animals. Few are happy alone. They need natural contact with their own kind, just as we do, every day. Turning out two or more ponies together is the same as playtime at school for you, a necessary part of the day – not just a treat for special occasions.

Exercise Nature designed ponies to be on the move most of the time. Exercise is just as important as feeding and watering – and **more** important than grooming and tack cleaning. Many privately-owned ponies don't receive enough exercise, either ridden or turned out.

Space Ponies don't like being cooped up. Give yours a large enough stable and daily runs in the paddock.

prepared surfaces, perhaps peat, sand, fine shale, straw, sawdust, shavings or wood fibre. Often (and this is the best method) there is an open barn or shelter they can use and in some cases the yard is roofed over but with open sides.

Obviously, they are fed like stabled ponies as there is no grass, but otherwise they have freedom. The pony is available when you want him, stays reasonably clean and can do very well on this system.

Everything considered, probably the most convenient systems for you and your pony are the combined system, keeping him out with a proper shelter, and yarding, if you can find the facilities. Whichever system you use, remember the six most important things he'll need on a daily basis: food, water, shelter, company, space for freedom, and exercise.

3. Foods, feeding and grassland care

Food versus energy

Nothing can live or work without energy, and ponies, like all other living things, obtain their energy from food. The energy is used by the body in the following ways: firstly, and most importantly, to keep a pony's body temperature at about 38° C (100.4°F). If his temperature varies more than a very few degrees either way, he becomes very ill and can die. Secondly, it is used to make body tissues such as muscle, skin, bone, teeth, horn, hair, tendon etc. Thirdly, it is used by the pony to put on weight, which means his body is storing food as fat. This can only happen when all the other requirements are fulfilled and he is getting more food than he immediately needs. Lastly, food provides energy for work and this means any movement at all – from jumping round a hunter trial course to keeping his heart beating.

If we don't give a pony enough food, he becomes listless and weak and loses weight because his food is being used to keep his body temperature at the right level. In winter, this obviously takes more energy than in summer. If we feed him too much he will put on weight, maybe too much, and might also suffer laminitis, colic or other disorders.

If a pony is thin, we obviously need to give more food than normal to bring his weight up to scratch; if he's too fat, we must cut it down. You should aim to keep your pony nicely rounded so that you can just feel (but

not see) his ribs under his skin. If in doubt, ask someone knowledgeable at your Pony Club, riding school, or ask your instructor.

If the pony's backbone is very obvious, if his hipbones stick out and you can count his ribs, he is much too thin and should not be ridden at all till he has been restored to good health and condition, otherwise he will be using up too much goodness from his food in making energy for work when he should be using it to put on weight. Check with your vet how much (and what) to feed a thin pony, as simply giving him as much as he can eat, or too many concentrates, can cause even more problems such as colic and laminitis, even in a thin pony.

On the other hand, a pony who is too fat cannot just be given nothing but water. His diet will, though, have to be very carefully controlled under expert supervision.

The digestive system

You already know that ponies in nature eat most of the time and that their natural food is grass. To keep them comfortable and ensure that their digestive systems are working properly, we must feed them a little food very often. If they're out at grass, this is easy. When they're indoors we can make sure they always have a supply of good hay in the stable, except for an hour before work. Ponies cannot work on a full stomach any more than you can. The stomach and lungs lie close to each other and if the stomach is full the lungs cannot expand and fill with air properly; when they try, they can press against the stomach and interfere with digestion. This can make the pony ill, usually with colic.

Ponies take in food with their lips and front teeth. Their tongues and cheeks move the food around so that the back teeth can grind it up and mix it with saliva, which starts off the digestion process.

Once swallowed, the strong digestive juices soak into the food and it starts to become more like a creamy pulp. The food travels on down the intestines, fleshy tubes which are divided into compartments and lined with blood vessels. The intestines squeeze the food along and mix it with other digestive juices which extract the goodness from the food. This is absorbed by the blood vessels and carried via the bloodstream all round the body, being used for the purposes already described. Any food not absorbed is passed out of the body as droppings.

Different types of feeds

Water

Although perhaps not strictly a food, water is absolutely essential to life: a pony can die in a very few days without water. Water makes up nearly threequarters of your pony's (and your) body. There is water in blood, digestive juices and mares' milk. When your pony sweats, he loses water; there is water in his droppings and, of course, in his urine.

Like us, ponies drink more in hot weather than in cold and during hard work than in light. Roughly, a pony could need between 22 and 45 litres (5–10 gallons) a day. So a constant, clean supply is most important.

Foods are divided into what are called roughage or bulk foods and concentrate foods, with an extra category called succulents or roots.

Hay

Hay is classed as a roughage/bulk food. As well as containing nourishment, it contains fibrous, woody material which bulks out the intestines and helps digestion. Good quality hay can provide all that ponies need, unless they are the sluggish type or are working very hard, when they need extra 'zip' from concentrates.

Hay is close to the pony's natural feed, grass, because it is just dried grass. Because of its fibre content, it needs chewing slowly and thoroughly, so apart from providing nourishment it also keeps ponies occupied and entertained during long hours.

Apart from an hour before working, stabled ponies should have a constant supply of hay so they can feed naturally and boredom is prevented. Most ponies eat only what hay they need and do not gorge themselves or become too fat (as they would if given too many concentrates) although there is the odd exceptionally greedy pony.

There are various types of hay and the best type for ponies is meadow hay. These days, natural meadow hay is almost impossible to obtain because so many of our traditional hay meadows have been given over to cereal crops. However, specially sown meadow hay is often available. A type of hay called mixture hay can also be good for ponies, especially if you explain to the merchant you are buying it from that it *is* for ponies and must not be a very 'rich' mixture, with high feeding value.

Types of hay to avoid are seed hay (some people call this racehorse hay) and clover hay, both of which are far too nourishing for ponies.

Hayage

Sometimes called haylage, this is also a roughage feed but moister than hay. It is a sort of cross between hay and silage, which is a very wet, green feed fed to cattle; it is made of grass, or other green crops, cut when

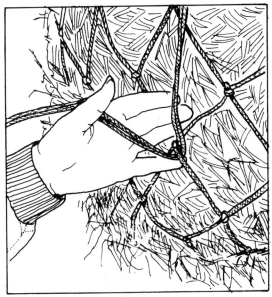
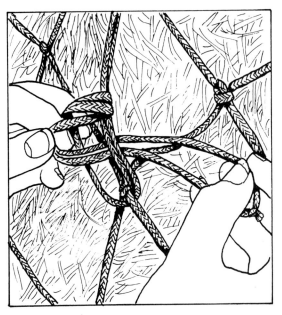
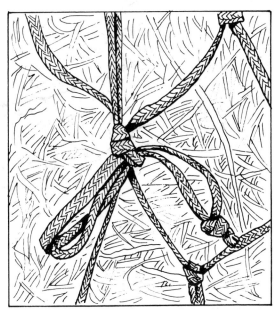

How to tie up a haynet: *Top left:* Thread the drawstring through your ring and pull it up as high as it will go. *Top right:* Pass the drawstring through one of the meshes about half way down the haynet. *Bottom left:* Hoist it up again, almost to the ring. Then pass the loose end of the drawstring behind the other piece and pull it through in a loop like this. Pull down with both hands . . . *Bottom right:* . . . and it will tighten into a half bow, like this. If you leave it like this the pony might be able to pull it down by fiddling with the loose end on the right, but if you pass this through the loop on the left you'll tighten it up (not too hard) and prevent this, yet still be able to undo it easily yourself.

young and sealed in special containers to 'pickle' in its own juice.

Hayage is sold under brand names such as Hygrass, Propack or Horsehage and comes in polythene bags. Its advantage over hay is that ponies allergic to hay (and there are a few) can usually eat hayage without any of the coughing or wheezing that their allergy brings on. In years when hay is hard to come by, hayage can be used as all or part of the ration.

To introduce a pony to hayage, first add a little to his usual hay ration and gradually mix in more, over two or three weeks, till he is eating all hayage.

This is molassed chop, which is tastier than ordinary chop. It is useful for mixing with concentrates to encourage the pony to chew his food properly, and to form the basis of a 'false' feed, perhaps mixed with sugar-beet pulp or grated or sliced carrots or apples, when a pony is not being fed concentrates.

Chop

Sometimes wrongly called chaff, this is hay and/or straw cut into short pieces, about 2 cm (1 in.) long, and mixed with concentrate feeds to bulk them out and add that all-important fibre. It also makes greedy ponies chew their food properly. You can either cut your own at home with a small machine or buy it ready-cut from a good merchant. (Bad merchants simply sell you sweepings from the warehouse floor, full of dust and dirt.) You can buy chop mixed with molasses (black treacle), which most ponies love, under the brand name, Mollichaff.

Straw

Yes, it can be quite all right to feed ponies straw! The best eating straw is oat straw and, although ponies will prefer hay or hayage, oat straw can be used to eke out hay or hayage when supplies are short.

In years when the hay crop is bad and you

have to feed straw instead, you may also have to feed a protein supplement. This is a product you add to your pony's food which will provide more protein, the part of his food which enables him to make new body tissues, such as skin and muscle. There is very little protein in most straws, so explain the situation to your vet and ask whether a protein product of some kind will be needed.

Now we move on to concentrate foods, called thus because they are more concentrated than roughage feeds as regards food content and contain only a little fibre.

Nuts or cubes
Pony nuts or cubes are popular and convenient to feed. A good brand will contain the right amounts of vitamins and minerals for your pony and will probably say on the bag how much you should feed your pony, depending on his size etc.

Coarse mixes
Like good pony nuts, these contain all the nutriments your pony needs and most manufacturers advise how much to feed either on the bag or in a booklet obtainable from your supplier or direct from them. With coarse mixes you can see all the different ingredients that go into the feed. Most ponies like coarse mixes whereas some become bored with cubes all the time.

Oats
Oats have been a traditional horse food for a very long time but they are not suitable for ponies as they can over-excite them, making them difficult to handle and ride, and can cause laminitis. Only very sluggish ponies,

This is coarse mix, a mixture of different concentrates in the same sack. You can spot here flaked maize, bruised barley, crushed oats and little pellets of dried grass. Different brands contain different ingredients.

those working really hard or out in bitter weather should be given oats, and then only about half a kilogram or a pound or two a day. This is especially important for small ponies.

Barley

This is a better alternative to oats for ponies needing something extra. It should be fed either cooked and flaked, or bruised or rolled, which means the whole grains have been crushed at the mill; this makes it easier for the pony to chew and digest.

Maize

Maize is obtainable cooked and flaked and looks like giant yellow cornflakes. It is made from corn on the cob. It is good for putting weight on thin animals or providing extra energy but is not suitable as a feed on its own as it is too starchy and can cause the same problems as oats.

Before feeding, oats should be crushed, like the sample above, as whole oats are often not chewed properly.

Right, above Bruised barley. Although this particular sample has been bruised rather hard until it is almost crushed, it is still acceptable for feeding. When barley is over-crushed, it becomes powdery and floury and ponies tend to swallow it without chewing it properly unless some fibre is added to the feed, such as chop.

Right, below Flaked maize. The seeds of corn on the cob are cooked and flattened into flakes. Flaked maize looks just like yellow cornflakes, but is harder.

Bran

Strictly speaking bran is a bulk food. It is the outside husk of wheat grains, left after the wheat has been milled to make flour. Many people feed far too much bran, which is inadvisable because it is not nourishing enough to be used as a food on its own and it

contains rather a lot of phosphorus, which can cause brittle, enlarged bones if overfed.

It is traditionally used to make bran mashes which are supposed to be suitable for ponies off work or on restricted exercise. It has a laxative effect when fed damp or in a mash and is said to be easy for sick ponies to digest. In fact, it is the other way round. It is *hard* to digest, so is certainly not suitable for a sick pony. It is also tasteless and not enticing to eat, and the reason it has a laxative effect is *because* it is hard to digest. The body wants to get rid of it as soon as possible, so moves it on down the intestines.

Bran is expensive, and good quality bran, with large, floury flakes, is very hard to find. It might be useful in small quantities (say a small double handful) to bulk out a feed or to damp with diluted black treacle for mixing with worming medicines, but generally, you and your pony can live without bran.

For novice pony owners, it is important to

A sample of broad bran. Bran is the remains of the wheat-grain husk, left behind after milling, and a little helps add bulk and fibre (roughage) to concentrate feeds. It should have broad flakes like this; the smaller and finer it is the worse its quality (and lower feeding value).

obtain good hay or hayage as the basis of the diet and to add concentrates, if your pony needs them in cold weather or during hard work, in the form of a good coarse mix or cubes. You can buy your feeds from an animal feeds supplier (look in *Yellow Pages* under 'Animal feed merchants') or ask your instructor or consultant where to buy. He or she can also give you detailed advice on what your pony is likely to need, too.

Roots or succulents
These are things like carrots and apples, both of which most ponies love. Some like turnips and most enjoy sugar-beet pulp.

This photograph helps to show the difference between sugar-beet cubes and ordinary pony cubes. The darker sugar-beet cubes are on the left and the lighter-coloured pony cubes are on the right. It is most important that you *never* mix them up. Sugar-beet cubes often look a little rougher than pony cubes.

This comes in cubes (which must *never* be confused with ordinary pony cubes) which are dark grey in colour, or in dry, grey shreds loose in a sack. Some have molasses in them.

You must soak sugar-beet pulp in *at least* twice its own volume of water for about twenty-four hours before use. Take a stable bucket and fill it no more than half full with beet, then top it right up with cold water and leave it till the next day. Squeeze out a good double handful for each pony and mix it with the ordinary food. Use it all up the same day or it might go bad.

For one pony, put a smallish double handful of dry beet in the bucket and fill it about a third full of water. Next day squeeze out the beet and add it to the feed. This way you won't have any waste. Some ponies also like to drink the water in which the sugar-beet has been soaked, but make sure you offer it *before* feeding, not after, thereby keeping to the rules of good feeding given later in this chapter.

A stabled pony should have about 1.5 kg (3–4 lbs) of roots a day added to his feeds. If he is receiving only hay, the roots can be put in his manger, say, at feed times, when other horses or ponies in the yard are being fed, so he doesn't feel left out.

Carrots must be thinly sliced lengthways so there is little chance of a piece choking the pony should he not chew it properly. Apples can be sliced or cut into small chunks and turnips can be given whole for the pony to scrunch on.

Roots take the place of grass for stabled ponies. Those on grass every day do not really need them.

How to tell good feed from bad

As ponies have such delicate digestions, they must only be given good quality food; anything else can make them ill.

One of the best ways to tell if food is fit to give is to take a good sniff. Food should smell sweet and appetising or else have little real smell at all. If *any* food – hay, coarse mix or whatever – smells sour or musty don't use it. Send it back to the merchant and don't pay for it.

Hay, in particular, should smell good. If it smells of nothing it is not necessarily unfit to feed but may simply be of low feeding value. Hay should look bright, golden to greenish in colour not dull, yellow or brown, with closed seed heads and plenty of leaf. It should feel springy rather than flat and lifeless. Most importantly, it should have no dust or mould in it. Mould will be seen as white, green or black patches and there might also be damp parts. If you shake out the hay and dust flies around, again this is a bad sign. It might make you cough, so imagine what it would do to your pony if he were to eat it.

Ponies often leave poor food unless they are very hungry, so apart from being dangerous it is also a waste of money and the pony loses weight.

Storage

To keep your feedstuffs in good condition, store them properly. Hay should be kept under cover in a dry, airy place, not exposed to the weather. Concentrates should preferably be stored in galvanised steel bins or plastic dustbins with lids tied on, so as not to encourage rats and so that the pony can't get into them by accident, which could make him very ill. The feed room should be cool, dry and airy.

Roots should be hard and crisp with no soggy, bad patches, and can be stored in a plastic mesh laundry bin where the air can get at them.

Some foods, such as coarse mixes and any foods containing molasses or other syrups which are sometimes added to pony nuts to bind the ingredients together, do not keep at all well in warm weather, which is why feed rooms should be cool. Molassine meal itself goes bad very quickly in warm weather, within a couple of days. It could be a good idea to have a large refrigerator in the feed room, with the shelves removed, into which you could fit perhaps a small sack of molassine meal and a sack of coarse mix. Sugar-beet pulp also often contains molasses, so this could be another candidate for 'fridge' storage.

Rules of feeding

Feed little and often. It is safe to feed a lot of hay all at once as the pony will eat it slowly, as described. Concentrate feeds, however, must be given frequently in small amounts, with no more than about 1 kg (about 2 lbs) in one feed. If the pony has only one feed a day, give it at night when he has most time to digest it. Never feed just before you ride. Allow at least an hour after feeding before working.

Water before feeding. If your pony has water constantly available, this is not so important as if he does drink it will be a small, harmless amount. If you have to provide water any other way, water first then feed, otherwise undigested food could be washed from the stomach into the intestines and cause colic. Also, too much water in the stomach dilutes the digestive juices and makes digestion less effective.

Make any changes in diet gradually. Sudden changes in foodstuffs, amounts or times of feeding can upset the digestion, so make changes over a period of days or weeks.

Use good quality food. As described, poor quality food can make your pony ill.

To be on the safe side . . .

- Don't give ponies concentrates unless absolutely necessary, for example if the pony is genuinely working hard or needs building up from poor condition.
- Keep your pony on poor-quality grazing, to help avoid laminitis and prevent him becoming overweight.
- Follow the golden rules of feeding, and especially always feed good quality food. Some merchants will try to palm you off with poor quality food because 'it's only for ponies'. Learn to recognise bad food, as described in this chapter, and refuse to pay for it. Certainly don't give it to your pony.
- If you are unsure what to feed your pony, always ask your vet or instructor. Don't take chances.
- Remember that ponies were meant to have a little food passing through their digestive systems most of the time. It is unnatural for them to become really hungry and it can cause colic. Except for an hour or two before work, make sure yours has hay or grass always available for him to nibble at when he feels the need, unless, for some reason, your vet advises otherwise.
- Another reason for not letting your pony become very hungry is because, in that condition, he's more likely to eat poisonous plants. If your paddock is very bare, feed him before turning him out, so he won't be tempted to eat nasty-tasting poisonous plants. And remove them from your paddock as soon as you can.
- It's safer, as far as concentrates are concerned, to feed too little rather than too much.

Do not work immediately after feeding. Always wait at least an hour if you possibly can. Half an hour is the very minimum, and then the pony can do only walking work.

Feed roots or succulents every day to stabled ponies to replace grass.

Feed according to work, weather and the pony's personal needs. Generally, the pony should have as much hay as he wants. Concentrates may not be needed for ponies. If they are, feed only as much as is needed to keep the pony nicely rounded but not fat. If he does put on weight, cut out concentrates and restrict spring and summer grazing by stabling part of the time.

Try to keep to a routine. This is less important for grass-kept ponies who always have access to food or, in winter, hay. Stabled ponies are more tying, but if they have a constant supply of hay, varying the feeding time by half an hour now and then won't matter. In general, though, it's better to keep to regular times.

How much?

Deciding how much to give a pony can be one of the most difficult questions to resolve, especially as ponies are all different and need different amounts. Ask your instructor or consultant, or the pony's former owner. Generally speaking, though, a small pony (say, under 12.2 hh) might need 2.5-3.5 kg (5-8 lbs) of hay a day, one of 12.2 hh about 4.5-5.5 kg (10-12 lbs) and one of 14.3 hh roughly 4.5-6.8 kg (10-15 lbs). Be careful with concentrates as it is so easy to overdo them with ponies. Small ponies rarely need any and should never have oats in any case. In very cold weather or if stabled and working hard, they might need 0.5 – 1 kg (1-2 lb) of cubes or coarse mix daily, plus succulents. At the other end of the scale, a 14.3 hh pony with some Arab or Thoroughbred blood, stabled and working hard or mainly out in cold weather, could need from 2.7-3.5 kg (about 6-8 lbs) split into two feeds, morning and night.

If the pony has grass in spring and summer, these amounts will probably need cutting down. Keep a close eye on the pony's condition and make sure you can always just feel his ribs beneath his skin. If you can't feel them, he's too fat; if you can see them, he's too thin. In winter, his long coat will hide his condition so push your fingers through all that hair and have a good poke about. He can be a little fatter in winter than in summer to help keep out the cold, but not too much. If in doubt, ask someone experienced for advice.

Preparing feed

All containers must be kept clean. Scrub and thoroughly rinse water and feed buckets daily, also portable mangers.

Have a pair of kitchen scales in your feed room and *always* weigh concentrates before feeding – don't guess, you can easily get it wrong. Hay can be shaken out and put into a haynet and weighed by hanging it from a spring weigher available from feed merchants. If you do not use nets, put the hay on an opened-out feed sack, hook the four corners to the weigher, then carry it in the sack to the pony.

Nuts or cubes are fed dry unless soaked beet is added, which will moisten them. Coarse mix is usually moist anyway, as it has molasses added. Other concentrates often benefit from being slightly damp as it is easier for the pony to chew them. Thoroughly mix feed with a clean stick or washed hands and give it in a strong plastic bucket or washing-up bowl, or tip it into the manger. Don't leave buckets, especially metal ones, in the stable or field as the pony might hurt himself on them.

Make a habit of changing your pony's water two or three times a day rather than simply topping up water which might be stale or dirty.

When feeding ponies in a field, always put out at least one more bucket of food than is needed so any timid ones always have somewhere to go if bullies chase them off their own bucket. With hay, hang up at least one more net than the number of ponies and try to feed it under cover (in the shelter). A long wooden hayrack (the cattle type) fixed at pony's head height along the back of the shelter is a convenient way to feed hay to outdoor ponies, but if there are any timid ponies give them an extra supply elsewhere in a sheltered spot.

With concentrates in the field, try to stay to see fair play and notice if any pony seems to be being bullied away from its food. This only takes about fifteen to twenty minutes and is well worthwhile.

Understanding feed labels

With brand-name feeds like cubes and coarse mixes, the scientific analysis (breakdown) of what the food contains will be printed on the bag, and the thing to look for is the amount of digestible energy the food contains. Digestible energy means how much energy ('action power' if you like) the pony will get out of 1 kg (2.2 lbs) of the food, and for ponies 8.5 to 10 MJ (megajoules – a scientific measure of power) per kg is right.

This information should also be on hayage, but you will not find it on hay, oats, barley, maize or bran. Your vet can give you an idea of what these foods contain, and also help you make up a suitable diet for your pony.

Grassland care

Basic grassland care is not difficult and, whether or not the land is yours, the condition of the pasture will affect your pony's health and well-being. If you have to inspect fields to find a suitable one for your pony, you need to know what to look for so that you don't put him somewhere useless or dangerous.

A field can contain much more than grass.

There are many different types of grasses for a start, also herbs, which are good for ponies, and poisonous plants, which are not. Ponies will have favourite grasses which they eat right down to the ground and will leave those they don't like. This means the field will become patchy after a few weeks, with long and short areas.

To make matters worse, ponies allocate at least one part of their field as a loo area where they do droppings. They will not eat the grass there so the whole area is wasted from a grazing point of view.

If ponies are kept on the same field for months on end, it becomes badly uneven. The favoured areas are constantly eaten and never have a chance to grow while the others are ignored. In time, this means that the field is hardly producing any grass and the ponies begin to get bored and hungry. This is when they often start chewing fences, jumping out if they can and experimenting with poisonous plants, even though most of them taste bitter. A field in this condition is called 'horse sick'. It becomes little more than an exercise area whereas, with a little care, it could be a varied dining table.

How much land do you need?

For one pony you need at least half a hectare (1-1½ acres) if you want your pony to obtain most of his food off it. For each additional pony add about a third to half a hectare (say, 1 acre). Ponies can become ill if on rich grazing, such as is used for milking cows. They are better off with poorer quality, but clean, grass over a larger area than on small, rich paddocks. The space helps satisfy their urge to wander and the poor quality grass will not put on too much weight or cause laminitis.

Orchards are not normally suitable for ponies as they often gorge on windfalls and, again, make themselves ill. Chemical sprays can linger there, too, with similar results. If the orchard is no longer productive,

however, it could certainly be better than nothing.

Different soils grow different types of grasses; also the lie of the land together with the type of soil decides whether it is well drained or not. Clay soils are heavy, sticky and usually badly drained, and they bake hard in summer. Peaty soils hold water but are not as gooey as clay. Loam and sandy soils are well drained and usually stay fairly soft in summer.

Improving land

Many land operations are very expensive but digging a ditch so the water has somewhere to drain is cheaper than installing drainage pipes underground, and can make a great difference. It is possible to greatly improve most fields quite economically provided the drainage is reasonable.

You'll need expert help and patience to improve any piece of land. If you ring the Agricultural Development Advisory Service at the Ministry of Agriculture, Fisheries and Foods, whose number is in the telephone book, they can send a specialist to inspect and test your land and tell you what it needs in the way of fertilizers, and treatments such as harrowing and reseeding. Ask for someone experienced with horse pastures, as the requirements are quite different from those for cattle. If the field is treated with nitrogen, ponies must be kept off it for quite some time and it should be grazed with cattle first, as the first growth of grass after treatment will be too rich for ponies.

The ADAS representative will also tell you how to get rid of poisonous plants, usually by spraying them and/or digging them up by the roots. Some, particularly ragwort, which look like tall dark-yellow daisies growing in umbrella-like clusters, are *very* persistent and can take years to eradicate. When poisonous plants are killed, they must be taken right out of the field and burned; when dead they lose their bitter taste and ponies may eat them and become extremely ill.

Although thistles, docks and nettles look unsightly in a paddock, they are not poisonous, so you don't really need to worry about them. They simply take up space which could be better occupied by grass. Like poisonous plants, they can be cut down and removed, or left in the field, but if you want to make the best use of all your land, don't allow them to grow.

Poisonous plants in hay are just as dangerous. The best way to learn which plants are poisonous is to have a lesson from someone who knows and can show you the growing plants. Otherwise, it would be worthwhile buying a copy of *British Poisonous Plants, Bulletin 161*, available from any branch of Her Majesty's Stationery Office (see your telephone book for the address). This has good descriptions and pictures of many poisonous things and will help you.

Some of the most common plants, shrubs and trees you should learn to recognise and watch out for are thorn apple, ragwort, hemlock (looks rather like cow parsley but has purple patches on the stem), bracken, bryony, buttercup, laurel, rhododendron, laburnum, oak, yew, nightshades, charlock, foxgloves, horsetail, iris, hellebores, purple milk vetch, lupin, lily of the valley, greater celandine, henbane, ivy, larkspur, wood anemone, rushes, poppy, privet, monkshood, meadow saffron and marsh marigolds. This list may sound formidable – and it is not complete!

Because most (not all) poisonous things taste bitter, ponies only eat them when they are very hungry, but some develop a taste for them. If your pony has enough grass or other food, he is less likely to develop that taste by experimenting with poisonous things. Check

Poisonous plants to watch out for. *Left:* Ragwort, which has bright yellow, daisy-like flowers in umbrella-shaped clusters, with jagged leaves. *Middle:* Deadly nightshade, which has dark green leaves and purple and yellow flowers. *Right:* Yew, which is a tree, not a plant. It has dark green, shiny leaves.

your field every week during the growing season for poisonous plants appearing, and be very careful where you let your pony graze for a break when out hacking. If you can't get rid of offending plants you'll have to fence widely round them so that ponies can't reach them.

If you suspect your pony has poisoning, call your vet at once. Don't delay or you could lose your pony. Signs of poisoning could include staggering about, unsteady gait, great listlessness, drooling, sleepiness, loss of weight, poor appetite, diarrhoea, constipation, colic signs, not wanting to get up and generally looking ill.

A land-management rota

To keep your land in reasonable condition divide it into at least two parts, remembering that ponies need access to shelter and water at all times. Let the ponies graze one part only for a few weeks. When it starts to look patchy, move them to the other part and try to put some cattle in to graze the untouched grass in the first area,

Cattle eat freely round the ponies' droppings and do their droppings on the ponies' grazing areas, which will not bother the ponies at all and will add valuable natural fertilizer there.

There is one other big advantage to this practice: worm control. The cattle will eat the worms which are passed out in the ponies' droppings and this kills them as they can only live in ponies. So this helps keep worms in check. (See also Chapter 10.)

If cattle aren't available, cut down the long grass and give the field a good harrowing to scatter the droppings. This helps dry up and rot them, and will root out old, dead grass and so air the soil. Then rest the land for a few weeks. (Ideally, droppings should be picked up every day to help stop the spread of worms, but few people do so.)

Return the ponies to the first paddock and give the area they have just left the same treatment. This way land is managed properly, rested and will grow more grass. It is cheaper to feed your pony this way than to neglect the land and buy food because your paddocks are bare.

If the land is not yours and you rent it on a short-term basis, you can still divide it up and use areas in turn. Cut down any long grass, pick up droppings or spread them, harrow the land if you possibly can and try to put cattle on it occasionally. This shouldn't be too difficult as in many areas where there are ponies there are cattle too. Their owner may be willing to harrow the land in return for free grazing.

If none of these things is possible, try to rent one field for each season, or at least two, one for summer and a drier one for winter.

Making hay

Many pony owners try to save on buying hay by making their own, but it is very often not a success. Making hay is an art. You must know exactly when to cut it (when the grass is young and leafy and before the seed heads open). One day late can be critical to the food content of the crop, so you have to be certain that whoever is going to cut the grass will come when *you* want and not when they can fit you in.

Unless you can have the hay barn-dried on a farm, it'll have to be turned regularly to dry in the sun – and if there is no sun, or even worse, it rains, the crop can be poor or ruined altogether. Making your own hay is not a good idea for most pony owners.

4. Bedding

If we did not have to provide ponies with beds we would be saved one of the hardest jobs in stable work. Mucking out, especially to those not used to it, is back-breaking work and it takes time. Because it is a hard, boring job droppings are often shovelled out hurriedly leaving dirty bedding behind or taking too much clean bedding out. New bedding is scattered higgledy-piggledy round the box, often covering up whatever the owner or groom cannot be bothered to clear out.

In reality, mucking out and bedding down are just as important as the more attractive jobs like exercising and feeding. Dirty bedding and a smelly stable will affect a pony's well-being very quickly. If he is forced to stand in his own droppings and urine-soaked bedding his hooves can become rotten and diseased and his skin sore and infected. The ammonia fumes, which soon start to rise from a neglected bed, are also liable to cause swollen, runny eyes, coughs and sore throats. A sore throat in turn, will make eating painful, put your pony off his food and cause him to lose weight.

Why do ponies need beds?

Stabled ponies need bedding for various reasons. Firstly it encourages them to lie down and rest. In the wild, they can find a soft, fairly dry spot to lie on in most weathers, but the flooring of a stable is usually a hard, cold and uncomfortable base.

Ponies can doze standing up; they have a 'locking device' in their elbows which helps prevent them falling over. In wild conditions, this ensures that they can be off and away with the herd as soon as danger threatens. Getting up from the ground takes a few seconds, and could cause a fatal delay if a predator were approaching fast.

When things seem quiet and safe, however, some pones *will* lie down whilst others doze on their feet, doing 'guard duty' around the edge of the herd. When it is time for 'changing the guard', the sentinel ponies come in, and may even nudge the others to take their turn, before lying down themselves. It seems obvious, then, that ponies do need to lie down and rest and will only sleep standing up when the occasion demands. Without lying down their legs would never get any rest, and for a wild pony four sound legs are essential to whisk him away from danger. Similarly, a domesticated pony also needs four sound legs if he is to work for a rider.

The second reason for bedding is to keep the pony warm, by protecting him from draughts or cold striking up from the stable floor. It also cushions bony parts like hips, legs and head from injury and helps to keep him clean and dry.

Finally, bedding should help to drain away or soak up urine, so that the stabled pony does not have to stand in puddles all day.

Ponies hate to splash themselves when they stale (go to the loo) and, without bedding, many will wait till they are absolutely forced before doing so, which is obviously both uncomfortable and bad for them.

What makes a good bed?

The qualities of a good bed are the same for ponies as they are for us. It should be dry, clean, soft, warm and inviting. You wouldn't like it if you got into bed one night and found it was damp or dirty, smelt horrible or made you cough, and your pony won't like it either.

Bedding should be thick, not only for the pony's health and comfort but, odd though it might seem, for economical reasons too. Thin beds are really useless as they neither absorb urine nor drain it away. They cannot prevent cold and draughts, they are easily scattered or scraped away to expose the floor, they do not protect the pony when he lies down and are more easily dirtied, making it impossible to save any for re-use. Bedding should be clean and dry, without any lumps of material which have not been properly broken up or shaken out. The material used should be warm and not dusty or mouldy, which is bad for your pony's wind (breathing).

All in all, if you don't fancy rolling around in it yourself don't expect your pony to either.

Suitable materials

There are five main materials used for bedding in Britain – straw (nearly always wheat straw rather than oat, barley or rye); wood shavings (sometimes called wood chips); sawdust; peat (two sorts – sedge peat which looks just like brown soil and sphagnum moss peat which is rather like dried moss); and shredded paper (again two sorts, long or short strips).

Straw

Wheat straw is the straw that is left after the grain has been harvested to make bread, flour and breakfast cereals. It should be shiny and golden, clean, dry and with no smell. If it is dull and yellow, damp, dusty or, worse still, with white or blackish-green mouldy patches and smells musty and sour, don't use it.

Wheat straw, combined with your pony's droppings, makes good manure for gardens, mushroom growers and nurseries. You should have no difficulty in finding a contractor to buy it from you, or you could sell it yourself by the sackful.

If you have any old books on stable management, they will probably describe straw as 'drainage bedding', meaning it drains urine away rather than absorbing it. Nowadays combine harvesters crush the stems, and straw is so mangled up and broken that some of the urine is soaked into the stems. It will still make a warm, inviting bed as long as it is good quality. One disadvantage of straw, for ponies who are prone to allergies, is that the chemicals which are sprayed on growing crops can cause skin irritations, or wind or digestive problems if your pony eats his bed.

Other kinds of straw used for bedding include *oat* (softer, finer and very likely to be eaten), *barley* (also soft and easily flattened into a thin lumpy bed, although you need not worry about the old complaint of prickly awns irritating the skin, as combine harvesters now remove them) and *rye* (good but very expensive).

Wood Shavings

Wood shavings are a very common bedding these days. Unlike straw, they are packed in polythene bales and can be stored outside. New shavings beds scatter easily and are not as protective as straw, but once the base has become established, after a week or so, this problem disappears.

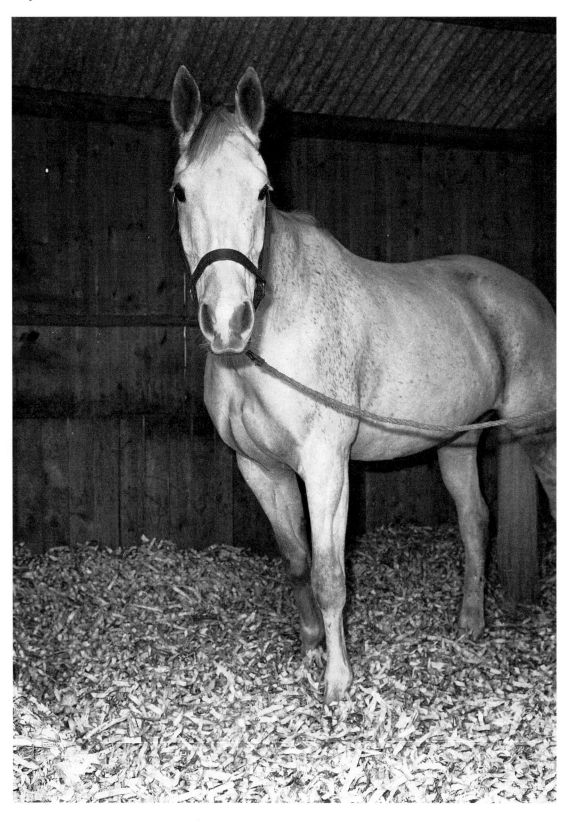

Shavings must be clean and dry without lumps of wood or nails which would injure your pony. They are not as popular for manure as wheat straw, but many contractors *will* take them, largely because so many people now use them that straw manure is becoming scarce. As trees are often sprayed with chemicals, shavings could again cause an allergy problem in sensitive ponies.

Sawdust

Sawdust is less common as a bedding but can be satisfactory if you use enough. Again, you might have problems disposing of it in some areas, and odd cases may also have chemical spray residues. Like shavings, sawdust is usually baled in polythene which is handy for storage. Some people say it makes a pony's feet hot (they should always be cool) and that the bed itself warms up and becomes smelly, but this can be avoided if it is kept clean.

Peat

Peat of both types, in my experience, does not make good bedding material. It is very absorbent, even more so than sawdust, and because of this I have always found it impossible to keep the bed dry. Unlike the other materials, it is cold (it may even freeze on top in a hard winter) and dusty, so it can make ponies cough and their coats look dull.

Paper

Shredded paper is an excellent bedding, particularly for horses and ponies with allergy problems. It is not at all dusty and has no chemical residues. As it is not widely used yet, there are problems in disposing of the resulting manure in some areas, although some makers may be able to advise you on this.

Watch out for metal staples which can

Left Shredded paper bedding, made by Diceabed International Ltd.

occasionally appear in some brands and which could stick into your pony. Again, this paper bedding is usually packed in polythene sacks.

Tools for mucking out

The right tools make any chore easier, and mucking out is certainly a chore. You should be able to buy your tools from a good saddler, tack 'supermarket' or farm goods supplier. Buy the best you can afford and *do* make sure they are small enough for you to handle comfortably. The job is hard enough as it is, and big, heavy tools make it worse.

You will need:

A long-handled **shovel** to pick up droppings and soggy bedding.

A four-tine (that is, four-pronged) **stable fork,** or a two-tine pitchfork for shaking and spreading straw or paper bedding.

A stiff-bristled **broom** for sweeping up the yard and stable. Choose the sort with natural bristles as plastic ones split and clog up.

A **wheelbarrow** for carrying manure to the muck heap. Two wheels are easier to balance and push than the one-wheeled types when full. They are also less likely to tip up!

A **rake** for spreading shavings or sawdust beds.

A **skep** (pronounced **skip**). Not essential but useful for removing droppings between mucking out sessions. They look like deep rubber or plastic trays, but you can manage just as well with an old dustbin lid, stable bucket or a plastic mesh laundry basket.

A pair of **rubber gloves** . Useful for picking up hidden piles of droppings, particularly from sawdust or shavings where they mingle with the bedding easily.

The wheelbarrow is the most expensive item, but you could do without it and use an opened-out feed sack instead. Shovel your

muck into the middle of it, gather up the four corners and you can then heave it over to the heap. You do need to be strong enough to lift it though, dragging it along the ground will wear it out in no time.

Different systems of managing a bed

There are three systems for coping with your pony's bed.

Full mucking out and bedding down

All the droppings and very dirty bedding material are taken out of the bed every morning. Clean and slightly soiled material is saved for re-use. The floor is swept, washed down if possible, and the bed relaid completely from scratch. This method is time-consuming if done properly, but keeps the stable clean and free from smells.

Mucking-out tools. *From left to right:* a three-tine pitchfork, useful for shredded paper bedding; a shavings rake; a four-tine fork for straw; a plastic crate used as a large-size skip with binder twine attached to drag it along the ground; a shovel; a yard broom and a wheelbarrow. The muck is heaped into a trailer (behind the tools) which can be towed away by a nursery contractor when full and an empty one left in its place.

Deep litter

The opposite system is called deep litter. Litter is just another word for bedding, usually straw or sawdust, 'deep' because bedding is not removed but simply added as a light top covering every day. This means, of course, that although droppings should be taken out as usual, the urine-soaked bedding stays in. It may sound dirty but, in a properly ventilated stable, the system works well, provided you are careful to remove all the droppings.

A pony does about eight lots of droppings in twenty-four hours. For a deep litter system to work properly these must be removed at least three times daily if the pony is stabled all the time. Otherwise he will trample on them and his bed will become too dirty. If the pony is turned out for some of the time, picking up the droppings twice a day may be sufficient. Unless the droppings are removed completely they will start to rot like a muck heap.

The urine will drain down to the bottom of the bedding which soaks it up and, in practice, you should get no smells or fumes from it provided you keep adding enough bedding and leave open the window and top door of the stable. If your stable is not well ventilated, only use this system in winter.

How often should you clear out a deep litter bed? Some people will say when the pony is in danger of hitting his head on the stable roof! The reason the bed does not build up tremendously is that the material at the bottom gradually rots away to nothing; you don't smell anything because of all the fresher material on top. However most owners remove the bed every six months, although occasionally it can be left for longer, providing the bed is soft, warm and springy, with no dampness or smells. These are the advantages of a well-managed deep litter bed, along with the saving on work and new bedding material.

When you do come to clear out the box, you will need adult help or a party of friends, because it will be a long, heavy job.

Semi-deep litter

This is an in-between system which many people find ideal. The droppings and the worst of the bedding are taken out each day, the bed levelled off and clean material spread on top. This works well provided you are careful to remove droppings frequently, and put in enough fresh material. It is useful if you are at school during the week and only

have time to muck out properly at weekends.

This system can be used with any bedding material, and is the normal way to manage shavings and shredded paper bedding.

Ventilation test

To check your stable ventilation, stand in the fresh air for a few minutes, then walk into the stable and take a long, deep breath. Notice whether there is much difference in the smell, 'feel' or temperature of the air. There should be hardly any difference at all. If the atmosphere feels warm or muggy, or there is a very noticeable smell of pony or mustiness, then the ventilation is poor and you are not managing the bed properly.

How to muck out and bed down

Straw bed

First pick up all the obvious droppings and put them in the wheelbarrow, checking for any piles that may be hidden in the bed. Some ponies have tidy habits and always dung in the same place in their boxes while others do droppings all over the place. Decide which is the cleanest corner of the box and pile all the clean straw there with the stable fork. Separate all the slightly soiled straw and pile it in another fairly clean corner.

You will be left with the really dirty, wet bedding and any droppings you may have missed. Shovel all this into your barrow.

Now, with the stable broom, thoroughly sweep every part of the floor, getting right into the two empty corners. Scrape up any stubborn dirt with the edge of the shovel, and leave the sweepings just inside the doorway.

You can now move your two piles of straw to the finished corners with the fork and sweep the last two corners clean. Shovel the sweepings into the barrow and cart it off to the muck heap, using the barrow to bring back new bedding.

The secret of successful bedding, whatever material you use, is to be sure you take out *all* the droppings, otherwise your box will heat up like an indoor muck heap.

Strictly speaking, the next job should be to rinse down the floor, scrubbing it as you go with the stable broom, but in many yards this is just done once a week. Disinfectant can be added to the water but is not essential.

Ideally, after sweeping, the floor should be left bare to air and dry while the pony is out, for exercise or in the field. If you can do this, open the windows and doors wide.

To bed down, spread the pile of slightly dirty straw evenly across the floor with the fork. Cover it with a second layer of the clean straw. Next, bring in your fresh straw and shake it out thoroughly so that there are no hard lumps or wedges, and spread it evenly on the top.

Finally, fork up the straw around the edges to make a cushion along the sides and into the corners of the box. This stops draughts and acts as a buffer when the pony rolls or lies down, bouncing him back into the middle of the box. If a pony gets stuck or 'cast' with his legs in such a position that he cannot get up again without help, he may well panic and struggle violently, knocking himself or even sustaining a serious internal injury. This is why it is very important to bank up the bed around the edges of the stable, even if it does seem an uneconomical thing to do.

Finally, smooth the bed with the fork so that the finished product looks as much as possible like a bird's nest, not a rough sea.

Deep litter straw

All you need to do is remove the droppings and lay fresh straw on top. Don't be tempted to dig over the bed as you will unsettle it and prevent it from stabilising.

Semi-deep litter straw

Remove all the droppings and the wettest of the straw. Using the fork, fill the spaces with clean straw from the bank round the sides, smooth the bed off evenly, and add new straw as necessary. Don't turn over the bedding or you will mix the clean and slightly soiled straw too much. When you come to muck out fully, at weekends perhaps, proceed as you would for ordinary mucking out – it will just take you longer.

Shavings, sawdust and shredded paper

These are usually easiest to manage on semi-deep litter, although, as mentioned earlier, sawdust can make good deep litter if you use plenty and remove all the droppings frequently.

For shavings and sawdust, as always, remove the droppings and soggiest patches and rake the top of the bed into the empty spaces.

When the floor is even, rake the clean material down from the banking and add new bedding to make a new bank.

For shredded paper, take out the droppings and wettest bedding. Separate the clean material into one corner and, using your fork, make a second pile of slightly soiled bedding in another corner, tossing it to help it dry out and air. Sweep the floor and re-make the bed as you would with straw. Leave it to dry off while the pony is out, then add fresh paper and make the usual bank round the sides.

What to do with the muck

The way you cope with manure depends on how you are going to dispose of it. If a contractor will take it, he will probably leave you a container to fill, replacing it with an empty one once a week, once a month or whatever you arrange.

If you are planning to sell your manure 'at the gate' to keen gardeners, who will only want to buy small amounts, you will have to do more work, but might make more money out of it. The simplest method is to put your muck straight into large polythene sacks and tie them firmly round the necks with binder twine from hay bales, or strong string.

If your customers don't want fresh manure for their garden compost heaps and prefer old, well-rotted manure to put straight on the ground, you will need three muck heaps; one that is old and ready to sell; one which is in the process of rotting and the third for fresh manure.

The heaps need to be convenient but also downwind of houses and stables, so the prevailing winds blow the smell away from living quarters. Otherwise the flies will be very unpleasant in summer and could be a health hazard, too. Place the heaps in a dip if you can, or run a ramp up to the top of them, so that you can simply tip your muck on to them instead of having to shovel it up by hand.

Beating the muck heaps down helps them

Tips and points to remember

• The secret of successful bedding is to keep it clean, as dry as possible, and plentiful.

• The bed should feel like a firm, springy mattress. If you can feel the floor under your feet, then the bed is not thick enough.

• Don't leave a bare patch at the door. A stabled pony spends most of his time looking out at the world and it is better for him to have bedding to stand on than a hard floor.

• Ponies do not like living in their own dirt any more than we do. Outdoors, they'll keep part of their field as a loo and stay away from it the rest of the time. When they are stabled, therefore, it is only fair to keep their bedding as clean as possible.

• Don't leave your pony with a thin 'day bed' as some people recommend. Thin beds do none of the jobs they are supposed to do and are a waste of money as well as being uncomfortable. A full bed should be the rule whenever your pony is indoors.

• Use an opened-out feed sack or your barrow to carry bedding to the stable to stop it dropping all over the yard.

• It's easier to deal with your pony's bed when he is out. Pop him into a neighbouring stable, do his box while he is turned out or tie him up outside unless it is very cold. If he has to stay in, tie him up and block the doorway with the wheelbarrow. Teach him proper stable manners so he moves out of your way while you work.

to rot, and keeping them neatly squared off makes them look tidy but during term time you may be better to spend the time attending to your pony.

Surrounding the heap on three sides with some kind of wall of old bricks, cement blocks or asbestos panels will keep in the heat produced in the rotting process, and make them tidier. Don't build your heap directly next to a wooden building as it will rot the wood in time.

Whether your pony is a show ring star or the kind you just hack around for pleasure, his well-being will be greatly improved if you recognise mucking out and bedding down for what they are – hard work maybe, but an important part of pony care.

5. Feet and shoes

You could be forgiven for thinking that your pony's feet are four hard, unfeeling blocks of horn because that's how they look from the outside. Horn itself *is* quite hard and because it doesn't contain blood or nerves, it *is* unfeeling. In fact, it is the same sort of substance as your fingernails.

But a pony's feet are not solid horn. You could perhaps think of them as horny boxes lined around the sides and on the bottom with sensitive fleshy tissues (which do contain blood and nerves), with bones in the middle.

When the pony has his hoof on the ground, the part you can see is the wall which grows down from the ridge at the top of the hoof, called the coronet (just as fingernails grow from the cuticle). If the coronet is injured, by a tread or knock, the horn growing from it can become cracked or weakened, sometimes permanently. It can take a pony about six months to grow a new hoof wall.

If you look at the underside of your pony's foot you will see that the rim of horn stops at the heels, which are like two fleshy bulbs. The underside of the hoof, the sole, is also horny but not so tough as the wall.

The outer rim of horn is the bearing surface, of the foot and carries most of the pony's weight. At the heels, this turns inwards in a v-shape to form the bars, two ridges with the space between them filled with rubbery horn, called the frog. Between the bars and the frog are two grooves called the lacunae (la-cun-ee). The frog itself has a groove down the middle, called the cleft of the frog.

The base of the foot (called the ground surface) is, therefore, not smooth but uneven, which gives a better foothold to the pony.

The frog is nature's shock-absorber and anti-slip pad.

The sole of the foot is arched slightly upwards and is of thinner horn than the wall, so it can be damaged fairly easily if the pony treads on, say, a broken bottle or sharp stone. The frog can be even more easily injured as it is not particularly hard.

Inside the horny wall, 'leaves' of horn called the insensitive laminae (lam-in-ee) run from the coronet to the sole. These interlock firmly with sensitive fleshy laminae which, in turn, are fixed to the outside of the pedal (pee-dal) bone, the crescent-shaped bone which gives the hoof its shape.

Fitted in behind the pedal bone is the navicular bone, and resting on top of the pedal bone and the navicular bone is the short pastern bone, which lies half in the foot and half out.

On top of this fits the long pastern bone, which is what we know as the pastern.

The cannon bone, with the two little sesamoid bones behind it, joins with the long pastern bone to form the fetlock.

Underneath the pedal and navicular bones

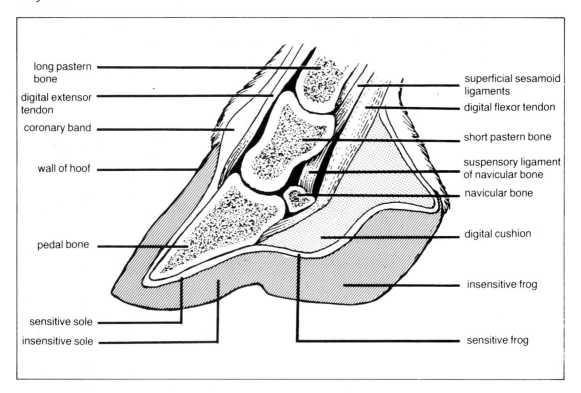

long pastern bone

digital extensor tendon

coronary band

wall of hoof

pedal bone

sensitive sole

insensitive sole

superficial sesamoid ligaments

digital flexor tendon

short pastern bone

suspensory ligament of navicular bone

navicular bone

digital cushion

insensitive frog

sensitive frog

are the sensitive sole and frog, with the horny sole and frog beneath them on the ground surface. Immediately over the heels inside the foot is a firm but squashy wedge of tissue called the plantar cushion which, like the frog, helps absorb jarring movement.

If you look at a pony's hoof on the underside without shoes, especially one freshly trimmed, you'll notice an area of whitish horn between the bearing surface of the wall and the sole. This shows the point where the sensitive laminae and horny laminae meet inside.

As well as these main structures, various ligaments, cartilages (gristle) and tendons attach to the various bones. Ligaments and tendons act like a pulley system, and enable your pony to move, although there is not space here to explain exactly how.

Why does the pony need shoes?

In the wild, ponies normally move over softer ground than a domesticated pony doing

This drawing shows some of the structures inside your pony's hoof. You can see how complicated the whole thing is; it is certainly not just a block of unfeeling horn.

roadwork, and their hooves wear down just enough to keep them in reasonable condition.

Domesticated ponies have to work harder and faster than wild ponies and with the additional burden of a rider. This causes the hooves to wear down more quickly, particularly on hard or rough ground. Unless shoes are fitted some working ponies soon become footsore. Therefore, many thousands of years ago, man invented horseshoes. The Romans used leather boots with lacing and the Arabs had metal plates with turned-up sides and a hole in the bottom for the desert sand to run out.

However, these ancient peoples soon realised that shoes prevented any wearing away of the horn at all, so they learned how to trim the overgrown feet so that the animals were still able to move properly and work for them. We still have this same problem today, of course. Nowadays, shoes are nailed to the feet through the insensitive horn and the farrier trims off any unwanted horn growth.

Different sorts of shoe

The type of shoe we have today was invented later and is a great improvement on the earlier styles. Formerly made of iron, shoes are now mainly of mild steel, forged into shape while the metal is hot and, therefore softer. Most farriers buy their shoes ready-made from a factory and simply alter them to fit individual 'clients' feet.

There are various kinds of shoes, from very light, thin aluminium racing shoes (called plates) for racehorses, to weighty solid shoes for working heavy horses.

In between comes the type of shoe most used for pleasure riding. It is called the hunter shoe. It is fullered (grooved) on the ground surface and concaved out (hollowed away in a curved shape) on the inside edge, so that the surface touching the hoof is wider than that touching the ground. The fullering gives better grip than a plain shoe and the concaving helps reduce suction in mud. The heels of the fore (front) shoes are tapered to a blunt point to lessen the chance of their being pulled off by the hind feet, and those of the hind shoes have shaped, thickened metal to give extra grip, the shaping on the

outside heel being called a calkin and the smaller one on the inside heel called a wedge.

In fact, calkins and wedges are not so much used now, since studs became popular. The former take some trouble to make, so most horses and ponies likely to be working actively in muddy conditions will have stud holes in the heels of their shoes (usually the hind and sometimes the front as well) so that the owner can screw or hammer in the sort of studs he or she thinks will help the pony best. Ask your farrier's advice on this.

The toes of the fore shoes usually have a raised piece of metal turned up against the wall, called a clip, to help keep the shoe on, and the hind shoes have clips at the quarters (sides). Hind shoes, particularly on traditional hunter shoes, often have rolled toes, that is, the metal at the toe on the ground surface is rolled or hammered back to lessen the chance of the fore heels being

A fullered, concaved shoe most used today for general-purpose riding. This is a front foot, so the shoe is almost circular in shape. It fits well and goes right back to the heels to support them without pressing into the frog. The frog, in this pony, is well developed and healthy. You can clearly see the cleft down the middle and the grooves down the sides, which should be carefully picked out twice a day with a hoofpick.

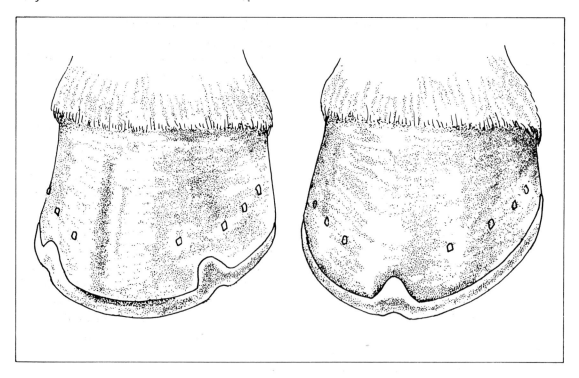

Can you tell which foot is which? The one on the left is a near hind foot and the one on the right a near fore. You can tell the difference by the positions and numbers of the clips and nails. The hind shoes have clips on each side of the toe, and the fore foot has a single clip at the front of the toe. As for the nails, there are usually four nails on the outside of a hoof and three on the inside.

trodden on and injured (called an over-reach).

This type of shoe is suitable, with and without studs, for most jobs. For showing, particularly at county level, light shoes, sometimes without clips, are used to enable a pony to lift his feet more easily and move smartly. Some people have heavy, thick shoes fitted for ordinary riding in the belief that they will last longer, but apart from straining the pony's legs and making it difficult for him to move well, they cause the feet to be put down harder and so, in fact, wear out quicker and jar the pony's legs at the same time. Light- or medium-weight shoes (if you do a lot of roadwork) are best.

How shoeing is done

There are two main kinds of shoeing – hot and cold. At one time, when farriers worked at their own forges, people took their horses and ponies to the forge and the animals were mostly shod hot. As the use of horses and ponies for work and transport declined due to the invention of motor cars and lorries, forges closed down and farriers started to travel to clients, taking with them portable forges or fitting the shoes on cold.

Hot shoeing is said to be better because the shape of the shoe can be more easily altered to fit the foot. However, provided your farrier knows your pony well he can make his shoes at home and obtain a very good fit cold. Unfortunately, if the shoes are *not* such a good fit, the farrier can do little to change them and this sometimes results in the foot being altered out of its natural shape to fit the shoe.

Before removing your pony's old shoes, a good farrier will ask you to walk and trot him on a loose rein so he can watch how he moves and consider if he can improve his action.

Next he will examine the existing shoes to see what sort they are and where the shoes wear most. After the feet have been trimmed, these shoes may be replaced if they are not very worn. This service is called a 'remove'.

First, the old shoes have to come off. When a shoe is nailed on (using specially shaped nails, not ordinary ones) the ends of the nails come out of the wall about 2 cm (1 in.) up from the ground and their long ends are twisted off with the claw end of a hammer. The remaining short stubs called clenches are hammered over to hook them down on to the wall and help grip the shoe in place.

To remove the shoe, these clenches must first be cut (straightened up); if the farrier tried to pull the shoe off without cutting the clenches, the hoof would be badly torn. He places a buffer, a wedge-like tool, under each clench and knocks it straight up by hammering on the buffer. There will

probably be four on the outer side of the hoof and three on the inner.

Next, he levers off the shoe from the heels using his pincers. He will then examine the shoe again. Then he will inspect the condition of the foot. He will cut away excess horn with a drawing knife or, if the feet are badly overgrown, with the pincers, clipping it off all round. Loose flakes of horn are trimmed from the sole and frog and the bearing surface will be smoothed level with a rasp, like a giant nail-file.

The rasp may be run round the edge of the bearing surface to remove any chipped or ragged bits of horn, but should not be used on the outside of the wall, which has a special covering, called the periople, which helps keep in moisture and natural oils. If it is scraped off, the quality of the horn could suffer.

Farrier's tools. On the top row, from the left, are the hammer, pincers and buffer. Under the buffer is the drawing knife, and along the bottom is the rasp.

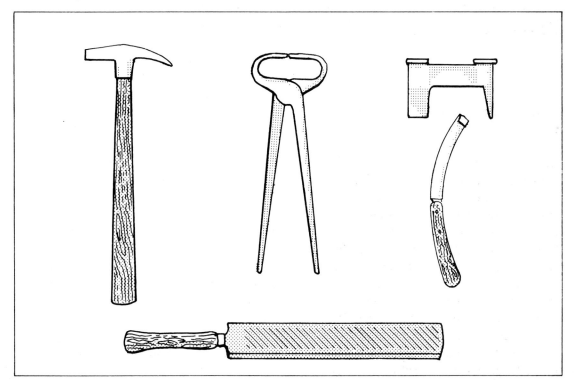

The farrier will measure your pony's foot and select the nearest size of shoe he has in stock, or make one to fit from a bar of metal. A ready-made shoe will be heated in the furnace till red hot and hammered to the correct shape on a special metal block, called an anvil. Nail holes will be inserted (stamped) and clips hammered out (drawn). Then, by sticking a pointed metal rod called a pritchel into one of the nail holes, he will carry the shoe to the pony and, while it is still very hot, press it lightly on to the bearing surface of the hoof.

The metal burns the horn (it doesn't hurt the pony) wherever it touches. As the horn has been rasped smooth, if the burn marks do not appear all round evenly, it means the shoe is not smooth. It will be carried back to the anvil and hammered into the right shape, then tried again. The farrier should *not* burn the shoe into the horn to make a 'bed' for a shoe that doesn't fit properly. This dries out the horn too much, then, when the hoof comes into contact with water again, the horn swells a little and becomes slightly too big for the shoe, possibly causing discomfort.

Some ponies are frightened by the sizzle, smoke and smell of burning horn and for nervous animals the farrier can shape the shoe while hot but cool it down (by plunging it into a bucket of cold water) before trying it. He'll then judge carefully where it needs altering, heat it up again before putting it right, cool it down and try again.

Once a good fit is obtained the shoe is nailed on, from toe to heel. Nails are kept away from the actual heel area as it is here that the foot expands or 'gives' most under weight.

The white line mentioned earlier is a guide to the farrier as to how far in to go with the nails and in selecting the right width of shoe for your pony. The nails ideally should only go into the bearing surface of the wall. They *can* go just into the white line if necessary, but if they go beyond it, they will probably penetrate the sensitive structures of the foot (known as 'pricking') or press against them (known as 'binding'), which will lame the pony. The shoe will then have to come off again and, in a bad prick, the vet called in.

The hammer used to nail on the shoe is called a driving hammer. As described, the

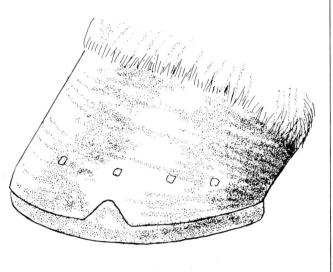

This drawing shows some features of a well-shod foot. The shoe fits the foot correctly; the foot has *not* been chopped about to fit the shoe, as so often happens, particularly at the front, and the shoe goes right back to the heels to give proper support there. You can tell this is a left back (near hind) shoe because there are four nails and the clip is at the front part of the side of the foot. Ther will be another clip on the inside of the shoe, where there will also be three nails. There is no 'daylight' showing between shoe and foot, which means the shoe will be steady on the foot, with even pressure.

claw end is used to twist off the clenches which are then hammered down. The clips are tapped into place and a little groove made in the wall just below the clenches to hammer them into. The clenches can be smoothed off with the rasp or pressed down with a device called a clencher. Finally, the edge of the rasp is run round the rim of the wall where it meets the shoe to round off the job and lessen the risk of cracking.

Some farriers finish off by applying hoof oil, but this serves no real purpose. Poor farriers oil hooves to disguise the fact that they have rasped the outside of the wall too much when tidying up a rough or hurried job.

After shoeing, the pony should be trotted up (led at the trot without a rider) on a hard surface such as a concrete path, to check that he is not lame. His lead rope should be fairly long and loose so that his head is not restricted and he can move naturally. Even a slight lameness can then be spotted, and the farrier can, if necessary, remove the shoe on the lame leg. Even a good farrier can very occasionally drive a nail too near the sensitive tissues inside the foot, which will cause lameness, but if the pony is trotted up after shoeing he can put matters right.

Studs

Depending on the work your pony does, he could need some sort of stud in his shoes, and this is something to discuss with your farrier. There are many different types of studs for different jobs: tiny needle-like studs for roadwork; chunky, square-shaped studs for cross-country in slippery muddy conditions; large pointed studs for hard, dry ground, and so on.

Shoes can have special holes put in the heels into which you screw the studs when they are needed. When the studs are taken out, the holes should be packed with oil-soaked cotton wool to keep them clean.

Some studs, such as tiny road studs, can be left in all the time but the larger ones must be taken out when not needed as they can alter the balance of the hoof when worn under ordinary conditions (the pony would feel as though he were treading on a stone all the time, which is obviously very uncomfortable).

Some people say studs should only be put in the outside heels of the shoes (that is, the left heels on the left shoes and the right heels on the right shoes); others feel it best to balance the feet by having studs in both heels despite the fact that, during fast work, the pony might strike into himself and a stud on an inside heel could cause a greater injury than would otherwise be the case. Similarly, some people never put studs in the front feet, only in hind ones. The whole subject is one which can only be decided after weighing up your individual pony's action, job and ground conditions. Your instructor and farrier should both be able to help you decide what studs, if any, your pony needs.

Going barefoot

If your pony works mainly on soft ground or *smooth* roads such as tarmac you could well manage without shoes, although the feet will still need expert trimming to correct any uneven wear and regular checks from the farrier.

If the pony is having several weeks' rest, it's a good idea to remove his shoes and let his feet get back to nature for a while.

Once horn has grown nothing can improve its quality. The horn is produced by the nourishment carried to the coronet band by the bloodstream – and that nourishment, as described in Chapter 3, gets into the bloodstream from the pony's food. Therefore, you can help ensure good quality horn by feeding your pony properly. Without good horn he cannot work without shoes. Poor horn breaks and cracks easily, is difficult for the farrier to nail shoes to, wears away quickly and makes for a footsore pony. Therefore, if you want to 'go barefoot' feed the pony properly.

The advantages of working without shoes are that the feet can work naturally, expanding and contracting fully and with full frog contact on the ground; many ponies stop slipping once they have no shoes on; unshod horses and ponies do not injure one another so much during skirmishes in the field and also the expense of shoeing is saved.

The disadvantages are that you cannot work the pony on rough ground such as stony tracks or roads treated with chippings. Smooth concrete, although harder than smooth tarmac, is all right provided you keep an eye on the feet and watch carefully to see that too much wear is not taking place. If the pony becomes footsore he might start taking shorter, pottery steps, going with his head lower than usual, dislike any pace other than walk and be generally unwilling to work; he might even start napping (refusing to go forward) and playing up. Watch for this behaviour.

If you and your farrier think your pony could go barefoot, the shoes are removed and the feet rasped smooth (but probably not have much horn taken away) and rounded off at the rim to help prevent chipping and cracking. Work gently on hard surfaces for the first few months so your pony's body 'realises' that harder horn must be produced. Gradually, the hooves will adapt if you work sensibly and produce tougher horn. Don't give up if he winces the first time he steps on a pebble. Be very careful where you take him, be considerate and persistent.

You may always need shoes in front for some ponies; ponies carry two thirds of their weight on their forehand so the front hooves take most wear and tear. This still leaves the 'kicking feet' bare, however, which may be a good thing if your pony is anti-social. However, should you want to work fast in muddy conditions, such as when hunting or cross-country riding in wet weather, you may find that he slips too much without shoes and then you'll obviously have to shoe him again.

For many people, however, going barefoot really can make sense.

General foot care for healthy hooves

Because feet are so important, learn all you can about them by reading good books, magazine articles, and the Pony Club leaflets. You will need a good veterinary book anyway and this will contain information on feet and their care.

Diet
The quality of horn your pony grows depends partly on his own constitution, in other words on what he produces by nature (some ponies, like people, have naturally good hair, skin, teeth, nails etc and others don't) and partly on how well he is fed.

A poor diet produces poor horn but overfeeding could give your pony laminitis, so the important thing is to get the balance right. Ask your vet to help you make up a correct diet containing the right amounts of all the different nutriments your pony needs. If he seems to have poor feet (your farrier will be able to confirm this if you are not sure), consult your vet. Sometimes a feed supplement can help, provided your vet advises it.

Picking out feet
Whether your pony is working or resting, shod or unshod, check his feet and pick them out at least once a day and preferably more. Make this a golden rule – many people neglect their ponies' feet and have trouble as a result. Never ride without first picking out the feet and quickly checking the shoes.

To pick out the feet, lift them as shown in the drawings on pages 98-99. Holding the hoof with one hand and your hoofpick in the other, scrape out all dirt, working from the heel to toe to prevent dirt being pushed under the loosest part of the shoe at the heels. Don't forget the lacunae and cleft of frog; go gently here but firmly enough to extract all the dirt. You can pick out into a dung skip to prevent debris falling into the bedding. Tie your hoofpick to your skip or basket (whichever you use) with a piece of binder twine about a metre (yard) long so you don't lose it.

Checking shoes

To check shoes look to see that the clenches are not sticking up as the shoe wears thinner, that the horn is not growing over the edge of the shoe, that the shoe is not being pulled forward from the heels by the growing horn, that the horn is not cracking and that the shoes are not loose.

To check for looseness put the tip of your hoofpick between the shoe and the hoof at the heel and see if you can move the shoe. If you can, or if you hear a clanking noise when the pony goes on a hard road, you have a loose shoe and must not ride the pony till the farrier has seen to it. A pony's hooves usually make a firm clip-clop-clip-clop noise as he walks; if, instead, you hear 'clip-clop-clip-clank' you know one of his shoes is loose. Watch and see which foot hits the ground on the tinny 'clank' noise to find out which one it is.

Loose shoes are dangerous. The reason you must not ride a pony with loose shoes is because they can easily become twisted out of place, either by the ground if it is muddy or by the pony himself treading on them with his opposite foot. A loose shoe can cut into one of the pony's legs, the pony can trip over it causing a nasty fall for you both, or the shoe can be wrenched off, either in mud or, again, by the pony treading on it in movement, and badly tear the foot which may take months to repair.

Co-operating with your farrier

You can't expect your farrier to care about your pony's feet if you don't. Most ponies need shoeing, or at least their feet trimming and the shoes replacing if not too worn, about every six weeks. Leaving it too long means the horn grows over the shoes causing discomfort due to uneven pressure. At the heels, this can cause injuries called corns (bruises to the sensitive tissues underneath) which can lame your pony. Check the feet daily so you can spot any problems before they become emergencies.

Make regular appointments with your farrier. When your pony is shod, the safest

The underneath of a hind foot needing shoeing. The horn has grown to such an extent that the shoe has been pulled forward and the heels, particularly the right heel, are pressing into the frog and sole in the area called the 'seat of corn', which can cause bruising (corns) and possible lameness.

thing is to book another firm appointment for six weeks ahead and make sure it is in both the farrier's and your diary. Give the farrier your telephone number and ask him to ring you if he wants to change the date. If you are businesslike and helpful, he'll probably be the same. Even if your pony doesn't quite need shoeing, it's safer to have him done than cancel and risk the farrier not being able to fit you in for another month or so. If your farrier genuinely feels your pony needs shoeing more or less often than six weeks, he'll probably tell you, so you can arrange appointments at the right time for you, the farrier and the pony. If you are efficient like this, when an emergency such as a spread (twisted) or lost shoe does happen, the farrier will be more inclined to help you out.

Forefeet in need of shoeing. The horn has grown over the edge of the shoes, the clenches have risen and the horn has begun to crack and chip away. The pony's left shoe, in particular, has worn very thin.

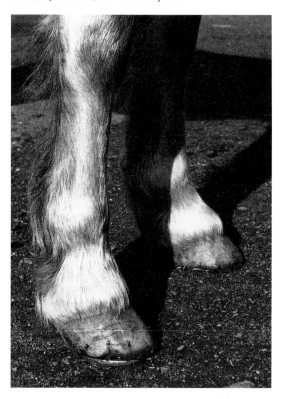

Remember that even if you don't have your pony shod, the farrier should still trim the feet and keep a professional eye on them. Don't ride unshod ponies on rough, stony ground or allow the feet to become very chipped, cracked, or badly worn. If and when you do decide to have the pony shod again, no farrier can be expected to keep shoes on feet in that condition as there will be not enough horn for the nails to hold on to.

Hygiene

Don't allow your pony to stand in filthy bedding and droppings. Keep his stable as clean as you can at all times; particularly, remove droppings as soon as possible to prevent them getting trampled in. Dirty bedding causes foot and lung diseases and sore throats. If you are at school and your pony is mainly stabled, try to get someone to skip out droppings during the day, and take the trouble to do so yourself before leaving the pony in the evening so the bed doesn't become any worse than necessary during the night.

Hoof oils

Don't spend money on hoof oils or other dressings unless you have been advised to do so by a vet or farrier. Most of them just coat the surface of the hoof with a greasy film that attracts dust and dirt – not really the effect you want.

Some hoof varnishes used for showing can dry out the hoof, so ask your vet about particular products before using them.

Stockholm tar is a product used for foot and horn diseases like thrush. It is not needed on an everyday basis and is not an ordinary hoof oil.

Remember . . .

● Your hoofpick is the most important part of your grooming kit. Use it frequently.

● Always pick out and check your pony's feet and shoes before and after riding. It only takes a couple of minutes and could save a nasty injury or accident.

● Keep your pony's bedding as clean and dry as you possibly can. Wet, dirty bedding can result in foot diseases.

● Don't wait until the last minute to ask your farrier to come and shoe your pony. He may not be able to call in at once and delay could mean badly overgrown feet and loose shoes.

● Even if your pony is resting without shoes, his feet still need proper trimming and checking every six to eight weeks.

● Don't have heavy shoes fitted thinking they'll last longer and save you money. They'll hit the ground that much harder and wear out just as quickly; also they could cause unnecessary jarring to your pony's feet and legs.

● If you use large studs for work in slippery mud, such as when hunting or riding across country in winter, always take them out as soon as work is finished. They unbalance the foot on ordinary ground and can cause problems.

● Remember, your pony's feet are not solid horn. If you ride over rough, stony going you could bruise his feet and lame him. If you do have to ride over this type of ground, walk and let him pick his way – don't rush him.

● The quality of your pony's horn depends on his food. Feed him well to encourage strong horn, but do not overfeed as this can cause laminitis, a serious foot disease.

6. Grooming and turn-out

Grooming is quite hard work and can be time-consuming, but it's one of those jobs where you can stand back and admire your handiwork because a well-groomed pony really looks a treat.

It's a matter of pride to have your pony reasonably clean and well turned out. If you are going to show, the pony will have to look smart if you want to be in the rosettes.

The skin and coat

The skin produces natural oils to help protect it and the coat from wear and wet. The skin is made of layers; the very thin, outer one is dead and comes off in flakes of dandruff. Ungroomed ponies build up grease and dandruff in their coats to help protect against the weather. Grass-kept ponies need much of this left in the coat as they are out in all weathers, but stabled ponies should have most of it removed because their skins are not rained on so much and can become dirty if not groomed.

Dirt encourages ticks, blood-sucking lice and skin diseases which give the pony sores and anaemia. It's unpleasant riding a dirty pony, and his skin, which is important to his health, works better when clean. The pony also feels better after a good grooming, and the very act of going all over the pony enables you to spot little wounds which might become infected if neglected.

Your grooming kit

The most important item is your hoofpick (a metal hook with a handle to clean the underneath of the hooves). The correct way to use it has already been described in Chapter 5. You'll also need a dandy brush which has stiff, fairly long bristles for brushing off loose hair and dried-on dirt and sweat; a body brush with finer, shorter bristles for getting through to the skin of a stabled pony's summer coat or clipped winter coat (it can't get through a long coat); a metal curry comb to clean the body brush and which is *never* used on the pony; a plastic or rubber curry comb to remove caked-on mud; a sweat scraper if you are going to be rinsing down or shampooing your pony (although you could use the edges of your hands); two sponges, one for the head and one for the back end; a stable rubber (not essential) which is like a tea towel and is used for a final polish; and a bucket for water. A water brush is useful for removing stable stains and damping down the hairs of the mane, forelock and tail – it's like a smaller dandy brush with softer bristles. If you are going to 'bang' your pony, you'll need a wisp (made of plaited hay or binder twine) or a stuffed leather massage pad.

Two other items which are not strictly grooming equipment but which are useful in trimming are a mane comb and scissors. Mane combs should not be used for actually

Grooming kit

Dandy brush

Body brush

Rubber curry comb

Water brush

Plastic-toothed curry comb

Hoofpick and brush combined

Metal curry comb

Hoof pick

combing manes as it is easy to pull out chunks of hair with them and so spoil the mane, and the same goes for the tail. Their correct use, and that of scissors, is described in the trimming section of this chapter.

Types of grooming procedures

Grass-kept and stabled ponies have the same basic grooming, but stabled ones are also body-brushed to remove excess grease from their coats.

A short form of grooming, called quartering, is used to tidy up stabled ponies before work. First the rugs are unbuckled and folded back off the forehand and the pony quickly dandied over. The rugs are then folded forward again while the back end is uncovered in the same way so the quarters and back can be brushed. The mane, forelock and tail are brushed so there are no bits of bedding in them, and the feet are picked out. The pony has his eyes, nostrils, lips, sheath or udder, and dock sponged clean, and is then ready for work.

Stabled ponies are groomed *after* work when their skin is warm (but dry), toned up after work and easy to clean. Grass-kept ponies are groomed before work to tidy them up; they do not need body brushing.

To groom a grass-kept pony

First pick out the hooves, then, with a plastic or rubber curry, scrub off all the dried mud in the direction the hair grows so you don't work it into the skin. Next, dandy him firmly but not roughly all over, working from front to back and top to bottom so you don't brush dirt on to parts you've already cleaned. If the pony doesn't like having his head done, do it with your hand, a piece of sacking or an old towel.

If you have a body brush, do the forelock, mane and tail next. This brush is the gentlest and helps avoid breaking the hairs, but a carefully used dandy brush will do. First unpick any knots in the hairs with your fingers. Lift the forelock and brush out a few hairs at a time from the roots. Push the mane over to the other side of the neck and, starting behind the ears, brush it back over from the roots, lock by lock.

To do the tail, hold it by the end of the dock in one hand straight out towards you. Again using the body brush, if you have one, release a few hairs and brush them down towards the ends, gradually working up to the roots. Release some more hair and carry on till the tail is completely brushed out. Separate the short hairs on the dock and brush down to the skin to get it reasonably clean.

Now for the sponging. Take a bucket of water (preferably warm in winter) and one of the sponges. Wet the sponge and squeeze it out well till just damp, then gently clean discharge and dirt from the eyes, inside the nostrils and around the lips. Now moisten the other sponge and clean the sheath (if the pony is a gelding) or udder (if she's a mare), between the buttocks and under the tail itself. In chilly weather, dry with an old towel to prevent chapped skin.

Finally, if you wish you can flatten the forelock, mane and tail with the water brush. Dip the ends of the bristles in water, shake hard and brush the hair flat. On the mane, flatten the hair right on the crest at the roots and down to the tips (difficult if your pony has a mane like a wire brush) and do the dock right from the root of the tail.

If the pony is wet you'll have to dry him before you can groom properly as brushing wet mud into the skin will make him sore.

This is done by 'thatching' him. Put a thick layer of straw all over his back and quarters and place a rug on top, fastening it just tightly enough to stop it slipping, and leave him stabled or standing under cover till he's dry, which, with a long winter coat, could take an hour or two. He will dry quicker if you put an anti-sweat rug on him rather than an ordinary rug, as the open mesh of these rugs lets the dampness rise up through the holes and away into the air.

If you have no rug you could open out an empty feed sack, preferably the hessian/jute kind or, failing that, the newer polythene type, and, using a friend's rug as a pattern, cut it roughly into a rug shape. Make holes for fastenings in the front and on the lower edges at the side where the surcingle would go, and tie on lengths of binder twine, which you can fasten with bows. You'll find this quite good enough for drying off. Once he's dry, carry on as normal.

If you have no straw, the anti-sweat rug mentioned above (which is a mesh rug, rather like a string vest for humans) can be used instead and another rug, or your 'sack rug' made from a feed sack, on top will do the job.

To groom a stabled pony

Pick out the hooves first, then dandy him. Remove stable stains with the damped water brush. Now take your body brush, putting your fingers through the loop on the back and holding it firmly with your thumb on the outside and, starting at the head, brush the pony all over, pushing the bristles gently but firmly right down to the skin.

On the neck and body, use the following technique. Hold your arm (usually the left arm for left side of the pony, right for right side) stiffly but slightly bent at the elbow, place the brush on the coat and lean your weight on it as you make long, sweeping

When grooming the mane, use the body brush and, having pushed the mane over to the wrong side of the neck, brush it back over from the roots, lock by lock.

strokes. This is less tiring than pushing with your arm and should ensure you have enough energy to do the whole pony.

Do about six strokes on one place and after about three strokes place the brush, bristles down, on the teeth of the curry comb and draw the brush firmly across to clean it.

Now and then, tap the curry on its side near the door or outside to dislodge the dirt.

Next do the mane, forelock and tail, 'lay' them with the water brush if you wish, then attend to the sponging. Finally bundle up your stable rubber, slightly damp, and wipe it over the coat to remove any dust.

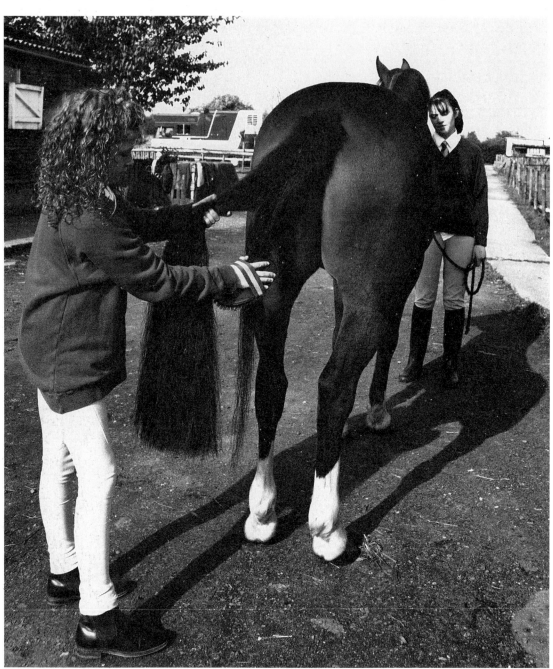

A pony on the combined system should be groomed as for a stabled pony, but with less body brushing.

The parts most often overlooked in grooming are under the jaw, inside the ears, under the mane and forelock, between the legs, under the breast and belly, behind pasterns and beneath the tail. Work out a routine so you do each part in the same order each time and don't forget anywhere.

Wisping or banging

This is a form of massage which stimulates the skin and works the muscles, so helping to

build them up. As stabled ponies don't tend to roll as much as grass-kept ones, it helps replace rolling to some extent.

To make a wisp, damp some hay or plaited binder twine and twist it into a rope about 2 m (2 yds) long. Form two loops at one end and thread the rest tightly through and round them. Tuck the end under the final twist and stamp on the wisp to flatten and firm it. (See illustration overleaf.) A good one should last several weeks or months.

Use the same type of motion as with the

Left To groom the tail, hold the dock at the end and brush out the tail a little at a time using the body brush. Start at the ends of each section and work towards the roots, gradually easing out the tangles.

To clean the body brush, hold the metal curry comb like this, with the handle pointing away from you, and pull the bristles firmly across the teeth towards you. If you hold the curry comb with the handle towards you and drag it across the brush, you can badly scratch the wrist of the hand holding the brush.

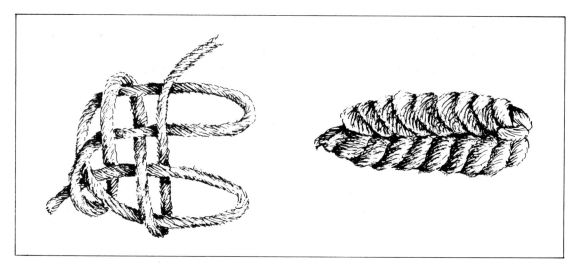

How to make a wisp. Using a twisted hay rope or plaited binder twine, form two loops, and thread the long, loose end through, backwards and forwards. Tuck the end under the last twist, and stamp on the wisp to firm it.

body brush but slap the wisp firmly (but not roughly) on to the muscles along the top of the neck, the shoulder and the quarters. Don't wisp bony parts or the loins (behind the saddle) for fear of injuring the pony. The idea behind wisping is that the pony flinches his muscles anticipating the slap, so working them and improving muscle-tone. The long stroke which follows the slap massages the muscles and skin.

Washing the sheath

Geldings need their sheaths washing occasionally to remove the build-up of greasy discharge (called 'smegma') which occurs naturally. If you don't do this, in a bad case the pony will not let his penis down to stale and his urine will run all over his belly, causing sore skin. Also, infection can set in on the penis and around the inside of the sheath sometimes.

You can wear thin rubber gloves if you prefer. You will also need two buckets of clean, quite warm water, one with a little Savlon liquid in it, your 'back end' sponge, some baby soap or a mild medicated soap such as Wright's Coal Tar soap (not perfumed cosmetic soaps which can cause skin irritation), an old towel and some almond oil or liquid paraffin from the chemist (*not* paraffin heating fuel).

If the pony is not used to this job being done, ask a friend to hold him and fuss him, and perhaps let him chew on a haynet, too, to keep him busy. If he really objects (which would be unusual), just do what you can, and gradually he will get used to you interfering with his personal areas. In any case, you should sponge the entrance to the sheath with a damp sponge during daily grooming, so he shouldn't feel *that* strange about it.

Soap your sponge well and gently put it right up inside the sheath and thoroughly soap all round. If you feel any lumps of smegma gently remove them with your fingers, but don't be rough or scratch the skin. Rinse the sponge thoroughly and, without squeezing it out, put it back up into the sheath several times to really rinse out all the soap. Use the water containing Savlon for the final two rinses. Dry off the outside of the sheath with the old towel and finally put some oil or liquid paraffin in the palm of one hand and smear it gently all around up inside the sheath. This will make the pony more comfortable, loosen any remaining smegma and make the job easier next time.

Some ponies will let you bring down the penis to be cleaned in the same way, but with others you have to wait for an opportunity to sponge it off, perhaps after he has staled or some other convenient time. Smegma can build up on the end of the penis in a hard 'bean', so you do have to keep an eye open for this.

Signs of a pony needing his sheath cleaning or having an infection or other discomfort there are: not letting down the penis to stale, frequent stamping with the back feet or swishing the tail when there are no flies around, and making a 'honking' noise when he trots. This sounds as though it is coming from his belly but, in fact, it is coming from the sheath.

Maybe this isn't a very pleasant job, and even slightly embarrassing if you're not used to it, but it *is* important, so don't avoid doing it. It should be done at least once a month.

Shampooing

Shampooing can save a lot of work and does not harm ponies provided they are not washed on chilly days and are dried properly afterwards. It's useful for very dirty ponies and for show preparation.

You'll need a good supply of warm water, a large sponge, and a medicated animal shampoo or mild washing-up liquid.

Avoiding the face, start behind the ears and thoroughly soap the pony all over, including the mane and tail. Rinse really well with warm water from a hosepipe or from your bucket. Clean the sponge in cold water first to remove the soap, and keep changing the rinsing water (if using a bucket). You must not leave any soap on the skin anywhere. Dunk the tail in the bucket and, holding it at the end of the dock, whizz the

hair round to remove excess water.

Use your sweat scraper or the edges of your hands to scrape off excess water and walk the pony in the sun to dry off, or stable him if it's wet. To hurry things along, you can dry him off with old towels and a hand-held hair dryer, but be very careful with the flex. Be especially sure to dry heels and pasterns very well.

One little tip. If you use straw or an anti-sweat rug to help dry off a wet pony, remove them while the coat is still *slightly* damp and rug up normally, otherwise the coat will dry with the pattern of the straw or mesh on it and you won't be able to remove it without damping the coat again. Putting on an ordinary rug just before the coat becomes completely dry will flatten and smooth it.

If a stabled pony finishes work muddy in winter you can hose off the mud from his belly and legs, provided you then dry them

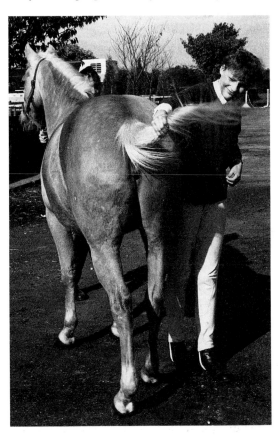

After washing the tail, hold it at the end of the dock, stand with your back to the pony's head, and whizz the hair round to remove most of the water.

really well and preferably bandage his legs with woollen stable bandages for warmth. Put knitted dishcloths under them to help them dry quicker.

Trimming

Even a grass-kept pony in winter can be improved by a little careful trimming, and a stabled one can be smartened up considerably even if not clipped.

Start with the ears. The hair inside should be left intact but if you gently close the edges of his ears together you can trim off with scissors any hair which sticks out, especially the tufts at the base. The hair under the jawline can be trimmed with hand-operated clippers or scissors and comb. Comb the hair the wrong way (up towards his throat) and snip off the hair that sticks out between the teeth of the comb.

The long 'feeler' hairs round the eyes and muzzle should be left on, in my opinion. Ponies need them to help protect their heads against knocks and for sorting out feed and grass. Unfortunately, it is still fashionable for them to be clipped off (*never* try to pull them out – the pain to the pony would be unbearable), but it is certainly kinder to leave them on. I have known horses and ponies become quite confused and reluctant to eat for days after having these important whiskers removed.

Before trimming the heels, remember that if your pony is turned out much he will need some heel hair to help protect against rainwater draining down his legs and against wet from the grass. Always leave a little tuft of hair on the point of the fetlock. Again, take your scissors (special rounded trimming scissors are available from saddlers to make fetlock trimming easier) and your comb and, as with the jawline, comb the hair up the wrong way and snip off that coming between the teeth.

If you have a pony of a registered breed, you may not be allowed to pull or otherwise trim the mane and tail if competing in breed classes where ponies are shown with 'natural' (but shampooed and groomed) manes and tails. Other ponies usually look smarter with trimmed manes and tails but, again, if your pony is out much go easy on the amount you remove as he needs them for protection.

To pull a mane

Buy a mane comb from your saddler and, starting behind the ears, hold the hairs at their ends with one hand and, using the comb in the other, push up the shorter top layer with the comb. Then put the teeth of the comb over the longer lower layer right at the roots, hold them against the comb with your thumb and quickly pull out just a few hairs, about six at a time is enough. Do this just a few times down the neck and, over a week or so doing this daily, you will notice an improvement in the length and thickness of the mane. Never try to do it all at once as you'll make the pony's neck very sore and he could become difficult about it in future.

When doing any pulling, you'll find dirty hair easier to manage as freshly washed hair is slippery. Also, pull straight after exercise when the pony's skin is warm and his pores open so the hair comes out more readily. It's also easier to do in spring and autumn when coat casting is taking place as all hair is 'looser' then.

Ponies with thin manes can have the ends shortened by simply snapping them off. Just take a few hairs between thumb and first finger and tweak hard sideways in a quick snatching movement.

If you feel you can't get the mane right or the pony objects strongly, buy a razor comb from the chemist. These fine-toothed combs have two layers of teeth and a sharp razor between them so you can't cut yourself. They are sold for trimming human hair. Just comb the mane from underneath right at the roots, carefully and a little at a time, and the

When pulling a mane, slide the comb up the hair, taking just a few hairs at a time (the amount shown here is plenty), right to the roots, pushing up the top hair. Then, holding the hairs against the top of the comb with your right thumb, pull quickly out from the roots.

hair will be cut off. With the ends, comb downwards on the top layer at the length you want the mane to be. You can get a very natural, even effect with these combs, but using ordinary scissors will give your pony a mane like a shaving brush.

To pull a tail

The idea is to pull out the hairs along the sides of the dock to about two-thirds of the way down the dock. Start right at the root (top) and twist about three hairs round your first finger and thumb and pull sharply and quickly downwards. Then do the same on the other side. Just make a few more pulls that day, and, again, over a week or so the tail will gradually take on more shape.

The tail hair on the dock is particularly important for a pony who is out a good deal, so it is kinder for these ponies to leave the hair full and practise plaiting it instead.

To trim a tail

To trim or 'bang' the end of a tail, you need a large pair of sharp scissors or proper tail shears. Ask a friend to put an arm under the pony's dock so it is raised as it is when he is moving, then grasp *all* the hairs in one hand

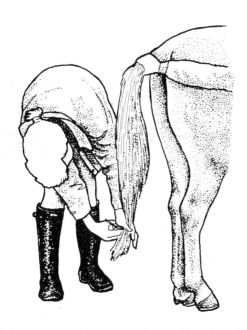

To bang a pony's tail so that it is in a neat line along the bottom, ask a friend to raise the dock to the position it adopts when the pony is in action, either with a hand (as shown) or by putting an arm underneath it. Hold the hairs together at the bottom, and carefully cut the hair off level, preferably in one snip.

at the end of the dock, run your hand down to just below hock level, hold the hair firmly and cut it off absolutely level with one firm cut. If you look at racehorses on television, you'll notice that most of them have tails that are full (unpulled) at the top and banged at the bottom and they look lovely. In fact, such a tail is called a racehorse tail.

To plait a mane

First be sure how many plaits you want. There's normally an odd number down the neck (traditionally seven) and one for the forelock. If your pony's mane is thick, he'll look better with more, smaller plaits, whereas a pony with a thin mane can have the traditional number. The mane should be about 13 cm (5 ins) long.

Damp the mane and divide it into the right number of sections with your mane comb, then separate each section with an elastic band round the middle. Make an ordinary three-strand plait from the roots right to the bottom, tight enough to look firm but *not* pulling, which can hurt the pony and even cause pain or numbness in the neck, which will affect his way of going.

Thread up some blunt-ended darning needles with button thread of a colour to match the mane and pin them in your jumper to keep them safe so they don't fall in the bedding. Lost needles are a nightmare and they could seriously injure the pony if he stood on them. Sew up the bottom of the plait, turn it under about a centimetre, wind the thread round twice and put the needle through again, then roll the plait neatly under up to the roots. Sew through the plait to fix it, wind the thread once round the whole plait, sew through again and knot securely on the underside.

Plaiting can be tricky and needs practice. A lesson can be very useful.

An alternative method for ponies with long manes is to use one long plait down the crest

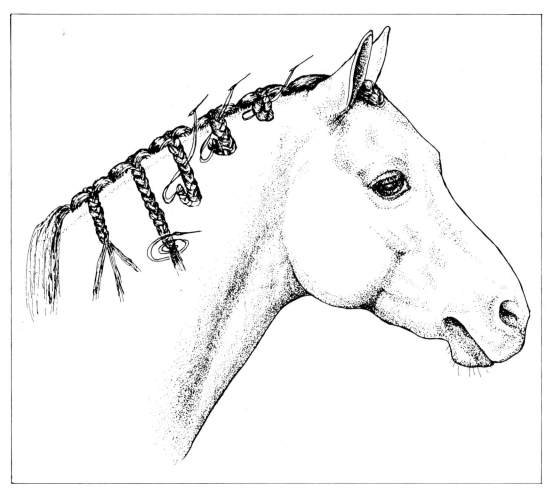

Plaiting a mane. This illustration has been drawn this way to show the different stages in making a single plait. You normally finish each plait before going on to the next, so your pony will never actually look like this. Starting from the left, comb the hair into locks according to the number of plaits you want. You can keep them separate with elastic bands, if you wish. Plait the lock down as normal, then, with your threaded needle, turn up the end, sew through it and wind the thread round to secure. Roll the plait up, passing the thread through it to secure it as you go. When it is rolled up to the top, sew through and round to fix the plait. Some people finish off with a knot on the underside, others just cut off the thread close to the plait and leave it.

of the neck. Plait the forelock, bringing it round and below the right ear, then plait into it a lock of hair from the top of the mane. Keep taking in more hair from the mane, making one long plait along the crest at the roots, and work all the way down to the withers. Plait the free hairs right to the very ends, sew and turn under the end and loop under again to the withers. Sew through here, wind round, and stitch down the middle of the loop so it is fixed into one doubled-up plait. Wind round the end again and knot the thread.

To plait a tail
Start right up at the root and take about six hairs from each side. Bring them into the middle and tie them together, fairly tightly, with button thread so there is one thin lock hanging down. Now take a few more hairs from each side and you have three strands with which to start. Plait firmly but not

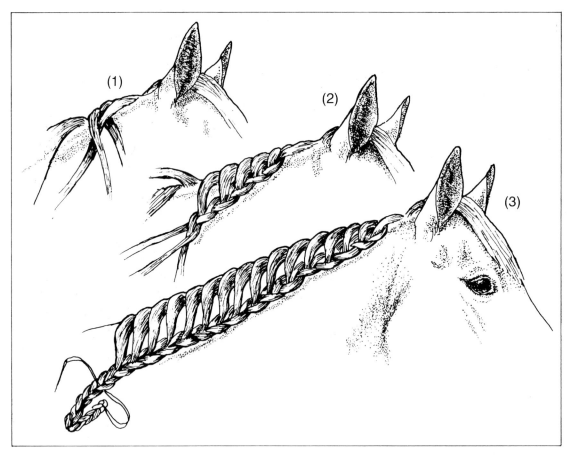

A way of plaiting a long mane which you don't want to shorten: (1) Start just behind the poll and make three locks. Begin a plait in the normal way, as shown. (2) Keep lifting another lock of hair from the mane to join with the left lock, as you plait on down the neck. (3) Finish at the withers by plaiting all the hair left into a free plait (as with a tail). Finish it off as normal by winding the thread round the end, sewing through, turning the plait back on itself and sewing down the resulting loop to make a 'sausage'. Wind the thread round the end twice, sew through two or three times and cut off the thread.

The forelock can be left free, made into an ordinary button plait or plaited into a long plait and brought round the right ear to join with the first lock of the neck plait.

tightly, taking in more hairs from the sides as you go and being careful to keep the hairs horizontal (in a straight line across the dock) rather than sagging so you end up with a v-shape down the dock, which looks terrible.

If you plait the strands under each other rather than over, you'll end up with a lovely raised braid down the dock. Plait to two-thirds of the way down the dock, being sure to keep the braid straight down the centre of the dock. Two-thirds of the way down, stop taking in extra hairs and plait on to the ends of the hairs. Finish off as for any plait – sew the bottom, turn under, wind round and sew again, loop up to where you stopped taking in hairs, sew through twice, sew the loop together down the centre and knot securely.

Plaiting really does need practice and quite a bit of it, so practise at home before risking it on the big day.

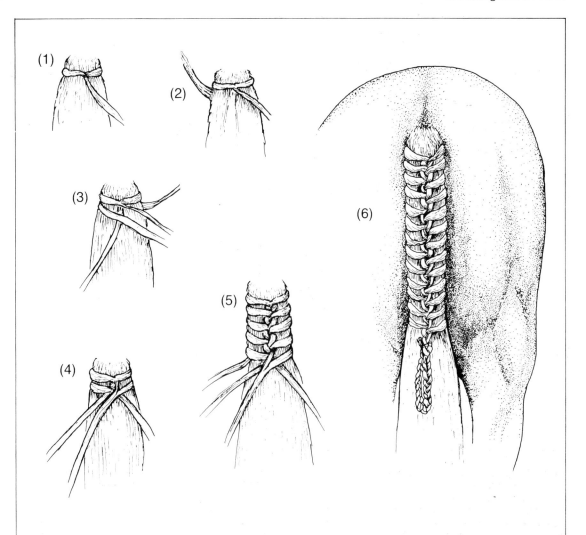

Plaiting a tail: This is a slightly different method from that given in this chapter. (1) Take two locks of hair from each side of the dock and tie them firmly together in the middle with button thread. (2) Take another few hairs from the left , , , (3) . . . and lift a lock from the middle. Cross the left lock over that and hold with your left finger and thumb. Now take a lock from the right and join it with the first lock you made. (4) Cross that over the lock from the left (which has now become your centre lock) to form a new centre lock. Take some more hairs from the left and join them with the lock on the left. Cross those over the centre lock again – and so on. (5) As you go on, you will see a plait forming down the dock. (6) This drawing makes the plaiting seem looser than it should be to show you the formation. When you have finished plaiting, turn up the plait as shown under itself, sew round the whole thing twice to fix it, then sew back down the centre of the loop, sewing the two parts of the loop together into one 'sausage'. Twist your thread round the bottom, sew through twice and cut your thread.

This method is a little trickier than the one described in the text. Because you are also taking hair from the centre, however, it is especially good for thin tails, making a fuller plait. Again, if you cross the strands under themselves rather than over, you get a raised plait which improves the appearance of a pony who normally carries his tail rather low, making it seem to arch more.

Two useful types of pony clip.
A trace clip, where the hair is
removed from the tops of the
back legs, the belly, the tops of
the front legs, the breast and
the underside of the neck. This
pony's tail, incidentally, is too
long for winter; it will easily
become clogged with mud and
snow on the end, and should be
shortened to just below the
hocks.
Right A breast-and-gullet clip.
The hair is removed from the
breast and the underside of
the neck (called the gullet).
This clip is excellent for ponies
doing no work during the week
as they can be turned out
without a rug, yet will be able
to do light work at weekends
without becoming too hot too
quickly.

It's better to plait on the morning of the show. If you leave a pony plaited up overnight he may well have rubbed undone all your handiwork in the morning and been very uncomfortable all night – not the best start to your day. As soon as you have finished your classes, undo your plaits by snipping the thread – and only the thread – with scissors and gently unravel each plait with your fingers. Brush out and wait for his curly look to die down. This can be helped by damping the mane.

Clipping

If your pony is going to do more than light hacking during the winter, you'll probably do best to have him clipped by a professional from your local stable or by a 'travelling clipper' who will probably advertise in your local horsy magazine. Clipping is not a job for a novice.

Ponies are clipped if working in winter because the work makes them sweat and a long, wet coat is difficult to dry. This means that the pony takes longer to cool down and could become chilled with serious consequences. Ponies made to sweat too much by being worked with a long coat also lose condition, so clipping helps prevent these things.

Remember, if you remove the pony's coat you'll have to replace it with clothing. If the pony lives out, he should only have his chest and the underside of his neck clipped. If he has a good field shelter, bedded down so he has somewhere dry to lie down, you could give him an Irish clip or, at most, a trace clip, but with the last two he'll need a New Zealand rug (see Chapter 8).

Most children's ponies, even hard-working stabled ones, are quite all right with a trace clip. If the pony is to be working hard and has a thick coat, a blanket clip can be given. Giving children's ponies hunter or full clips can cause problems; the colder they feel

Points to consider

- Although it's nice to have a sparkling clean pony, don't worry if you haven't time to groom thoroughly every day. Grooming is not as important as some other tasks, such as exercising, watering and feeding.
- If you are not riding, the mud can stay on a grass-kept pony and no harm will be done. In fact, a coating of dried mud helps protect grass-kept ponies from the wind.
- The most important parts of grooming are picking out feet and then sponging clean the eyes, nostrils, sheath or udder and dock. Do these jobs each day, even if you haven't time to groom more thoroughly.
- On the other hand, don't forget that a dirty skin, especially in a stabled pony

not exposed to the rain, can harbour disease and that daily grooming helps you keep an eye out for such things as ticks and lice. Especially with a stabled pony, it helps stimulate his skin and makes him feel better.
- Don't put tack or harness on top of mud or dried sweat, or you could make the pony's skin sore from rubbing.
- If you clip your pony he will be easier to keep clean and dry but harder to manage as he will need more clothing and shelter. Don't clip any more than is really necessary. Most ponies do very well with no more than a trace clip. If the pony lives out, clip his chest and the underside of his neck, otherwise he could be too cold.

Two useful containers for keeping your grooming kit tidy. Left: a plastic tray-type grooming box with handle and compartments; right: a canvas bucket with rope handle. If you do not have a proper grooming tidy, a plastic shopping bag or denim tote bag is quite adequate.

the more they play up to keep warm and the extra feed needed also encourages this. Generally, the less they are clipped the better.

The pony must be clean and dry before clipping starts otherwise the blades will soon become blunt, pulling the hairs, and causing the machine to overheat, both of which will make your pony difficult to clip in future.

Put up a haynet for him to munch on as clipping is a long, boring job. Have a blanket or rug to put over him as clipping progresses to stop him feeling chilly. When it's finished, groom him quickly, rug him up and give him a feed. He'll need more food if he's clipped

to help stay warm, and you'll have to check regularly that he has enough clothing.

Feel the base of his ears and his loins – if they are cold so is he, so put on an extra blanket or under-rug.

Care of equipment

You cannot clean a pony with dirty brushes. Brushes can be washed in warm soapy water, rinsed *very* thoroughly in cold water and dried, bristles down, in a warm but not hot place. Keep your kit together in a proper grooming box, a canvas bag or small plastic bucket, kept covered over by a stable rubber or old tea-towel. Your plaiting equipment, if any, should be kept in a separate small compartment or in a partitioned drawer in the tack room or at home, since it is not used every day – unless you are doing that all-important practice.

7. Handling your pony

Have you ever been dragged round the stable yard by a pony who wanted to go somewhere you didn't and realised just how weak and powerless you were to stop him? If so, that will have given you some idea of just how strong ponies are and how impossible it is with ordinary handling methods physically to force one to do something he doesn't want to. Even a small pony is too strong for a large man, in terms of physical strength.

It's obvious, then, that as ponies are so strong they can also be very dangerous if they are not handled correctly or if they are frightened. A pony in a panic thinks only about protecting himself and getting away from whatever is hurting, frightening or confusing him. Some are more nervous than others – what upsets one will not bother another.

Unfortunately, ponies can sense when people are frightened, either of them or of something else. Because they are herd animals most of them need leadership, which must come from you with kind but firm handling. But, as in the herd, there are bosses and underlings and some ponies, like some humans, try to boss people and other ponies about.

Most ponies will 'try it on' with new people to see if they can be bossed. In such cases, a firm voice, but *not* a shout, and maybe a slap on the shoulder or belly reminds the pony that *you* are the boss.

Good horsemen are always quiet, gentle and firm, with an air of confidence which gives the ponies and horses confidence, too, and they do everything smoothly and gradually because they know that sudden movements can startle even the quietest animal. They speak to their horse a lot, making requests or indicating their intentions by running a hand over the part of the horse they want to work on. This is the sort of behaviour you should try to develop till it becomes second nature. People who treat ponies roughly are, underneath, frightened of them and are trying to cover this up by showing their strength. Also, people who lose their tempers easily have no place around horses, especially if they are the type who take it out on the animals.

Treating him fairly

Most ponies are willing to please when they understand what you want. If you are constantly having trouble getting your pony to do a particular thing, either from the saddle or the ground, seek expert help before you turn the pony into a confused, nervous wreck.

If the pony does something he knows is wrong (and you are sure he knows), you must tell him off *at once* so that he associates your cross tone of voice with what he is doing. You have to let him know immediately or he won't understand what he is being told off for and you will simply confuse him.

If a pony does keep doing something wrong, be sure you reprimand him *every* time he does it. If you do so one time and not the next, your inconsistent reaction will confuse him. When he is good, praise him immediately; when he is bad, tell him off immediately; otherwise he can't hope to learn.

Teaching commands

Ponies learn quickly if you make everything clear to them, and once they have learned something they never forget it – this goes for unpleasant experiences as well as good ones. If you once lead your pony through his stable door and the door swings or blows on to him, frightening and perhaps hurting him, he will remember it for ever, and might become difficult about going into stables in future. Surprisingly, although they'll remember such incidents most ponies continue to behave correctly but will be on the lookout for trouble.

Ponies who fall when jumping, for instance, are not bound to refuse to jump for ever more, but they *will* remember, especially that particular jump, or jumps of that type or colour or in that place, so always try to calm a pony who has had an unpleasant experience and take extra care in future.

Ponies are just as good as dogs at learning commands. They learn simple phrases best rather than whole sentences, each always said in its own tone. Watch an experienced instructor lungeing a pony and note how he or she always gives commands by using one or at most two words and always in the same way.

Ponies should ideally learn their own names and come to call, but not many really do. The first word you say to him on approaching him in the box or field should be his name. If you have a titbit, call his name and make him come to you for it; he'll soon associate his name with going to you.

Ponies should learn 'walk on', 'trot', 'canter', 'whoa' and 'back'. They should also know 'over' (to move over in the stable), 'easy' or 'steady' to calm them down, 'no' (in a cross tone as a reprimand) and 'good boy' in a pleased tone. Always use the right command at the right time so he always knows what you mean. By all means have a running conversation with him if you are out hacking or grooming him, or whatever, as the sound of a calm human voice has a confidence-giving and quietening effect on ponies, but when you actually want him to do something, use only the correct word on its own, not in the middle of a stream of conversation when he can't possibly pick it out. Remember, your words are just sounds to him – he doesn't speak English! He associates particular sounds and tones with particular actions; the actual words mean nothing to him.

For example, to teach the pony to move over in the stable, put your hand firmly on his side where your leg goes when riding, and *at the same time*, push and say 'over'. Repeat if necessary, and maybe use two hands in the same spot; push hard and keep saying 'over' in the same voice, and pretty soon he'll catch on. Don't keep up a constant pressure. Just push and say 'over', then stop, push again and say 'over', and stop. If you are having no luck at all, get someone to help you, and the *instant* he moves even half a step praise him with 'good boy' and stroke him.

Soon, all you will have to do is touch him gently in the right place and say 'over' and he'll move at once. Never forget to say 'good boy' when he does.

It is best to try never to stand or walk immediately behind a pony unless really necessary. If something beyond your control startles him he might kick out instinctively and hurt you. If you do have to go right behind him, stay in close as then the kick won't be at its strongest when it hits you.

Teaching him to stale

We read a lot in pony management books about getting the pony to stale as soon as he comes home, but it's much better to get him to stale *before* so he's not bursting to spend a penny when you are in the middle of the show ring or on the road.

The usual methods are to whistle and shake straw under him or rustle fresh bedding.

Notice when he usually stales. Most ponies do it after they have been lying down, when they come home from a ride and on fresh bedding. If he is kept out after a ride he will usually trot off when turned loose, roll, shake and then stale.

Whenever you notice him staling, whistle softly to him in a certain way and use this way of whistling only for when he stales. He will gradually associate that whistle with staling. When you notice the pony straddle his legs and lift his (or her) tail to stale, whistle at once, and keep it up while he is staling. Then say 'good boy' and fuss him.

The next stage is, after about a week, as soon as you come in from your ride, untack him and lead him to his box or field, holding his rope if he is in the field, then stand back and whistle, perhaps shaking bedding under him. He will very likely cotton on and stale. Praise him the moment he shows an inkling of doing what you want.

Next, try it before you tack up or during a rest on a long ride, remembering always to choose soft ground as ponies hate staling on to a hard surface for fear of splashing themselves. Don't worry if he doesn't take to this new time at first, but really make a fuss of him when he does.

You can give your pony plenty of opportunities to stale during a long day out and be quite sure that he is never in great discomfort because he badly needs to stale. Eventually he will actually expect to stale before going out.

Picking up feet

To pick up a forefoot, stand at the shoulder, facing the tail. Put your nearest hand on the shoulder and run it down the back of the leg. When you reach the fetlock hold it round the inside, lean against the shoulder and pull the fetlock upwards, saying 'up'. It sometimes helps if you press your elbow behind his knee. Hold the hoof under your fingers at the toe as then the pony will not be able to put any weight on you as he will not feel steady.

To pick up a hind foot, stand at the hip, facing the tail. Put your nearest hand on his quarters and run it down the back of the leg. When you reach the hock, pass your hand round in front of the hock and down the inside of the leg to the fetlock; hold it round the inside and pull it upwards, leaning against the pony's thigh to put his balance off that leg. Always use the command 'up' as you pull. The pony may try to hold his hind foot too far under his belly so try to gently push it back (but never sideways which can hurt his hip joint) so you can get at it easily.

Hold a back hoof with your hand cupped round the wall and have your arm in front of his leg so if he kicks backwards he won't pull you with him. Do not rest a hoof on your knee as if he moves his legs you could be pulled or knocked over and maybe trampled on. Your farrier may do it, but he needs two hands and is trained to cope with difficult ponies.

Leading a pony

Ponies should be led and handled from *both* sides, not just the left as is often done, otherwise they tend to become 'one-sided', in other words they will not lead properly from the right-hand side. Whether the pony is wearing a headcollar and lead rope, a webbing or rope halter or a bridle, the procedure is the same.

If he is wearing a bridle, bring the reins over his head and use them in the same way as a rope.

Hold the rope or reins about 15 cm (6 ins) from his head with the back of your hand upwards. With your hand like this (instead of the more usual way, palm upwards) you have more control over the pony. If he pulls away, simply twist your wrist round away from yourself and draw the rope back towards you; you would otherwise have to give a direct pull, which is not so strong.

It is always a good idea to lead in gloves and have a knot in the very end of the rope to help prevent its being pulled through your hand should the pony play up. When leading with reins, never loop your arm through the buckle end or you could be dragged if something upsets the pony.

The spare end of the rope/reins is held in your other hand to keep it from trailing dangerously on the floor. Never wrap a rope round your hands or wrists thinking you have a better hold. It is very dangerous as you could be dragged if the pony really took off.

Be at the pony's shoulder, give the

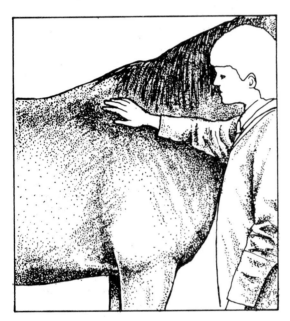

Never just grab your pony's foot and try to lift it, as you might startle him. Start at the shoulder and run your hand down his leg, then hold the back of his fetlock and pull it upwards, giving the command 'up'. If he resists, lean on his shoulder with your own shoulder and push his knee forward with your elbow. Hold the hoof at the toe as shown; he will find it uncomfortable to put weight on it and is less inclined to lean his weight on you while you work with your other hand.

command 'walk on' and encourage him to walk forward with you, not trail along after you, when he might push you over with his head or tread on your heels.

If he won't walk on, have a long schooling whip or twig in the hand furthest from the pony and as you give the command to walk on tap him smartly on the flank behind your back. He'll soon get the message – be ready for him to step smartly forward and don't

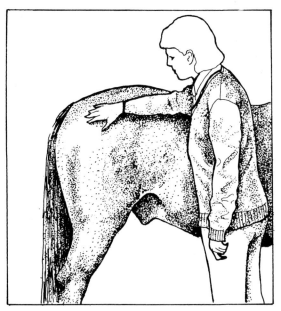

To pick up a hind foot, first put your hand on the quarters, and run it down the inside of the hind leg. Hold the fetlock underneath and on the inside, pull upwards and give your command. Hold the hoof at the toe with your arm on the inside of the leg, like this. If a pony kicks, he is

more likely to kick backwards than forwards. If you have your arm on the inside of the leg you can simply let go and be safe. If your arm is on the outside of the leg holding the hoof, you could more easily be pulled over.

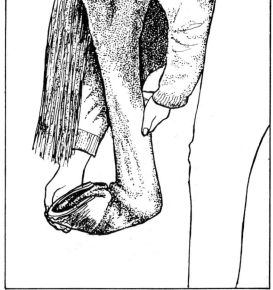

yank him back, accidentally or otherwise, with the rope or he won't understand what on earth you *do* want.

If you regularly lead a strong pony, you might find it worthwhile to buy a proper lungeing cavesson and fasten your rope to the front ring on the noseband. This gives more control than a headcollar and saves wear and tear on your bridle. If you need to give a couple of sharp tugs on the rope to keep him back, it won't hurt him, but doing that with a bridle will surely hurt his mouth and could make matters worse.

Turning round

Always push the pony away from you to turn him, walking on the outside of the bend so you are less likely to be trodden on; also the pony will be able to keep his hocks under him, his head up and remain balanced.

When turning a led pony, walk on the outside of the bend and push him round away from you. This way he'll stay better balanced and is less likely to tread on you.

Tying up

Use a quick-release (half-bow) knot which can be pulled undone with one tug on the loose end in an emergency, such as the pony panicking. Never tie up even a quiet pony and go off and leave him, as something could easily happen in your absence to frighten him and a bad accident could occur.

Most people recommend tying a loop of string to a tie-ring and tying the pony's lead rope to that, then if he does pull back for any reason the string will break and he will be free, rather than struggling to release himself with the risk of injury to himself and people near by, or of damage to the building.

The risk of horses and ponies getting free when being handled is the main reason why stable yards should always be firmly enclosed by walls or fences. You can imagine what a horrific accident could occur if a pony who had broken free got on to a road. If he got on to open land instead he could still be injured or cause damage to other people's property, apart from the difficulty in catching him again. A pony can travel a long way in a short time if he is galloping in excitement or fear.

Catching a pony

There are few things more infuriating than a pony who won't be caught. This is a serious fault in a pony because it means he can only be kept stabled and, if grazed at all, must be tethered on a long rope to a strong stake properly embedded in the ground, or else grazed in-hand. All these things are time-consuming, inconvenient and not particularly good for the pony.

Tethering has a code of practice (recommended guidelines) and ponies must be tethered on a stake with a swivel so they don't wrap their rope round and round the stake till they are tied up impossibly short; they must be within reach of shelter and water and out of reach of vandals. Also, they should be out of reach of other ponies who might attack them or trip over their rope. Tethering is a poor way to keep any pony except in an absolute emergency.

The right way to do it

Take your halter or headcollar and rope into the field and call the pony. If your pony has learnt his name (as described earlier) and is a perfect angel he'll trot up obediently and stand still while you put on his headcollar and lead him away.

If he isn't quite perfect, you may need to wave a titbit at him before he'll come sauntering over to casually enquire what you want or what you've got. While he's

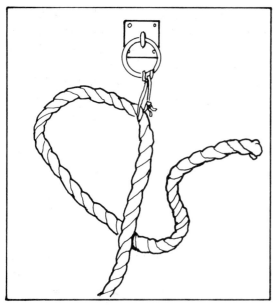

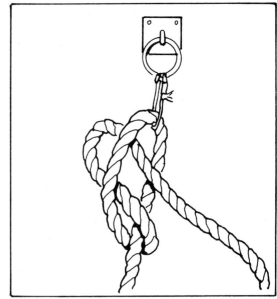

How to tie a slip-knot, sometimes called a safety knot. *Top left:* Pass the end of your headcollar rope through the loop of string on the tie-ring. *Top right:* Feed it back through in a loop, as shown. *Bottom left:* Pull down on the loop with one hand and it will tighten. In an emergency, just pull hard on the free end and the knot will come undone. *Bottom right:* If your pony has a habit of untying the knot himself by playing with the free end, place it loosely through the loop, like this.

However, keep an eye on him because if he pulls it tight it is no longer a safety knot and will not come undone with a pull on the free end – it will just pull tighter. If your pony makes a habit of playing with this knot, buy a special metal safety clip (available from most saddlers) for the end of your rope, which will come undone with one hard pull but which the pony will be quite unable to fathom out. The secret is that you pull downwards on the clip, whereas the pony will almost always pull sideways, when the clip will stay put.

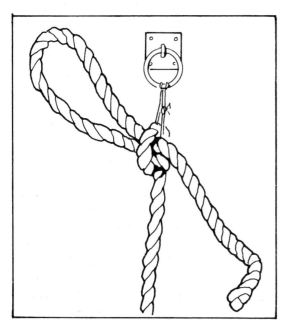

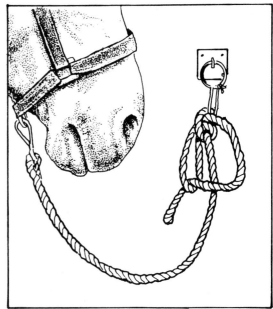

munching, you can put on his headcollar and lead him off.

If he's quite plainly not perfect, walk up to his shoulder, speak to him and hold out your offering. While he's eating the first piece and wondering if it's worth hanging around for more, slip your rope behind his ears and catch it together under his throat so you have hold of him. Give him another piece, put on the headcollar and off you go.

With a pony who always plays hard to get and grabs the titbit but won't let you lay a finger, much less a rope, on him, you'll save a lot of trouble if you always turn him out in a well-fitting headcollar (preferably leather which should break if he gets it caught up on a hedge, his own hoof or anything else – nylon headcollars are too strong to be safe for this job). To the bottom ring of the headcollar under his jaw, firmly tie a piece of binder twine about 15 cm (6 ins) long. If it is any longer than this he might tread on it when grazing and frighten himself when he feels the pull on his head.

When you offer your titbit, put out both your hands. As he takes the titbit off one, quietly and quickly get hold of the twine with the other then clip on your lead rope. Don't hold your hands right out in front of you but make the pony come in quite close in case he starts to move away again at once.

Obviously, when he comes, say 'good boy' and stroke him.

Ponies who are difficult to catch

If difficult ponies make up their minds not to be caught there is little you can do about it. Even a group of hefty men with a long rope cornering the pony doesn't always work because a determined pony will charge at them, knocking them down and risking injury all round, although some do give up when cornered.

There are various ruses that work such as having a squeaky toy in your pocket which so strains the pony's curiosity that he can't resist coming up to see what the noise is; sitting in the middle of the field (or standing if it's wet) with a large white rustly bag full of his favourite peppermints which *you* are eating; walking round and round him in ever-decreasing circles, ignoring him till he regards you as part of the furniture and you eventually casually pass so close you can just grab the binder twine and take him with you; leading his best friend out of the field; bringing another pony into the field or anything else which you've discovered arouses his curiosity.

A permanent cure seems like a dream come true, but next school holidays (because you'll need plenty of time for several days in a run) you might like to try this one which has cured several animals I know.

Move the pony to a field with no water or cut off the supply he has. The field will need fencing strong and high enough to thwart any attempt to break or jump out in search of water. Take water to the pony in a bucket but *do not let him drink* till he has let you catch him. Splash your hand in the bucket so he knows it is water, and stand by the normal water source, if there is one.

If he will not come after a few minutes, take the bucket away. Grass contains water so he'll come to no harm at this stage.

If he does let you catch him, take him somewhere where he can drink his fill (after praising him thoroughly) then turn him loose again without working him. If catching *always* means work it's no wonder some ponies become difficult.

If he won't come the first time, take the bucket back two or three hours later and try again. No catch, no water! Try once or twice more that day, then leave him for the night. Try again early next morning, by which time he will be quite thirsty. If he will, let him lick your wet hand and swoosh it in the bucket but be firm about catching. Give him several minutes each time to decide whether to be caught and have a drink, or otherwise.

On this second day, you must go to the field every hour or so till he gives in, which he almost certainly will on the second day. After all this time without water he must not be allowed all he wants now. Let him have half a bucket as a reward, then return about an hour later with another half bucket and gradually build up to leading him away to drink as much as he wants.

In a very short time, he will be resigned to the fact that unless he is caught he cannot drink. You'll probably soon find that after just a few days of this treatment he will come trotting up waiting to be caught.

Once he allows himself to be caught readily, restore his water supply and try catching him with titbits. Grass-kept ponies don't go so much for carrots, but prefer things like coarse mix, mints or cubes.

If he goes back to his old tricks, put him back on the no-water routine for a few days and I think you'll find that, like other ponies who have been given this treatment, he becomes a changed character. Always praise him when he lets you catch him – but don't always work him, so he never knows what's coming.

If there are other ponies with him they must not be made to suffer for his stubbornness and must be caught up and led to water at least twice a day, being allowed to drink their fill (which they will probably do in two stints, so don't lead them away when they lift their heads the first time). This may well annoy your pony, especially if he can see them drinking, and might speed up the cure. Always try to catch him at the same time; it just might work.

Turning loose

The ideal way to do this is to have a friend open the gate for you, wide enough for you and your pony to pass through without bumping into gate-posts and to prevent the gate from swinging or blowing back on to you, perhaps hurting and frightening the pair of you and maybe allowing the pony to get free on to a road. Your friend can also keep back any other ponies in the field and prevent them escaping.

If you're on your own, however, try it this way. Hold the pony in the hand nearest the gate-post and open the gate with your free hand, allowing enough room for you and the pony to pass through without being knocked by the gate or bumping into the gate-post and keeping hold of the gate all the time. It helps to have a properly hung gate which opens and moves easily with one hand. Keep a firm hold of the pony's lead rope and bring his head back towards you, saying his name, when you are through, so making him do a turn about the forehand to face the gate again as you close it firmly behind you.

Any ponies already in the field, who may try to get out as you come in, will have their exit blocked by your pony on one side and by you and the gate on the other. Lead the pony a few steps into the field, turn him to face the gate again and make him stand still. Do not release him immediately or he could get into the habit of refusing to wait, dashing off with the lead rope still attached and bringing himself down by treading on it.

Instead, pretend to straighten his forelock or stroke his neck and talk to him for just a few seconds. Then, standing in front of and to one side of his head, unclip the rope or unbuckle the headcollar, say 'good boy' and step back the instant you let him go.

If he spins round now (which he will do on his hind feet) and gives a kick and a buck as he charges off, you will be well out of reach of those heels. If he had been facing into the field when you released him, he may have knocked you over or kicked you as he charged past and away.

Bringing out of the field
Again, hold the pony in the hand nearest the gate-post and open the gate with your other

hand, wide enough for you both to pass through without injury but leaving little room for any ponies following to squeeze by. As your pony goes through, be ready to bring his head back towards you and, at the same time to step across into the space where his quarters were, keeping firm hold of the gate all the time, to block the escape route of other ponies. Fasten the gate properly.

It helps to shoo other ponies away from the gate if you can. Use their names in a cross tone and be ready to give a slap on the muzzle to any pushy pony who tries to boss you around. You have to *seem* confident even if you aren't!

Head-shy ponies

A pony who does not like having his head handled is known as 'head-shy'. Some ponies may hold their heads sky high because they don't like the slight discomfort of being bridled or having their heads attended to in any way, but others are actually frightened of the bridle or bit.

First of all, see that the bridle and bit fit properly and are not rubbing or pinching anywhere. If the bit has become roughened or the stitching is coming undone causing a turned-up end of a strap to come away and rub the pony's face, this will certainly hurt or irritate him, for example. If the bridle and bit don't seem to be the trouble, there is a chance the pony's ears, sinuses, mouth or teeth have some disorder and a vet should examine the pony. Another cause is simply that those who handle the pony are not gentle enough or careful enough when handling his head. With a proper examination of the cause, and improved handling, the problem should disappear.

With ponies who are set in the habit, you can still put a bridle on them usually by unbuckling the reins at the hand end and passing them up the shoulders from under the neck, right rein up the right shoulder and left rein up the left shoulder.

Buckle them together again on top of the withers and slide them up his neck to just behind his ears, then you should be able to control his head and put on the bridle. Taking a strong box or bucket into the stable to stand on also helps small people handle head-shy ponies.

In a particularly stubborn case, put the bridle on by taking it to pieces and putting it together again on the pony's head as if you were reassembling it on its bracket after cleaning. Put the headpiece into place by sliding it up the pony's neck from behind. Fit together/add on all the other pieces and insert the bit last. Making sure it is not upside down or back to front, fasten one side of it to the correct cheekpiece, say the left, then put your finger in the right side of his mouth and tickle his tongue, when he will almost certainly open his mouth. Bring the bit carefully up into place and fasten it to the remaining cheekpiece.

Restraint

Sometimes you'll need to keep a restless pony still for some kind of treatment, say veterinary or clipping. At times like this, holding him as normal with a headcollar or bridle is not always sufficient. For a firmer hold with a headcollar, clip the rope to the offside dee, pass it under his chin and through the nearside dee, then when you pull on the rope his nose will be held in a tightened grip all round.

You can hold up one of his legs on the side opposite the one on which the vet is working. If the near hind leg is being treated, you could hold up the off fore, for example.

You could try passing the headcollar rope through his mouth – but you must *never* do this with a chain. If the pony becomes really difficult, do get expert help and advice before trying any stronger method, and/or risking injury to all concerned. Your vet will

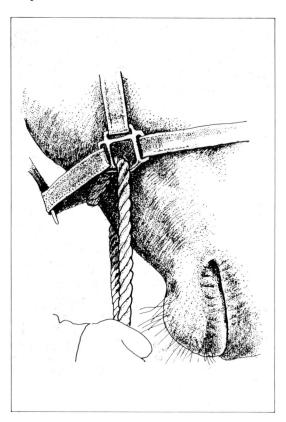

know what to do, as will your instructor. In any case, *never* allow anyone to beat up the pony, shout or bawl at him or get rough. It will not help matters as it will frighten the pony even more and he will be worse next time. If this happens, tell them to stop and call an adult to help you sort things out.

Learning pony language

This isn't a section on how to neigh and whinny but on how to understand what ponies are telling us or each other by their different facial expressions, body positions and vocal sounds.

You'll be familiar with the interested look

You can obtain stronger restraint with an ordinary headcollar and rope if you unclip the rope from the back ring, where it is usually fastened, and pass it through the side dees. If you pull on the rope the noseband will tighten and help restrain the pony more.

Don't forget . . .

● Even a small pony is stronger than a big man. Ponies are best handled with **firm kindness**. If you are rough with them they often fight back and usually win.

● If you are having problems handling a pony, seek expert help before the situation gets out of control and dangerous. Some things ponies **have** to learn to submit to, such as having their feet attended to. Being kind doesn't mean letting them have all their own way. Like us, they have to learn discipline if they are to get through life, and sometimes that discipline can best be taught by someone more experienced than ourselves.

● Beating up a pony never does any good and neither does losing your

temper. A frightened or angry pony does not learn anything, except how to resist and fight. Again, if you are having trouble, ask an expert to help you.

● Speak often to your pony. Ponies take comfort from a quiet, confident human voice. Speak before approaching him, either in stable or field, to warn him you're there, and speak to praise him or correct him, so that he knows where he stands with you.

● If you have to tell your pony off for something, it has to be done **immediately** he has done wrong or whilst he's in the act. If you leave it two seconds, it's best not to bother at all because he will not be able to connect the punishment with the wrong-doing after that time.

a pony has when you walk towards him with a bucket of food or a titbit. The most noticeable thing is that his ears are pricked sharply forward. His ears are one of the most important signals to help you understand how he is feeling, what he is thinking about or what he is going to do.

Ears are usually pricked towards whatever the pony has his attention on. When you are riding, his ears would normally be pricked more or less in the direction in which he's going. If he's bored with his work, his ears will be at 'half mast', flopping sideways and he'll have a fed-up expression on his face (although you'll be unable to see that from the saddle).

If you give him a command from the saddle with your voice, one or both ears will flick back towards you to listen. Some ponies do this when leg aids are given and most will press both ears back harder if you use your whip because whips can hurt and flattened-back ears show dislike or anger.

If you are jumping and your pony's ears are not pointed towards the jump yet he is bowling along quite gaily, he is probably not concentrating and may not see the jump or refuse at the last minute or even bump into it. However, if his ears are forward but he is *not* bowling along gaily but going very reluctantly, he is probably thinking of refusing or running out. This signal is a combination of ears and way of going.

Another example: when the pony's ears are back, his head goes down and his back 'humps' beneath you, a buck is on the way very soon and you should bring his head up and kick on if you want to stay on board. He can't buck so hard when he is moving forward, so get him going.

Ears flopping sideways can indicate boredom, relaxation, sleepiness or tiredness, but they can also mean illness. If the pony perks up when you approach and looks interested he's probably all right, but if he pays no attention and has a dull look about

This horse is looking really fed up, with floppy ears and a bored expression on his face. He's probably thinking: 'When is someone going to let me out?'

him he could well be ill, especially if he is in the field and not moving about much and keeping away from other ponies.

The eyes, like ours, express feelings, too. Gentle, calm eyes indicate a relaxed, content pony; wild, wide-open eyes show excitement or fear; and dull, sunken eyes might mean illness or generally being run-down.

Your pony's top lip is very sensitive. He uses it to root out his food and to investigate strange objects. If he raises it and curls it up and back showing his teeth, this is called 'flehmen' (flay-men), a German word for which we have no real translation. It means the pony has smelled something either strange or unpleasant, but in stallions it can mean they have scented a mare in season, as mares give out different smells at that time.

107

This pony is entitled to look cross, with ears back and nostrils wrinkled up and back. He is being brushed roughly on a sensitive part of his body. Always groom gently, but thoroughly, otherwise your pony could become difficult about it.

When ponies yawn they also draw back their upper lip and show their teeth, but they open their mouths (like we do) and close their eyes.

At the other end of his body, his tail can also give you a good idea of what's going on inside his head. A slightly arched tail is usual for most ponies and means normal interest and energy. A flattened tail, clamped between the buttocks shows anger, discomfort or dislike; a swishing tail, anger or dislike, and a highly raised tail, great excitement. Ponies with a lot of Arab blood sometimes arch their tails backwards, right over their quarters, when extremely excited.

Facial expressions are something you'll develop a feel for the more you work around ponies. The nostrils can help you decide on what a pony means, as well as the eyes and ears. If the nostrils are flared it means excitement or a pony greatly out of breath, and you'll surely be able to tell the difference. If the nostrils are wrinkled up and back it means bad temper or pain.

How would you interpret your pony's signals if he came towards you, with his ears pressed flat back, a cross expression on his face, his nostrils wrinkled up and back, his head stretched out towards you and maybe his teeth showing? You'd be pretty safe to assume he was going to bite you! If you're working on him in his stable and you notice a cross expression plus the tail raised and maybe swishing and a hind leg waving about, I'd say a kick was on the way. Incidentally, ponies find it hard to kick with their tails down, so pull hard and down on the tail and you could stop or lessen the kick.

If you are watching horseracing on television or gymkhana games, you might notice that the horses/ponies have their ears back hard when galloping. This could mean that they don't like what they're doing, but it usually means they are trying their best as it is a sign of all-out effort.

Stamping feet can indicate excitement at meeting a strange pony (sometimes ponies will strike out at each other with their forefeet in these circumstances) or the pony could be stamping to dislodge flies. However, it can be one of the signs of colic, the others being patchy sweating, tail swishing, the pony trying to bite or look anxiously at his flanks, general restlessness and unease with a worried expression and maybe getting down to roll.

When ponies roll to scratch their skins, they have a good shake when they get up again. If they do *not* shake after rolling, it could be a sign of internal pain.

As well as these signs which ponies use to 'speak' to other ponies and to humans (they expect us to know what they mean) ponies do, of course, use their voices, which are as individual as ours. A soft whicker means 'welcome and have you got anything for me?' a louder one means excitement, usually at seeing a feed bucket coming, and a loud neigh either great excitement, worry or uncertainty, or an anxious call to distant friends. Ponies squeal to each other when playing in the field or when standing still and talking to one another, usually with nostrils flared and pressed nose to nose.

I find it very interesting watching ponies talk to each other – with practice you can learn not only what they are saying between themselves but what they mean with voice, face and body signs when communicating with you.

8. Tack and clothing

The word 'tack' is short for tackle and includes saddles, bridles, martingales, girths, stirrups, and so on. It also includes horse clothing such as rugs and bandages.

The variety of tack is enormous and can be bewildering. Much of it is useful, some is essential and some is actually harmful, especially in novice hands. Tack can also be very expensive but cheap-quality equipment can put your life at risk. If you have to watch the pennies, or rather pounds, it is better to buy good quality secondhand tack.

What you and your pony will need

Saddles

Your saddle will be the most expensive single item. There are various sorts but the most useful for all-round riding (flat work and jumping) is a general-purpose saddle. The flaps, on which your legs rest, are set moderately forward to allow room for your knee when you have a shortened stirrup for jumping, but are still suitable for the longer stirrup used for riding on the flat.

Most saddles are made of leather, although there are some made from synthetic (man-made) materials on the market. The frame on which your saddle is made is called the tree and is normally made of wood and metal. Assuming the saddle fits you and your pony (we'll come to that in a minute), the most comfortable saddle will

have a spring tree rather than a rigid tree. This means there are springy strips of metal running from front to back of the tree, so that when you sit on them the springing absorbs your weight and makes it more comfortable for you and, provided you are riding properly, your pony, too. Spring-tree saddles are more expensive than rigid-tree ones, but I would rather have a good, secondhand spring-tree saddle than a new rigid-tree one for about the same price.

Good quality, well-cared-for tack lasts a lifetime and longer and you'll get many more years' wear than you need out of a good, used saddle.

Details of saddle fitting and saddling up are given on pages 125-129.

A general-purpose saddle. It has a moderately forward-cut flap and a fairly deep, comfortable seat. The stirrups have been run up the leathers and the spare end of the leather has been put through the keeper (or loop) on the flap, so that it doesn't get in the way. The girth is draped over the seat with its inside touching the leather of the saddle. This keeps the girth in good shape and, if muddy, prevents the dirt scratching the saddle seat. A saddle arranged like this is said to be 'put up', the way it would be kept on the saddle rack in the tack room. The type of girth shown here is a Balding girth. It is specially made to be narrow behind the elbows (where the separate pieces of leather cross) so there is less chance of it causing discomfort or girth galls.

Girths

You'll need a girth to keep the saddle on.
This buckles to the long straps under the
flap called girth tabs. Some straps reach well
below the bottom of the flap to allow you to
use a short belly girth instead of the longer
kind which buckle higher up and sometimes
cause an uncomfortable lump under your
leg. Your girth can be made of leather or
fabric such as lampwick or mohair, or of
cotton or nylon string. The string ones aren't
so good and tend to cause sores called girth

111

A general-purpose saddle showing what is underneath the flap. The knee roll (on the right) acts as a support to the knee during jumping. There are three girth tabs and the girth is buckled to the first two, as normal. It could be buckled to the last two if the pony's comformation demanded that the saddle sit further forward than normal. (This is something to discuss with your instructor.) The leather flap on the tabs above the buckles should be pulled down to cover them and prevent the saddle flap being damaged by the buckle tongues.

galls. Any girth can cause them if too tight, too loose or caked with dirt, but string ones seem particularly prone to problems. Some girths are made of nylon or acrilan and seem good, but natural materials such as lampwick or mohair are my favourites because they absorb sweat and seem more comfortable for the pony, if kept clean.

Stirrups and leathers

You'll also need stirrups and stirrup leathers. The best kind of leathers are the (virtually) unbreakable rawhide ones; the stitching is not guaranteed to last for ever but, as with stitching on all your tack, keep an eye on it every time you clean it and you should not be caught out. If it is worn or coming undone, do not use the equipment, but take it to a saddler to be mended.

It is most important that stirrup irons should be the right size and type. Always buy stainless-steel stirrups, never nickel, which is weak and dangerous. The inside of the bottom of your stirrup should be 2.5 cm (1 in.) wider than the sole of your boot at its widest point. If wider than this your foot could slip through and in a fall you could be caught by the ankle and might be dragged, which could kill you. If it is narrower, your foot could get jammed in the stirrup with the same result. Stirrups come in many sizes so

Under the little skirt of the saddle is the stirrup bar over which the stirrup leather is looped. In this picture the small catch at the end of the bar is up, the idea being to keep the stirrup leather in place. In fact, when riding, the catch must always be down, so that in the event of a fall and your foot becoming caught in the stirrup, the leather will be pulled off the bar and you will not be dragged. If you ride with the catch up as shown, you stand a good chance of being dragged by the foot should the pony gallop off, and could be seriously injured or killed.

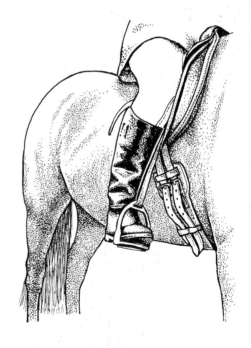

Right This saddle has a short belly girth, a type used mainly for dressage saddles. In dressage you need a close contact with your horse and a short girth like this removes the buckles from under your leg, enabling you to get closer to your horse or pony.

you will have no trouble getting the right one.

The width of your stirrup leather is dictated by the eye-hole at the top of the stirrup. The leather should pass through easily but should not be *much* narrower than the eye as narrow leathers are uncomfortable against your shin. They come in varying lengths so tell the saddler how tall you are and you should get the right length.

Rubber treads which slot in the bottom of your stirrup help keep your feet in place and do keep them a bit warmer in winter.

Numnahs

A numnah (a saddle-shaped pad) to put under your saddle is not essential but can absorb sweat when the pony is working and help keep the underside of your saddle cleaner longer. It should not be used to pad the back against a badly fitting saddle but simply to provide extra comfort for the pony. Again, natural materials are a safer bet than fabrics like nylon or acrilan fleece. The numnah should be shaped to fit the pony's backbone. If you fold one down the back where it goes along the pony's backbone you should see a definite lift at the front for the withers. A useful type of numnah is quilted cotton with cotton filling. These are absorbent and easily washed.

Bridles

Bridles usually come in pony, cob or full sizes, with occasionally small pony sizes. They are adjustable within their sizes, anyway, so you will not have much trouble getting a good fit. If you tell your saddler the pony's size you should get the right one.

The width of the cheekpieces should suit the pony's head. For most ponies 13 mm (½ in.) is about right. If the pony has a very small head you could have narrower leather, and a little wider for a bigger head.

The browband can, if you wish, be coloured, especially for shows, and you'll see a wide range of patterns and materials on saddlery stands at shows and in shops. If you can afford only one bridle you could buy a special browband for shows and use a plain or fancy-stitched leather one for everyday riding. The colour is important and a matter of taste, and you can carry on the colour scheme in your show clothes. Grey ponies look nice, I think, with burgundy or blue browbands, chestnuts with green or blue, whereas bays and browns can wear almost any colour.

There is a wide variety of nosebands and some of them are rather rough means of making up for poor schooling or bad hands on the part of the rider. A good child's pony should not need anything but an ordinary cavesson noseband, which is just a strap going round his nose, held up by another going over his head. It doesn't actually serve any purpose unless the pony needs a standing martingale to keep his head down, which a child's pony should not need anyway. (A standing martingale is a strap passing from the back of the noseband to the saddle girth, held up by a strap round the base of the neck). Most people feel, however, that a noseband finishes off a pony's appearance, and as they can be decorated with fancy stitching, they do give a smart effect.

A commonly used noseband is the drop noseband. This, again, is held up, like any noseband, by a strap going over the head. The strap over the nose goes only very slightly lower than that of a cavesson, but the underneath strap is 'dropped' (hence its name) under the bit, in the groove just above the pony's fleshy chin (the chin groove), not behind the straight jawbones; it is the back or underneath strap which is dropped, not the front.

These nosebands are supposed to keep a pony's mouth closed should he try to open it to evade his bit (often the rider's fault, anyway, for being too heavy-handed). They are often seen wrongly fitted with the front nosepiece much too low, near the nostrils, which interferes with the breathing to some extent. Ponies cannot breathe through their mouths and if they are not allowed to breathe freely might justifiably feel suffocated and panic.

Never buy anything other than a cavesson noseband unless your instructor advises it, and certainly not because your favourite showjumping or event rider uses one. Your pony may need something quite different from their horse and you could do more harm than good with the wrong noseband.

You will also need a pair of reins, of course. There are various lengths but a good saddler will sell you a pair the right length for the size of bridle you have bought. As for width, if they are too narrow you could find yourself clenching your fists; this will make your hands heavy and unfeeling, a very bad riding fault. If the reins are too wide, though, you will have trouble holding and using them correctly. Hold different widths in the tack shop to see what is comfortable – about 13 mm (½ in.) should be all right for small children and about 17 mm (⅝ in.) or 19 mm (¾ in.) for older children.

Plain leather reins are fine for showing but not very practical for everyday riding, jumping or gymkhanas as they slip, especially when wet with rain or sweat. Rubber-covered ones do not slip even when wet and neither do plaited cotton ones. Nylon is rough on the hands and slippery; plaited leather stretches easily but laced leather reins (with little loops of leather stitched through plain reins in a V pattern) are quite good.

Details of how to fit, put on and remove a bridle are given on pages 129-132.

Bits

There is an old saying which says there is a key to every horse's mouth. This means there is a bit to suit every horse or pony, and has led some people to think that if they find the right bit the pony will suddenly, as if by magic, be transformed into a perfect mount who goes superbly, looks wonderful, is instantly obedient and will win everything he enters. This is perfect rubbish.

Far more important, within reason, than the bit itself is the way you use it. In other words, to be a good rider you need good hands, which usually only come from years of practice and good instruction. Even the mildest bit can hurt your pony if you jab his mouth, haul on the reins or use them to keep your balance.

Bitting (the study of and use of bits) is a vast subject with which your instructor will help you. Most children's ponies are bitted with some kind of snaffle bit, that is, a bit with a ring at each end of the mouthpiece (the part which goes in the pony's mouth), to which are fastened the bridle cheekpieces (to hold it in place), and the reins (to give you direct contact with the mouth).

If you pull on the reins (gently, please!) with a snaffle bit, the pony feels the pressure in his mouth as if the reins were a continuous loop going from one hand, through his mouth and up to the other hand. The mouthpiece may be 'broken' i.e. with a joint in the middle or, more rarely, with two joints, or it may be an all-in-one, straight, round bar. This bar can be curved slightly, when it is called a half-moon or mullen-mouth snaffle.

A bit your pony does not like will obviously not make for a co-operative relationship between you. It could make him seem awkward or disobedient when all he is trying to do is get away from the discomfort in his mouth, especially if you are handling the bit roughly. In your disappointment you might punish him quite wrongly. The right bit could avoid this, so it is as well to try to understand a little of how the bit works and feels to the pony.

A jointed snaffle, especially those with only one joint, is generally felt to be more

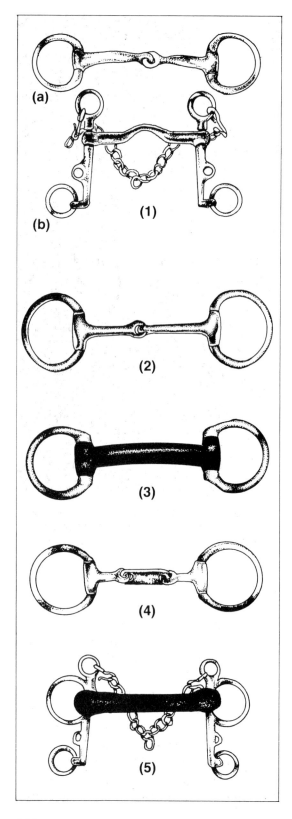

(a)

(b) **(1)**

(2)

(3)

(4)

(5)

severe than a half-moon snaffle as it has a squeezing action on the bars of the mouth when the reins are used. (The bars are the toothless part of the gums where the bit rests). It also presses on the corners of the lips and the tongue.

This squeezing action is less severe with a double-jointed snaffle.

The straight-bar snaffle is not very comfortable for the pony as it allows little room for his tongue, which can be squashed under it. The half-moon snaffle is more comfortable. It has no squeezing action on the bars and so is milder than a jointed snaffle, but some ponies tend to lean on it, making them 'dead' to the bit and heavy in your hands, resulting in an unpleasant ride and a pony who may be harder to control. Such ponies would probably be better in a jointed snaffle.

Many ponies prefer a jointed snaffle, anyway, as they can move them about in the mouth and play with them more easily; also the joint leaves more room for the tongue. It is good for the pony to play with his bit as this produces saliva to keep the mouth moist and soft; a dry mouth is not so sensitive. But if you see a pony actually frothing at the mouth it means his bit (or his rider's use of it) is worrying or hurting him and he is moving it about constantly to try and get away from it.

The way the mouthpiece is joined to the rings can also affect the feel of the bit to the pony. If there is simply a hole in the ends of the mouthpiece through which the rings run, this is called a loose-ring snaffle if the rings are just like flattened circles, or a wire-ring

Some bits in common use:
(1) The two parts of a double bridle: (a) the bridoon or bradoon and (b) the curb or Weymouth, with chain.
(2) Single-jointed eggbutt snaffle.
(3) Rubber eggbutt snaffle with a mullen (half-moon) mouthpiece.
(4) Dr Bristol snaffle.
(5) Vulcanite pelham, with chain.

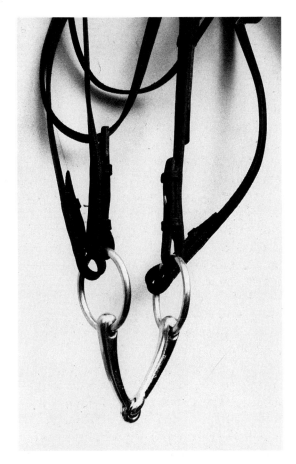

A wire-ring snaffle bit attached to a bridle. The mouthpiece can run up and down the rings and gives the pony a freer, looser feel in the mouth which encourages him to play with the bit. Many ponies prefer this type of bit, which feels less stiff and fixed than an eggbutt.

This snaffle bit has been put into the bridle upside down – a common mistake with beginners. It would be very uncomfortable for the pony, as it is curving the wrong way.

snaffle if they are of rounded metal. If the mouthpiece forms a fixed hinge on the ring, it is called an eggbutt bit. This means the pony's lips cannot be pinched between the mouthpiece and the rings, but also that there is less play in the mouth. Loose- or wire-ring bits allow the pony to play more with the mouthpiece, but if such bits get worn at the hole (as nickel bits will) the lips can be pinched, which is obviously very painful indeed.

For this reason, apart from the usual one of quality and strength, always buy stainless-steel bits if you are getting metal ones.

Some people feel that softer, less cold materials than metal are better, and you find half-moon bits in rubber, vulcanite (like hard rubber), and nylon. Jointed bits can be rubber-covered and half-moon *and* jointed bits can be leather-covered.

Never buy any bit with a grooved, roughened or twisted mouthpiece. Just because they are on sale in a tack shop does not mean they are good for your pony. Smooth mouthpieces are best – and always check your bit daily to see it has not become

117

roughened, chipped or cracked, which could be not only painful for the pony but dangerous if it broke, leaving you with no control.

You will have seen horses and ponies in showing classes and advanced dressage competitions wearing what are called 'double bridles'. These carry two bits in their mouths, a thin snaffle and a curb or Weymouth bit.

A curb bit has one mouthpiece but it has metal cheeks (rods) at each end of the mouthpiece, and looks like a capital H with the middle line (the mouthpiece) too far up. At the tops of the cheeks are rings for the checkpieces. There are two hooks fastened to the top rings on which is hooked a chain called the curb chain. The reins fasten to rings on the bottoms of the cheeks and when they are used the cheeks act like levers, pulling the chain into the chin groove so the lower jaw is held in a vice or clamp between the chain and the mouthpiece. The idea is that the horse will relax his jaw to escape this feeling and so flex nicely to the bit – once he has been patiently taught. These bits are much more severe than a snaffle and are not suitable for any but well-trained riders and ponies.

With a double bridle the pony has two different sorts of action to think about and the rider has two pairs of reins to handle. It is certainly not the bitting arrangement for a first pony, a novice or a very young rider. When your instructor thinks you and your pony are ready to progress to a double bridle, he or she will tell you; in the meantime, don't be afraid to ask questions, just for the sake of learning, if you want to know more.

One bit which tries to combine the actions of a double bridle and an ordinary snaffle is the pelham. This, too, is shaped like a letter H with the middle bar too high, but as well as rings at the tops and bottoms of the cheeks there are larger rings for the snaffle reins right next to the mouthpiece. The pony has

A pelham bit being used with only one rein by means of roundings, the leather loops fitted to both top and bottom rings of the bit.

only one mouthpiece in his mouth which combines, through two sets of reins, the direct action of the snaffle with the indirect, lever action of the curb.

In use, pelhams are not so exact as double bridles. The two pairs of reins can be reduced to one by two leather loops, one each side, going from the curb rings on the cheeks to the snaffle rings, the single rein being fastened to the loop. The loops are called roundings (or rounders).

Many ponies go well in a pelham but they are usually the headstrong sort who need some controlling. Again, your instructor should be the one to advise whether or not a pelham is needed.

Further notes on fitting a bit can be found on page 131.

Neckstraps

One very useful piece of equipment not mentioned so far is a neckstrap. This is a piece of leather which runs around the pony's neck, and is attached by little straps to the front Ds (little metal loops) on the pommel of your saddle. Neckstraps are very handy to hold on to when you perhaps don't feel too safe, such as when learning to jump or if the pony is playing about. You can hold the reins in one hand and the neckstrap in the other so you have both control and security.

The neckstrap adjusts to fit snugly round the base of the pony's neck, by means of a buckle, which is fastened on the outside so that it doesn't rub the pony.

Never be ashamed to use a neckstrap, even if you have to improvise with one made of soft, thick rope or an old rein. Almost anything is better than jabbing a pony in the mouth – a very bad thing to do and something he will never forget. He can't understand that you didn't mean it, and if you make a habit of it he will soon lose confidence in you. Using a neckstrap shows knowledgeable people that you are a sensible, considerate rider.

Headcollars

A headcollar and lead rope for leading your pony about and tying him up will also be needed. A headcollar looks like a heavyweight bridle without bit or reins and usually without browband, although a browband is an advantage as it stops the headpiece slipping down the neck and

A neckstrap is useful to hang on to to help when you want to keep your seat! It is kept in place with short straps or leather loops fastening to the saddle dees.

causing an indirect and uncomfortable pull on the nosepiece.

Headcollars come in leather and nylon webbing. The best have buckles on both sides of the head to adjust the height of the noseband; cheaper ones have only one buckle but are quite good enough. The buckle is usually at the top of the left cheekpiece and the headstrap, which fastens to it, comes up over the head from the off (right) side. Some headcollars also have a buckle on the noseband to give a better fit.

There is a ring under the jaw for attaching a lead rope; they usually clip on with a dog-lead type of fastening.

Details of how to fit and put on a headcollar are given on pages 132-133.

A well-fitting leather headcollar. The noseband is about mid-way between the corners of the mouth and the sharp face bones. If too high it could rub the bones, if too low the pony could rub it off down over the muzzle. The 'dog-lead' clip on the lead rope enables the rope to be quickly and easily attached or removed.

Rugs

Depending on the type of pony you have and your system of management, you may not need rugs to keep him warm. Hardy, native-bred ponies often live out all year round and are never rugged. Ponies with even a little Arab or Thoroughbred blood, however, will probably need rugging indoors especially at night in winter, and may also need a New Zealand (waterproof) rug outdoors, especially if clipped or during wet weather. Any pony, regardless of his breeding, will need a rug if he is clipped much.

These days, most rugs for everyday use are made of synthetic materials such as quilted nylon or the new 'breatheable' fabrics which allow moisture from the body to pass through the fabric and so discourage sweating or clamminess under the rug.

Some rugs are still made from traditional, natural fabrics such as jute or wool. Jute is a rough, beige-coloured material used for night rugs. Woollen materials are used for day rugs and look very smart with matching or contrasting bindings and owner's initials. Jute rugs can be washed whereas woollen ones are better dry-cleaned and so are not as practical for use when they might get dirty.

However, although washable, jute rugs *are* bulky, heavy and difficult to launder. They also take a long time to dry. Much easier to use are the modern synthetic rugs which wash easily, dry quickly and are lighter for your pony to wear; they are also often warmer than jute rugs. They can be used for day or night wear but many people like their animals to have a different rug for night and day, even if only to give them a chance to air and freshen up. Also, you still have one rug available when the other is in the wash.

You can also buy woollen blankets or synthetic under-rugs if one rug is not enough to keep your pony warm.

Night rugs, day rugs and the modern synthetic stable rugs are not suitable for turning your pony out. For this you need a

New Zealand rug (it was invented in New Zealand) which is waterproof and heavier quality to withstand the wear and tear of ponies galloping about and rolling in the mud. Traditional ones are made of heavy canvas and are lined with wool but modern ones are of synthetic fabrics which are lighter and can be just as tough if a good make.

You can still buy New Zealand rugs which are kept on by a surcingle (belt) round the pony's girth area but these are old-fashioned, uncomfortable for the pony and can cause back problems; they also tend to slip round leaving him partly uncovered, and with the rug trailing on the floor for him to tread on and maybe bring himself down.

The surcingle passes over the backbone and, if fastened tight enough to keep the rug on, causes pressure which can give the pony a sore back. A padded surcingle (known as a

A quilted nylon stable rug. This rug fits well, coming in front of the withers (not pressing on top of them) and extending well back to the tail for warmth. The surcingles are the type which cross under the belly and keep the rug in place without causing pressure on the spine or an uncomfortable tightness round the pony's middle. These rugs can be quickly and easily laundered at home in an ordinary washing machine.

roller) helps remove the pressure on each side of the backbone, but this arrangement is still not as good as the modern method of fastening with leg straps or narrow surcingles criss-crossing under the belly.

Leg straps are most often found on New Zealand rugs but can be used on stable rugs, too. There is one strap on each side which is usually buckled on the side of the rug behind where your leg would go when riding. At the

A modern, shaped New Zealand rug from Hydrophane Laboratories Ltd, correctly fitting *in front* of the withers and extending just past the root of the tail. It has two adjustable breast straps. If the crossed surcingles were fastened a little more tightly there would be less chance of the horse's leg becoming caught in them.

other end of the strap is a clip which snaps on to a ring on the back edge of the rug. The straps are adjustable.

Another important feature of a good, modern rug is that it will be shaped to fit the pony's body. In other words, the back seam of the rug will follow the up-and-down line of his backbone, with a rise for the withers, a slight dip for the back, another rise for the croup on top of the quarters and another dip towards the root of the tail. There may also be tucks or darts behind the elbow and in front of the stifle to take up any slack

material, and maybe on either side of the tail for the same reason.

Some New Zealand rugs also have a drawstring sewn inside the back edge of the rug over the quarters, which you can pull snug (but not tight) to improve the fit.

All rugs fasten at the front with one or two short straps and buckles at the breast. Some have a fillet string, or strap, behind the thighs to help keep the back of the rug in place, although with leg straps this is not necessary.

There are even rugs for summer use, put on simply to keep the coat of a stabled pony dust-free. These are usually made of cotton or linen and are called summer sheets. They are useful for show ponies but are quite unnecessary otherwise.

Notes on rug fitting and the correct method of putting on and taking off are given on pages 133-135.

Bandages

Under this heading come stable bandages and exercise bandages for legs and tail bandages. None is essential but all can be useful. (Details of how to apply the different bandages are given on pages 135-139.)

Stable bandages are for drying off wet legs or providing extra warmth for a stabled pony in winter. Obviously, they would be useless on a grass-kept pony as they would be soaking wet all the time. The best are of thick, soft woollen material which is warm and moulds itself to the shape of the leg. Stable bandages are best in dark colours as wool will not stand the hot washing needed to remove stable stains.

Exercise or work bandages are made of elasticated material or sometimes from a knitted cotton material called stockinette. Strangely, many people use these bandages without knowing why. They can help lessen the force of any knocks taken by the pony on jumps and protect his legs from scratches and thorns during cross-country work. They do *not* support the legs, as many people believe, but might just lessen the effect of jarring on hard surfaces. The fact is, though, that your pony should not be working fast in such conditions anyway and if his legs need supporting he shouldn't be working at all.

Exercise bandages are tricky to put on properly and it's best to have a lesson from your instructor if you really want to use them. It's safest to put them on over padding such as gamgee tissue, felt or foam-filled pads so that any unevenness may be lessened. You'll probably find it easier to use boots if you want to protect your pony's legs.

Boots

There are various types of boots designed to protect the leg from injury. Brushing boots and the slightly longer speedicutting boots have protective padding on the inside of the leg and straps fastening on the outside, pointing backwards. Fetlock boots are short felt boots fitting just round the fetlocks. Over-reach boots are plastic or rubber bell-shaped boots, which either pull on (with some difficulty) over the hoof to protect the coronet and heel, or strap on round the pastern. Hock boots are designed to protect the pony's hocks during travelling, although you can now buy all-in-one travelling boots which cover the legs from the coronet to the knee or hock. Knee pads strap on above the knee, have a hard pad covering the front of the knee and a loose strap below to keep the pad down. They are used for travelling or for exercising ponies on roads to protect the knee in case of a fall.

Further information on boot fitting is given on pages 139-140.

Where to buy

It is always safest to buy your tack and clothing from a saddler who is a member of the Society of Master Saddlers, so you know you are getting good quality equipment and will be able to obtain expert advice. Such firms will display this fact on their brochures, letterheadings and billheads and there may be a crest or other notice inside the shop too. Not only can you buy new and secondhand equipment from them, but also you can take in equipment for repair or checking. If you want to change any item the saddler will usually take it in part exchange for something else, and generally offer you a good, all-round service.

If you buy tack from private sellers, you have no come-back if the items turn out to be not what you wanted or even not what the seller said they were.

Buying tack at auctions can be extremely risky for anyone but the most experienced. Those who think they will save money this way, often end up with useless, dangerous, worn-out equipment which costs a lot to restore and may not even be suitable afterwards. If you do go to an auction, be sure to take an expert adviser with you.

When buying secondhand tack look first at the condition of the leather. It doesn't matter if it is as stiff as a board because this can be put right with leather dressing, but there must be no cracks in the leather as these weaken it, make it dangerous and cannot be repaired. If the stitching is worn or coming undone, it must be sewn before use; any metal items or fittings should preferably be of stainless steel, not bent or cracked, and any bits, especially, must be quite smooth.

To find your nearest saddlers, look in the *Yellow Pages* under 'Saddlers and harnessmakers' and ask them if they are members of the Society of Master Saddlers. If you're having trouble finding a good firm, write to the Society at the address given in the Appendix and ask for members in your area.

Where to keep your tack

Tack is expensive and therefore valuable to you and to thieves. There is a flourishing trade in tack, so take care of yours and keep it under lock and key whenever you aren't using it. A tack room needs to be fairly warm and dry. Cold, damp, or conversely, hot, humid conditions will weaken and ruin leather and rot the stitching, too.

Saddles can be hung on the walls on special holders which support the padded part of the panel under the seat; do not sling the saddle on a rope or pole which goes up into the gullet as this will stretch the seat from underneath. Bridles and headcollars should be hung on semi-circular holders by the headband; a shaped block of wood nailed to the wall will do, as will an empty saddle-soap tin. Don't use a hook or nail, as the headpiece will eventually crease and crack and be ruined.

Rugs can be hung from special wall holders, folded and stored in drawers, baskets or on shelves, or hung from a rack on

a pulley, suspended from the ceiling. Bandages and other bits and pieces should be kept in drawers or boxes.

As well as keeping your tack in a safe place, join one of the tack security schemes run by the British Horse Society and Pony Club or by some saddlery firms. Here, your tack is indelibly marked with a special code number, your post code or National Insurance number (if you are old enough to have one). The data is placed somewhere you cannot immediately see it, so the tack is not marred, but anyone checking its ownership could easily find it. Usual sites are under the flap of the saddle or under the

It's best. . .

● To buy good quality second hand tack rather than poor quality new tack.
● To buy from a member of the Society of Master Saddlers so you know you are buying reliable equipment and that there is a qualified person on the premises to give help and advice should you need it.
● To buy stainless-steel stirrups and bits. Nickel is softer and can bend and break much more easily.
● To keep your tack simple. Don't buy anything unless your instructor says your pony needs it.
● To clean your tack after every use, but most people don't have time. At least wash your bit after each ride, and run over the underside of your bridle and saddle if you possibly can to help prevent a build-up of dried sweat and grease, which could rub your pony sore in time.
● To use the mildest bit to which your pony will respond. It is not clever to use a severe, complicated bit; it simply shows that the pony is poorly trained or ill-behaved and that the rider is not good enough to handle him using basic equipment.

headpiece of a bridle. Bit rings (*not* mouthpieces) can be engraved with the number, as can stirrups.

You can obtain details from the British Horse Society and Pony Club.

In some areas, your local police will mark your tack, usually with your post code followed by your house number, if you have one, for precise identification. However, if you move house, this can cause complications and it may be better to have things marked with your own or your father or mother's National Insurance number, which is a permanent number held for life no matter where you live.

At shows, don't leave your equipment lying around unattended. Lock it in the boot of a car, the cab of a horsebox or make sure someone stays with it. If you keep your pony at a stable other than your home and there is no suitably secure room for your tack, it's well worth taking your saddle and bridle home with you for safety's sake, unless it's needed by the staff to exercise your pony.

Never keep your tack in the stable with your pony. The slightly humid atmosphere will ruin it and if the pony can reach it he is almost certain to chew it.

How to fit and use your tack and clothing

Saddle fitting

The fit of your saddle is most important if you want your pony to be comfortable and go well. If the saddle is uncomfortable or even hurting him he could play up and become difficult to control, causing an accident, apart from which, of course, it is cruel to subject him to pain and discomfort.

Saddles come in different lengths and, usually, in narrow, medium and wide fittings. Tell your saddler the height of your pony and seek an expert opinion on his build (that is, whether he is narrow, medium or wide in the back). Some saddlers have a leaflet showing you how to take various measurements to help in determining the correct size.

The most important point is that the saddle must not press on your pony's withers or backbone *anywhere* when a rider is mounted. The rider should lean forward and back, and all the time a clear channel of daylight should be seen from front to back down the gullet, along the pony's backbone. There should be three fingers' width (vertically) between the pommel (front arch) of the saddle and the withers when the rider is in the saddle, and the same at the cantle.

The saddle must not rock too much from side to side. You should just be able to slide the flat of your fingers between the withers and the pommel at the sides to check there will be no pinching and bruising or rubbing.

The panels must not hamper the movement of the pony's shoulder blades. His foreleg should be picked up and held stretched straight out in front by the point of the hoof. You should be able to place your hand easily between the top of the shoulder blades and the front of the saddle.

The saddle must also not be so long that it reaches back and presses on the loins or kidney area, just in front of the hip bones.

If it still fits after you have ridden round in it for quarter of an hour to let it settle, it should be all right.

To see if the saddle fits the rider, you should wiggle well down into the centre of the saddle without stirrups, legs hanging straight down. Adjust the stirrups so the base of the irons comes just above the ankle bone Now put the feet in the stirrups, keeping the heel down but relaxed and directly under the hip joint in a good riding position.

If the knee is pushed forward off the flap or very near the edge and/or the rider's bottom is less than a hand's breadth from the cantle, it is too small. On the other hand, if the knee comes nowhere near the front of the flap and there is more than a hand's

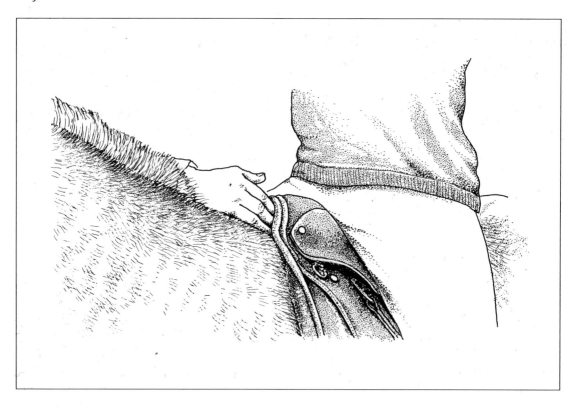

With the rider in the saddle, there should be three fingers' width at least, between the pommel and the withers, and the same at the cantle. The saddle must not touch the pony's backbone anywhere.

breadth in front of and behind the rider, it is too big.

Telling the saddler your height and inside leg measurement will help him give you the right size.

New saddles in particular often need restuffing after a few weeks or months of use as the stuffing becomes compressed; restuffing may also be necessary if your pony loses or gains weight. Keep an eye on saddle fit daily and ask your saddler to make any necessary adjustments.

Saddling up
Before you put your saddle on the pony, the stirrups should be run up the leathers, by pushing them up the back part of the loop

Remember

Correct fit is extremely important. It doesn't matter how expensive or smart your tack is, if it causes your pony discomfort or annoyance because of poor fit, it is no use. Think how uncomfortable you are when wearing clothes or shoes which pinch or chafe. The pony can only react by rubbing at them or trying to tear them off. If that fails, he might react more strongly by bucking, rearing or becoming in other ways difficult to ride and control – and then he becomes dangerous, all because he is trying to tell you his tack or clothing doesn't fit. If he feels comfortable he'll usually be willing to co-operate with you – so check the fit of everything before you use it, and every time you use it. It doesn't take long and is well worthwhile.

(they'll stay put on their own), or crossed over the saddle seat, and the girth should be placed over the seat, too. This is so nothing gets caught under the saddle, annoying the pony.

Hold the pommel in one hand and the cantle in the other and place the saddle well forward of the withers, then slide it back to its normal position. If you slide it back too far don't push it forward but lift it off and start again. Otherwise you'll ruffle the hair and the pony could feel uncomfortable.

If you are using a numnah with your saddle it's best to put it on at the same time as the saddle. When positioning the saddle hold the numnah underneath it, at the pommel and cantle and into the gullet between the padded seat panels, so that it is not pulled down tight on to the withers or backbone once the saddle is in place. Make sure it is not rucked up under the saddle panel, but smooth and comfortable.

If the girth is not already fastened to the offside girth tabs, buckle it on, usually to the first two straps if there are three, and make sure it is hanging straight, not twisted. (You can put your saddle on from either side, but if you put it on from the offside you are already there to check the girth and make sure the panel is not tucked up under the tabs.)

When you have buckled up the girth on the off (right) side, pull down the girth protector, the little leather flap which slides up and down the girth tabs (see photograph page 112) so that the buckles do not wear a hole in the saddle flap. Buckle the girth to the nearside tabs fairly loosely at first, so it just touches the pony. Ponies *hate* being girthed up tightly straight away and doing so can make them difficult to tack up and handle.

Put the bridle on, then come back and girth up another hole. Pick out the feet, then girth up another hole if necessary, so the process is gradual. Before mounting, slide your fingers (flat) between the girth and the

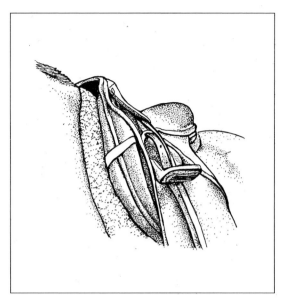

This numnah is touching the withers and spine and so is fitted wrongly. When the rider is mounted, the saddle will press it down quite hard and the pony's withers could easily be badly bruised as a result.

pony's skin – you should *just* be able to get them in without actually being able to pull the girth away from the pony's side.

Now go to the front of the pony and pull his forelegs forward from the knee to smooth out any skin wrinkles beneath the girth, which could cause pain and girth galls (rubbed sores). The pony must get used to this, so if he objects at first be patient and persistent without upsetting him and he'll eventually get the message.

Finally, lead the pony out of the stable (if indoors) and pull the stirrups down the leathers. To check they're a reasonable length for you, put your knuckles (or fingertips if you have long legs) on the safety bar and check that the base of the stirrup iron reaches your armpit. Now you can mount.

After you have been riding for five or ten minutes, check your girth from the saddle by leaning down and sliding your fingers behind the girth from the front and seeing how far you can pull it away. An experienced friend

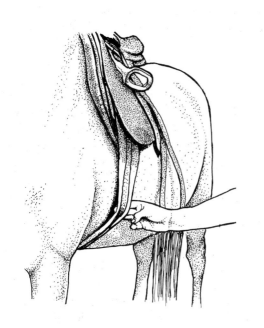

or your instructor will help you recognise what is too loose and what is too tight: a too-tight girth can cause girth galls (sores) just as easily as a loose one. Your weight in the saddle will obviously push the saddle down on the pony's back, loosening the girth a little, then it will become looser still as the pony, during exercise, relaxes and lets out any excess air he may have held in – called 'blowing himself out' – as a protection against your girthing him too tightly and quickly. Therefore, you are almost certain to need to tighten your girth a hole or two.

Don't forget finally to pull down the girth

Left To test the tightness of the girth before you mount, slide your fingers behind the girth and pull it away. This girth is too loose. The saddle would probably slip round if the rider tried to mount.

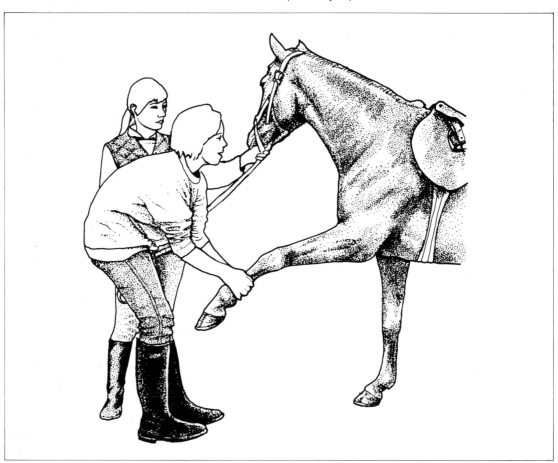

protector on the near (left) side after checking your girth as above.

Unsaddling

To unsaddle, first run the stirrups up the leathers, unbuckle the girth, put one hand under the pommel and one on the cantle and *lift* the saddle off the pony's back. Slide it on to the arm near the pommel and bring it towards you, catching the girth with your other hand. Lay the girth across the seat, muddy side upwards so it doesn't scratch the leather, and take it to the tack room. If you have to put it on the floor for any reason, stand it on its pommel resting on the inside of the girth to help protect the leather; in this position, the inside will air and the panel and flaps will not be folded up but remain straight. You can leave the saddle over the stable door or field gate, if you wish, while you finish off the pony.

Putting on and fitting a bridle

First see that the throatlatch and noseband are undone. Take the headpiece in your left hand and the buckle end of the reins in your right and stand on the near (left) side by his head with your back to his tail. Don't stand in front of him as he might accidentally give you a thump with his head, maybe knocking you over.

Put the reins over his head and rest them just behind his ears so if he moves you can catch them together under his throat and control him. If he is wearing a headcollar, now is the time to remove it. Pass your right hand under his throat and hold the two

cheekpieces together, resting them and your right hand on the front of his face so you can control his head. Let go of the headpiece and bring your left hand under the bit. Open your hand and rest the bit across it, bringing it *gently* between the pony's lips and pressing lightly where the top and bottom teeth meet, when he should open his mouth. If he doesn't, put your left thumb in the corner of his mouth and tickle his tongue. He is then almost sure to open his teeth and you can bring the bit up into his mouth by raising your right hand, still holding the cheekpieces, and guiding the bit between his teeth with your left hand.

Next take your left hand back to the headpiece, holding the bit up with it, and with your right hand gently bring his right ear under the headpiece, then his left ear, finally slipping the headpiece into place behind the ears. Smooth out the hair under it, bring the forelock out over the browband and buckle up the throatlatch, making sure it's not twisted.

Fasten the cavesson noseband (*under* the cheekpieces) and see it is even. If it is higher on one side than the other, do not yank on the high side till it is level; adjust it from under the bridle headpiece by easing the strap up and down with your fingers, till the band is level across the nose.

Adjust the browband so it is comfortable, just below the base of the ears, and see the bit is level in his mouth, just touching the corners of the mouth. See that all the straps are straight and in their keepers (those leather loops stitched just below the buckles) and runners (the loose ones which run up and down the straps). Flapping strap ends look very amateurish.

The fitting of the bridle is very important. Starting with the browband, the purpose of this is to stop the headpiece slipping down the pony's neck. It must not pull the headpiece up against the base of the ears and should not touch them itself. You should be

Left After tightening the girth for the last time before you mount, make sure the skin under it is smoothed out (on both sides) to help prevent rubs and girth galls. Stroke your pony's shoulder and run your hand down to just below his knee, then lift his leg and pull it gently outwards like this. If the pony resists at first, gently persist. He'll soon get used to it.

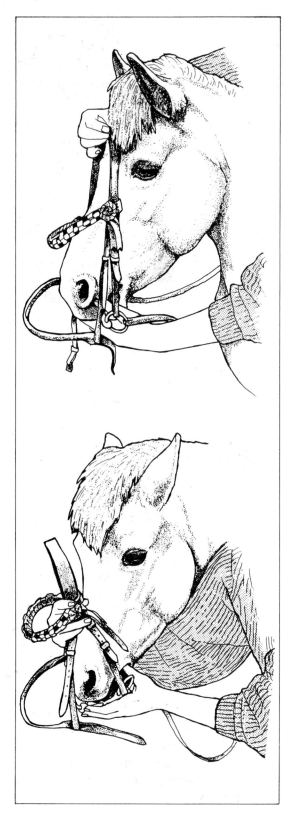

able to slide one finger comfortably under the browband. If you can't, it is too tight, but if you can get more than one finger easily under it, it is probably too long and could gape away from the forehead, looking untidy, or flop about and annoy the pony. Browbands are not adjustable, so you will have to change it if it isn't right.

The throatlatch helps stop the bridle being pulled off over the head in a fall. You must be able to put the full width of your hand outwards between it and the pony's round jawbone. If it is too tight it will cause a choking feeling and be most uncomfortable, interfering with his breathing.

The cavesson noseband should come mid-way between the corners of the lips and the sharp cheekbones and you should be able to put two fingers' width between it and the nose. The band round the nose has a buckle fastening on the nearside just under the jaw and the strap holding it up buckles on the nearside of the face, so you can adjust it.

The cheekpieces should be long enough to hold the bit snugly in the corners of the

Two ways of putting on a bridle. *Above:* Stand on the pony's near (left) side. Hold the headpiece in your right hand and have the bit resting on your left palm. Bring the headpiece up to the poll, at the same time gently pressing the bit against his teeth where they join. *Below:* For ponies who are slightly difficult, hold the cheekpieces together in front of his face, with the bit on your left palm. Bring your right hand up his face and press the bit gently against his teeth, as with the first method. If he doesn't open his mouth, put your left thumb into the corner of his mouth (where there are no teeth, so you won't be bitten) and tickle his tongue. He'll almost certainly open up then, so you can quickly slip in the bit and hold it up in place by means of the cheekpieces in your right hand. Then swap hands. Hold the cheekpieces with your left hand and bring your right hand back towards you under his thoat. Then quickly but gently put the headpiece on with both hands.

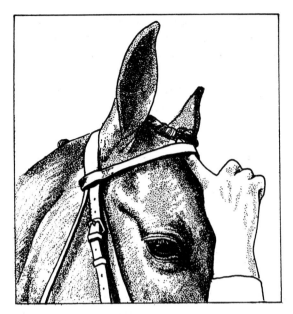

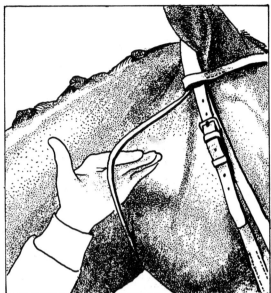

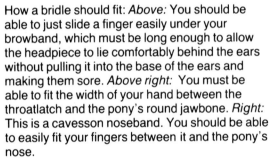

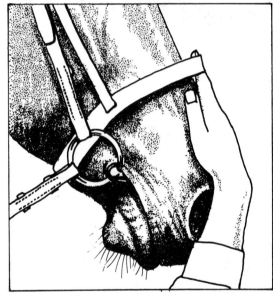

How a bridle should fit: *Above:* You should be able to just slide a finger easily under your browband, which must be long enough to allow the headpiece to lie comfortably behind the ears without pulling it into the base of the ears and making them sore. *Above right:* You must be able to fit the width of your hand between the throatlatch and the pony's round jawbone. *Right:* This is a cavesson noseband. You should be able to easily fit your fingers between it and the pony's nose.

mouth, or *just* wrinkling them, depending on the fit you can achieve with your cheekpieces. The holes on the top halves of the cheekpieces should be level with each other all the way down otherwise you will not be able to adjust them evenly and the bit will always be lopsided. To check this (before you put on the bridle) hold the two top holes exactly together and put a matchstick or piece of wire through them. Now look down all the other holes seeing that they are level.

It is important that your bit should be the right size for the pony's mouth. It should stick out about 7 mm (¼ in.) each side of his mouth to be comfortable.

Thin mouthpieces seem to feel less comfortable than wide ones. Snaffles with chubby mouthpieces are commonly used

now and are called German snaffles; they come in both eggbutt and loose- or wire-ring types.

Taking off a bridle

As soon as you dismount bring the reins over the pony's head and put your left arm through them at the buckle end so they are looped over your arm. Then you have both hands free to unsaddle him but you still have hold of the pony.

131

This pony is wearing a wire-ring snaffle bit. Many ponies like the looser feel these bits give, but you must watch for wear. He is wearing a flash noseband, which is an ordinary cavesson with another strap from the front passing under the bit along the chin groove. It aims to discourage the pony from opening his mouth too wide and evading the bit (like a drop noseband), but cannot interfere with breathing. Don't have it too tight. You should be able to slide a finger under it all round.

If the pony is going to be tied up for a while, indoors or out, don't take the bridle off and *then* put on the headcollar, as the pony will be free for a few seconds and might get away. Instead buckle the headpiece of the headcollar round the top of his neck, allowing the rest of the headcollar to hang under his throat (in other words, not on his head). You can then either hold the lead rope or tie the pony up while you remove the bridle.

First undo the bridle noseband, then the throatlatch and, with one hand behind each ear, gently ease the headpiece over the ears and allow the pony to let go of the bit in his own time. *Never* pull, snatch or drag the bit out of a pony's mouth as this can really hurt him and make him difficult to handle in future. If he doesn't let go, put your thumb in the corner of his mouth to encourage him to open up. You can also hold one of the bit rings and guide the bit out of his mouth if he seems nervous about it hitting his teeth.

Drape the bridle over your saddle seat (if the saddle is on the top of the stable door or fence rail) rather than dump it in a muddy patch or on concrete where it might be scratched. Otherwise, lay it over the door or fence or put it on a clean piece of grass while you finish off. Don't put it on the floor in the stable where the pony might tread on it.

Now (if the pony is to be tied up) you can easily unbuckle the headcollar headpiece and put the headcollar on properly without actually letting go of the pony. If your headcollar has a buckle on its noseband, you can undo this, put the noseband round the nose and buckle it again without having to undo the headpiece.

Putting on and fitting a headcollar
The headcollar should fit closely without being tight. The best headcollars have a browband to keep the headpiece in place, and a buckle on the noseband to adjust the fit so that you can place two fingers' width between it and the pony's nose. Most headcollars are fitted with the noseband far too loose. The top of the noseband should come about 2 cm (1 in.) below the sharp face bones so it doesn't rub them but cannot be scraped off by the pony or easily caught in a hedge or anything else if the pony is turned out in it.

To put the headcollar on, stand with your back to the pony's tail and hold the left cheekpiece in your left hand and the right one in your right hand, with the headstrap falling away over your right hand. If the noseband has a buckle, it's all right for it to be fastened. Bring the noseband up over the pony's muzzle and flick the headstrap over behind his ears with your right hand, buckling it on the left. To take it off, just undo the buckle and slide it off downwards.

Rugging up

Rugs have to be comfortable as well as warm, because the pony will be wearing them for many hours at a time. Apart from buying a correctly shaped rug, as described earlier, the rug must be deep enough to reach down to the pony's elbows and long enough to come in *front* of the withers, not on top of them, going right back to the root of the tail, not finishing halfway up his bottom.

The neck of the rug should permit you to slide the flat of your hand easily round inside, especially over the withers, but it should fasten tightly enough so it cannot be pulled back (or slip back) on to the withers, as if it presses there it could eventually cause sore withers. There should be no pulling on the points of the shoulders.

To put on a rug, hold it with the front in your right hand and the back edge in your left and stand on the pony's offside. Gather it together and put it quietly over the pony's withers. Do not fling it on like a tablecloth as you might startle him. Holding the front of the rug at the withers with your right hand, take the back edge (in your left hand) back to the tail making sure the seam lies exactly along his backbone. If there is a fillet string, bring his tail out over it. Fasten the crossed surcingles so that they *almost* touch the pony underneath. With a good, shaped rug, this is quite tight enough; the rug needs to be able to move and right itself as the pony moves about his box and gets up and down, to stay in the right position.

If the rug has a single surcingle or roller round the girth, fasten this on the nearside fairly high up on the pony's back so he doesn't lie on an uncomfortable lump (the buckle) when he gets down. You should not fasten it as tightly as a saddle girth, but should just be able to pull it away from the pony's side. When he lies down he will 'spread out' and if the girth is too tight he'll be very uncomfortable. Smooth out the rug under the surcingle and, holding it at the bottom edge, give it a little forward pull to take up any slack at the back and give more room for the shoulders. Smooth the hair at the withers under the rug so it is comfortable, and fasten the breast strap.

To take off a rug, unfasten the breast strap, then the surcingles, roller or whatever and, holding the front of the rug at the withers in one hand and the back at the tail in the other hand, slide the rug off and down over the tail. Fold it in the middle and rest it on the manger or in a clean corner on the floor until you can put it away. You can hang it over the stable door unless it will be exposed to rain.

Don't fold it inside out with the lining showing as it will pick up bits of hay and bedding which you'll have to remove before rugging up again, otherwise they'll irritate the pony.

If you want to use an extra layer under the rugs you will need a clip-in under-rug for a rug with crossed surcingles, and either a shaped under-rug or an oblong blanket (of wool or acrilan usually) for a rug with a single surcingle or roller.

The under-rug goes on just the same as the top rug, but a blanket has to be laid lengthwise on the pony so one edge is just behind his ears and the other just at the root of his tail. Put your rug on, as described, then fold the front edge of the blanket back to just in front of the rug, then fold the doubled thickness back again over the shoulders, like a rolled coat collar. Some people fold the front edge right back over the saddle area and fasten the surcingle on top of it to keep it all in place. Make sure there is no creasing or pulling around the neck which could cause discomfort.

New Zealand rugs should be a little roomier than stable rugs; they, too, must come in front of the withers, but at the back should go on past the root of the tail for a few centimetres for extra warmth.

To fasten the leg straps, first make sure they are not twisted, then take the left leg strap and pass it between the pony's back legs out behind him and clip it to its ring on the left side of the back edge. Now take the right leg strap between the back legs, linking it through the left one, and clip it to its ring on the right side of the back edge. This way,

the straps hold each other away from the sensitive skin inside the pony's legs.

When fastened, you should only just be able to see the straps below the bottom edge of the rug. This is most important. The rug will be only slightly longer than a stable rug. If the straps are too short they will pull and annoy the pony, but if they are too long, he might get both legs down inside one leg strap when playing about or getting up from rolling, trip himself, panic and break a leg. This, sadly, is quite common simply because people do not know how to adjust the leg straps correctly.

If you are in any doubt on any aspect of fitting tack and clothing, ask an instructor to

This is an ordinary woollen blanket used under rugs kept in place with surcingles or rollers. It can be folded back like this, the rug put on and then folded back again over the front of the rug, like a rolled coat collar. Another way is to spread the blanket right out, up to the pony's ears, put on the rug, fold back the blanket over the rug (smoothing out wrinkles at front and shoulders), then put on the roller on top of the blanket and fasten it. This method secures the blanket better and helps prevent it slipping back under the rug.

show you exactly what to do as it really is very important.

The breast straps on a New Zealand rug should be fastened just tight enough to keep the rug on but so that the pony can put his head down to graze in comfort. Usually, the top strap is best fitted a hole looser than the bottom one, to allow this.

To take off a New Zealand rug, unfasten the breast straps, then unclip the leg straps from their back edge and clip each one to its buckle on the side of the rug so they don't dangle down. Then simply slide the rug off like a stable rug.

Bandaging
Bandaging is something you have to practise and it is important that you do – a lot of damage is done to ponies' legs by wrongly or carelessly applied bandages. Practise on a table or chair leg first. Once you acquire the knack it is not so difficult, although you always have to take care.

Most bandages have a straight end and a pointed end. The tapes are sewn to the pointed end. Fold them neatly across the top and roll the bandage, sewn side inwards, so you end with the tapes in the middle and the straight end on the outside. Roll firmly but don't stretch the fabric.

Exercise bandage
Exercise bandages should always have plenty of padding under them otherwise if used alone they can create uneven pressure

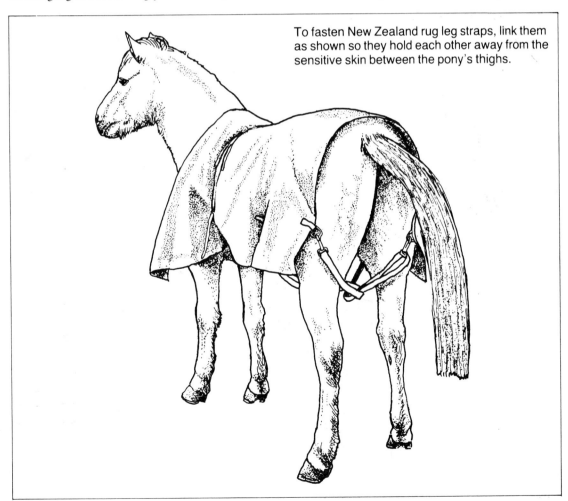

To fasten New Zealand rug leg straps, link them as shown so they hold each other away from the sensitive skin between the pony's thighs.

on the leg, interfering with blood flow and causing problems such as soreness, swellings, lameness and permanent lumps. Elasticated bandages, particularly damp ones, have a self-tightening effect and if put on too firmly can certainly cause discomfort. Padding helps lessen this. Leg bandages must *always* be put on dry and removed as soon as possible if they become wet.

No bandages at all are far better than those put on wrongly.

Cut your chosen padding to cover the pony's legs from knee or hock to fetlock, and wrap it round the leg evenly with the most thickness over the tendons at the back.

(Never kneel down near a pony's legs, crouch instead so you can jump to your feet quickly if anything happens.)

If you are working on a nearside leg, take the bandage in your right hand with the loose, straight end, away from you, and opening to the left. With your left hand, take the straight end and unroll about 20 cm (8 ins). Place this diagonally across the leg with the free end highest and the roll just under the knee or hock. Take one turn round the leg anti-clockwise (to the right, round behind the leg to the left, back again towards you, and to the right). Let the spare end piece drop down the outside of the leg and continue bandaging down the leg and over this spare piece. This acts as an anchor for the bandage and helps prevent slipping.

Roll firmly but not tightly, stretching the material slightly as you go. At each turn, cover half the width of the previous turn. When you reach the fetlock, turn up the remaining spare end and bandage once over it.

Ideally, take the bandage down over

How to put on an exercise bandage. Put your padding in place and have the rolled bandage in your right hand with the loose end in your left, for a left leg. Pass the bandage round the back of the leg and back over the loose end, which you then allow to drop down. You can either bandage over the end now or leave it loose while you bandage

down the leg. Roll back up the leg and try to finish just below the knee. The end of the bandage will point backwards, which makes it less likely that twigs and things will catch in it. Tie the tapes smoothly round the leg, *no* tighter than the bandage itself, tie a firm bow and tuck in the ends.

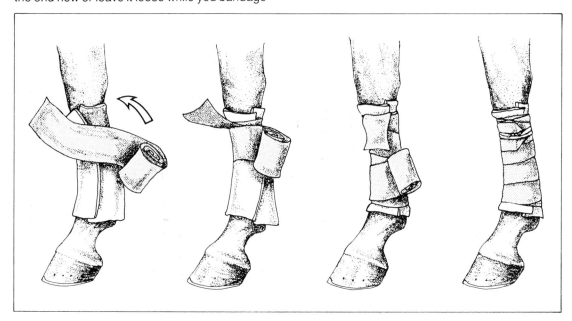

and half under the fetlock at the back for two turns (the padding should go well down over the fetlock) but leave it up at the front. This will protect his fetlock at the back if it sinks down to the ground, as often happens when galloping and jumping, and give a certain amount of protection without pressing into the bend of the joint in front.

Go back up the leg till you come to the end of the bandage. Try to finish with the end on the outside of the leg pointing backwards, so branches and twigs are not so easily caught in it. Take the tapes round the leg, seeing they are not twisted, and fasten them on the outside in a firm bow or reef knot, and tuck in the spare ends. With scissors, neatly trim the excess padding over the front of the fetlock.

To do the offside legs, simply reverse the words 'left' and 'right' in the instructions.

The tapes must not be fastened tighter than the bandages themselves but at the same pressure. If they are tighter they will

How to put on a stable bandage. The procedure is the same as for the exercise bandage but you have longer padding and take the bandage right down to the coronet for extra protection.

interfere with the circulation, and if looser the whole lot will unravel and could cause a nasty accident. Tapes must always be fastened on the outside of the leg so the pony cannot kick open the fastening. If you fasten over the bone or tendons the knot might cause a painful lump, despite the padding.

In professional yards, bandages are often secured by sewing. Another way of securing the fastening is to go over it and right round the leg with wide adhesive tape.

Stable bandages

Stable bandages are put on similarly but not so firmly. You need only half as much spare end. These bandages go right down over the fetlock to the coronet and heel, where they take a natural turn upwards again. Most stable bandages are too short and many people have to sew two together to get the right length, but for ponies, as opposed to horses, you'll probably be able to manage with horse-length bandages, if your saddler sells different lengths.

Removing bandages

To take off leg bandages, untie them and pass them quickly round the leg from hand to hand, making no effort to roll them. Take off the padding and put it with the bandages,

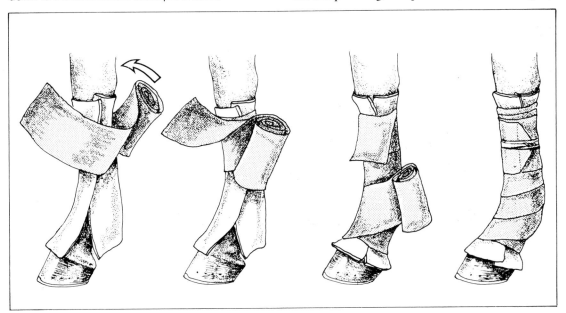

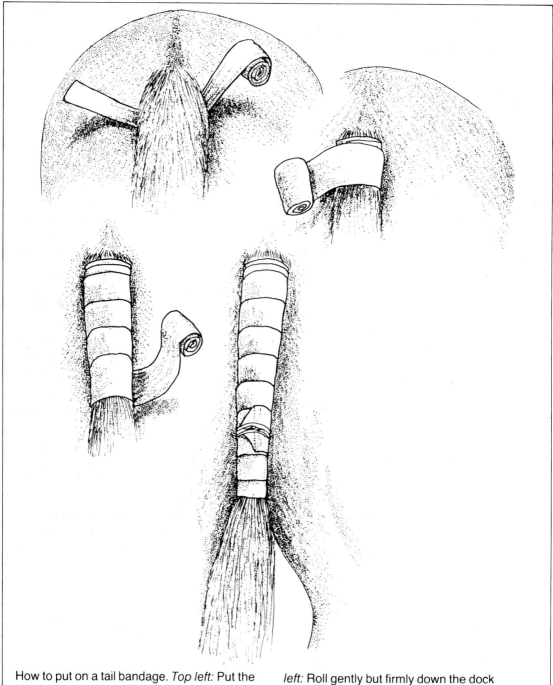

How to put on a tail bandage. *Top left:* Put the bandage under the tail with a short length on one side and with the roll, facing downwards, on the other. *Top right:* Wrap the loose end round the top of the tail and bring the roll end the opposite way over it. Make sure that the bandage is smooth with no creases which could irritate the skin under the tail. *Bottom left:* Roll gently but firmly down the dock almost to the end. Then continue rolling back up again till you come to the end of the bandage. *Bottom right:* Tie the tapes smoothly round and round the dock, *no tighter than the bandage itself.* Finish with a bow, and tuck in the loose ends. Finally, bend the tail back into a natural position for the pony.

not in the bedding where they will pick up bits, but on the door or manger. Now rub the legs briskly with the palm of your hands to restore circulation.

Tail bandages

Tail bandages need practice, too, to make a good job. They are usually put on without padding, but I believe this is wrong as the underside of a pony's tail hasn't even got hair to protect it. Padding (gamgee tissue works best for tails) also prevents ring-marks on the hair in the direction of the bandage – a sure sign of a bandage applied carelessly and too tight, as are white hairs in the tail and hair breaking or falling out.

First measure out your gamgee to extend threequarters of the way down the dock; one thickness is enough. Damp (not wet) the hair with your water brush or a sponge. Do not wet the bandage or it will shrink on the tail and become too tight.

Wrap the gamgee smoothly round the dock and take your bandage, again with the straight end away from you, although it does not matter whether you roll to left or right. Leave a little spare end. The first turn will probably not be very good but you can secure it by doing the next one above it. Roll down firmly but not tightly almost to the end of the gamgee. Wrap the tapes smoothly round and tie them, again only as tight as the bandage,

to the outside. Gently bend the tail back into a comfortable, natural curve.

To remove, place both hands firmly round the top of the tail and slide the whole lot down and off without untying.

Fitting boots

Protective brushing or speedicut boots are worn with their protective shielding on the inside of the leg and the straps on the outside, pointing backwards. Place them carefully round the leg, making sure there is no dirt or straw inside and that the edges are not turned under, and buckle the bottom strap first, working up. If you start at the top the boot might slip down over the hoof, especially if you have to let go for any reason. The pony might then tread on it and damage it or trip and panic. The boots should fasten firmly enough to keep them from slipping but should not be tight. They rub less and are more comfortable if put on over a layer of padding. To remove them, start at the top and unbuckle downwards, laying them inside up to air.

Pull-on over-reach boots are almost impossible for a child to stretch on and off singlehanded so you will probably need an adult to help. Pull them on over the hoof, and make sure the top edge is curling outwards and resting round the pastern.

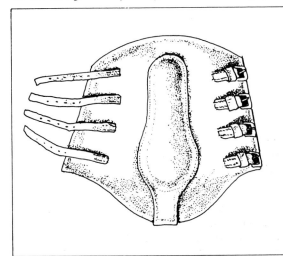

Brushing boot (*left*) and over-reach boot.

They are easier to pull off from the heel than the front.

There are some new over-reach boots available which buckle round the pastern and are made of strips of tough synthetic material, which also means they cannot turn inside out while on, as is sometimes seen.

Caring for your equipment

Tack cleaning is a job that should be done regularly rather than just on rainy days or when your pony cannot be ridden. Tack is expensive but can last many years *if* properly cared for. Also, hard, dirty tack can make your pony sore and tends to crack and break, causing nasty accidents.

Your saddle and bridle are supposed to be cleaned after every use but most people don't have time for this. After each wear, however, try at least to wipe over the underside of the leather (which touches the pony) to keep it reasonably dirt-free and soft, and clean it properly after every two or three times. Using a numnah under your saddle not only helps absorb sweat, it also helps keep your saddle clean, too.

Your tack will collect not only mud and grime but also grease from the pony's skin and coat. A muddy bridle, stirrup leathers and girth can simply be washed by swishing them in a bucket of water. Your saddle, though, which is padded, cannot be washed like this and will have to be sponged. Grease, in any case, has to be sponged off other items, too.

To restore neglected secondhand tack or make stiff, new tack supple, treat it with a leather dressing, such as the Hydrophane one (which doesn't make it slimy like neatsfoot oil). Follow the directions on the tin and don't use it too much or too often. It also darkens new tack to a lovely mellow colour and protects it before you even start to use it.

Ordinary cleaning involves washing off mud and grease with a sponge and just-warm water with one or two drops (not squirts) of washing-up liquid in it, and then rubbing in saddle soap to condition and protect the leather. Do not use hot water as this can take out of the leather too much natural oil and preservative and cause cracking and discoloration.

Metal parts, except the bit mouthpiece, should be cleaned with metal polish every now and then.

Many people take bridles to pieces to clean them but others do them while they are buckled together. It is important to clean the leather next to buckles as this is particularly prone to cracking from wear and neglect, but you can do it by simply moving the buckles a hole or two, then putting them back again.

You will need:

Two buckets of just-warm water, one for washing the leather and one for damping the soap.

Two flattish sponges, one for washing and one for soaping – and don't mix them up. Big car sponges are no good.

A tin or bar of glycerine saddle soap. (Glycerine soap is by far the best for protecting your leather.)

Chamois leather (imitation will do) for drying.

Metal polish and cloths. Duraglit wadding is good for cleaning, with a separate cloth for polishing.

Stable rubber or old tea-towel for holding clean metal so you don't finger-mark it.

Take the stirrup leathers and girth off your saddle and wash the saddle thoroughly all over. If there are any hardened little bits of black grease, scrape them off carefully with a *blunt* knife or the edge of a coin. If you haven't got a proper saddle horse (that is, a stand specially for cleaning and storing saddles), you'll find it easiest to sit on a chair and clean the saddle on your knee.

Dry the saddle with the chamois leather, then take your soap sponge and rub it with your bar of soap which you have dipped in clean water. If you are using tinned soap, damp the sponge and squeeze it out very thoroughly. If the soap lathers on the leather, the sponge is too wet. Rub it in, using a circular movement, all over, especially underneath, till you have a lovely sheen.

Now take the stirrup leathers and hang them by the buckle on a convenient hook – perhaps a bridle-cleaning hook, if you have one. Wrap the washing sponge round the leather and, holding one end of the leather so it is taut, rub the sponge hard up and down it. Use the chamois and soap sponge in the same way as you did on the saddle.

During the washing process, frequently rinse your washing sponge and when soaping apply more soap as necessary. You need plenty and must rub it well in.

Clean the buckles and stirrups with the metal polish.

If your girth is fabric, scrub it with soap (the ordinary kind, not saddle soap) and warm water and rinse it very thoroughly. Clean the leather parts, and finally the buckles, then hang it up to dry.

To clean tack properly you will need these items as a minimum: a good size plastic bucket with a soft cloth, a stable rubber (with the stripe), a bar of glycerine saddle soap, two sponges and a tin of metal polish.

Put the leathers back on the stirrups by threading the pointed end of the leather (inside up) through the eye of the stirrup, going away from you. Bring the pointed end over the top of the stirrup towards you and pass it down through the buckle, fastening it as usual. Now the fastened buckle should be at the top of the loop of leather, with the spare leather hanging down nearest you and the stirrup on the bottom.

It's very easy to get in a muddle with stirrup leathers till you are used to handling them.

Change the leathers round when cleaning your tack, so that the leather which was on the right is now on the left, and vice versa. This is so that they will stretch evenly during use (particularly mounting) and you don't end up with one longer than the other.

The same procedure – washing, drying, soaping and cleaning buckles – is used for the bridle. Just clean the leather parts of rubber-covered reins. Fabric reins can be cleaned like a fabric girth.

Metal polish should not be allowed to touch leather; if it does, wipe it off at once. Obviously, never let it get on to the bit mouthpiece, which should be simply washed in clear water. You should do this after each ride, in fact. Dried saliva, grass or food left on the bit is unpleasant and unhygienic.

Never dry any leather in front of a fire or other strong artificial heat as this will dry out the leather and weaken it. Whether it is wet from rain or washing, rub it with the chamois leather, soap it and let it dry naturally. Dressing with oil is seldom necessary for tack cleaned regularly with a glycerine saddle soap.

If your tack is not going to be used for a long time, oil it, smear the buckles with oil or Vaseline and keep it covered with a large, old cloth in a reasonably warm, dry place.

Clothing (except for expensive woollen day rugs) can be washed in a washing machine – or in the bath or a tank in the yard if you enjoy hard work! Washing powder *other than* biological ones can safely be used (biological ones can cause terrible skin rashes) but give plenty of rinses. Spin out the worst of the water then hang on a rack, hedge or fence, inside up, to dry off, to avoid bad creasing. Thoroughly oil leather straps before and after washing, and you'll have no problems with them. Fabric conditioner in the last rinse can help keep rugs and blankets soft and in good condition, too.

New Zealand rugs can be washed this way if they are the modern synthetic kind. Heavy canvas ones should be hung up by their strap rings on the back edge and hosed down, then scrubbed with water and a yard broom. The insides of all rugs should be vacuumed before washing. Woollen linings should be scrubbed gently with baby soap and lukewarm water and rinsed very thoroughly with water of the same temperature, otherwise they might shrink.

You might need to reproof your New Zealand rug occasionally. Some saddlers sell their own reproofer or you can use tent reproofer from camping shops.

Your numnah can probably be put in the washing machine with your bandages, or washed in the tack room or kitchen sink. Bandages remain fairly untangled if you put them in an old pillowslip and sew up the opening loosely.

Make a habit of checking all stitching, especially girth tabs and stirrup leathers, at every cleaning. Repairs should be carried out by a qualified saddler rather than botched by an amateur in an attempt to save money.

Keep your tack cleaning equipment in good order. Your washing sponge should be thoroughly washed with ordinary soap and rinsed in clean water after each use. Leave your soap sponge as it is; when it starts wearing out just get another. Don't put it down in a dirty place where it can pick up dirt and grit which will scratch the leather. Your chamois leather can be rinsed in warm water plus a little vinegar, and kept in a plastic bag to keep it moist.

9. Organising the day-to-day care

Establishing a routine

One of the problems of owning a pony is that some parents don't accept that his welfare is just as important as your schoolwork and homework. Most insist that homework comes first and that you can go and 'play' with your pony only after it is done.

This misguided attitude can seriously affect your pony's well-being and your peace of mind. You will be unable to concentrate on schoolwork if you are worrying about your pony, so the very schoolwork your parents are concerned about will suffer.

But it *is* possible to organise yourself so that both your pony and your homework receive proper attention. Unlike bikes and other toys, ponies aren't playthings. Like any family pet they need proper, regular attention, as you'll realise by now. Because you love your pony (otherwise you wouldn't have him) the jobs involved are not chores but responsibilities, and accepting responsibility is an important part of growing up. Your pony is part of your education for life.

Ponies do take up a lot of time and you will probably have to give up some other hobbies, such as watching too much television or playing with friends. The most difficult times of year are when the days are short – November, December, January and February. These sixteen or so weeks of the year will be a struggle but for three of those (the Christmas holidays) and two more

(half-terms in the autumn and spring terms) you'll be on holiday anyway. That only leaves eleven bad weeks out of fifty-two.

I strongly advise you to keep your pony on the combined system or at least out with a shelter because this will cut down on your work and ensure that your pony gets enough exercise and freedom to stay happy and healthy. Stabled ponies can suffer greatly from lack of exercise and boredom. It is very wrong to keep a pony in with no proper exercise because not only will he be driven crazy with boredom and maybe start crib-biting, wind-sucking, weaving, box walking, tearing his clothing or kicking his stable – all classed as stable vices – but his health will suffer, too.

When he finally does get out he is likely to go crazy with relief and excitement, to the extent that he becomes a danger to you, himself and anyone round about.

If your present yard has no turning out facilities for winter, look for somewhere else to keep him, for all your sakes.

You may be able to obtain help from your family, friends or others who keep their ponies or horses in the same yard. It is unlikely that your parents will leave you entirely on your own to look after your pony so you may already have a help-each-other system going.

Apart from morning and evening visits, someone should check the pony before bedtime if at all possible. Remember, if you are bringing your pony in at about 4.30 – 5 pm and not seeing him again until 8 – 8.30 am next day, he will be without supervision for about fifteen or sixteen hours. Anything could happen in that time – he could die of colic without anyone knowing it.

Let's look at the sort of things that need to be done and how they can be achieved.

Someone will have to visit the pony in the morning to check that he has not hurt himself during the night, to feed and water him and turn him out for the day. It will take a pony about fifteen minutes to eat his breakfast and during that time you can, working quickly but without rushing, have the box mucked out, the floor swept and any clean bedding left over piled in a corner with the half-dirty bedding in another. Leave the floor bare all day to give it a chance to dry.

After his feed, take the pony to the field and turn him out, preferably with a supply of hay (in a rack or net to prevent it blowing about or getting trampled in the mud) if there isn't much grass. All this will take about half an hour. You can pick the droppings out of his feet but don't bother brushing him as he'll get filthy again in no time unless he wears a New Zealand rug.

If you finish school at 4 o'clock and can be at the stables by 4.30 pm you'll obviously be there sooner than someone who works till 5 pm or 5.30 pm. Why not offer, say, to bring their horse in from the field ready for them to ride, or to bed down its stable, or fill haynets etc, in return for their seeing to your pony in the mornings. This could save you one trip a day to the yard and will help them, too. This is only one example of how people can help each other to the benefit of all concerned. See how many more ways you can think of.

In the evening, you'll have to bed down the stable, put feed, hay and water ready and bring the pony in. He might be wet and muddy but if he grows a typical pony coat and is not clipped much, you may not need to dry him off. Carefully part his hair and see if he is soaked to the skin; you might be surprised to find that he isn't, so you can leave him stabled without fear of his getting chilled.

If he *is* wet through you'll have to thatch him and come back later to remove it so he doesn't get hot and sweaty, and then get chilled again when you turn him out next morning.

This will usually only happen with a finely bred pony who doesn't grow a thick, native-type coat, and you may feel it worth getting a New Zealand rug for such a pony. When he comes in at night, all you'll have to do is take off the rug, check the pony over as normal and put on his night rug if it is cold.

Before you go home (to do that homework), fill the haynet or rack and make up the pony's feed for morning to save time. Don't damp it or it will go sour overnight.

Try to arrange a late-night check. Your pony is going to be in for many hours and won't sleep away the night like we do, so he'll need enough hay and water to last that time: two buckets of water and a crammed-full haynet. Remember, what hay he doesn't eat can be used next day, but if he gets hungry he will start eating his bedding or chewing his stable. A pony's digestion needs some food passing through it all the time to avoid hunger.

So, if you finish your evening jobs by 5.30 pm you could be home and having your meal by 6 pm and doing your homework by half past; that's plenty of time to concentrate on doing it well, knowing your pony is tucked up and munching his hay.

If you go straight to school from the stables, take your school clothes in a large shopping bag and change out of your mucking-out gear at the stables or at school. This saves you making extra trips home to change.

If you have free periods at school, use them to do your homework instead of fooling around, but don't do it during break times – you've got to relax some time. Most schools have about an hour and a half for lunch, so you could do a bit of work then. If you go home for lunch, perhaps you could find time to, say, clean your bridle or saddle or wash some bandages. It's surprising how much spare time you can find and use profitably and still not feel overworked.

If you have to keep the pony stabled, try to exercise him in two stints, one in the morning and one in the evening, otherwise he'll get bored stiff. Quarter him quickly in the morning and get him out before feeding so you don't have to wait for his food to go down. See to his bed when you return (he'll need a good bed down all day) and feed, hay and water him before you leave.

Light work, such as he'll be getting now, calls for few, if any, concentrates but as much nice hay as he'll eat instead, to prevent such things as laminitis, filled legs and crazy behaviour when he *does* get out.

How much exercise will your pony need? As much as you can give him. During term-time, it will be difficult to give him too much, or even enough. An hour a day is the absolute minimum, and that isn't sufficient really.

However, if he's being turned out during the day you don't *have* to exercise at all during the week unless you want to work him hard at weekends, then he'll need at least two days working under saddle to help keep him fit, in addition to being turned out. Make these days, say, Tuesday and Thursday, to break up the work.

Only you can decide how to manage your pony according to your own school times, homework and facilities. However, here are some suggested routines which show that it *is* definitely possible to go to school, get your homework done properly and also give your pony the care he needs and deserves.

Use your head and discipline yourself to work to a time-table. You do it all day at school, after all, so you only have to extend it a little for outside school hours.

A sound routine ensures that everything that has to be done actually is done. Because you know what you should be doing at a certain time, you don't worry how you are going to fit everything in – you *know* it will all get done so you can relax and get on with it.

The stabled pony

This routine is the most time-consuming, winter and summer, but will be more or less the same throughout the year. Exact times will have to be adjusted depending on how far your home, stables and school are from each other, but the time-table below should give you some idea of how to proceed. I have assumed that you have arranged for someone to feed and skip out your pony at lunchtime. This routine is fairly gruelling and would be suitable for a teenager but not a young child.

6.30 am	Get up, cup of tea, dress.
6.45 am	Leave for stables.
7.00 am	Arrive at stables; check pony, quarter and pick out feet, muck out and leave floor bare to air (if on straw or paper). Otherwise (and if saving time by using semi-deep litter during the week) just remove droppings and worst of bedding.
7.15 am	Tack up and exercise.
7.55 am	Bed down; water and hay up; rug up (if worn); feed. (You will have prepared a filled haynet and mixed a feed the night before to save time. Just add a little water, if necessary, to feed now.)
8.10 am	Leave stables.
8.25 am	Arrive home to wash, change and have breakfast.
8.40 am	Leave for school.
4.00 pm	Leave school.
4.15 pm	Arrive home, cup of tea and biscuits. Change.

4.30 pm	Leave for stables.
4.45 pm	Arrive at stables. Check pony, pick out feet, quarter if messy.
5.00 pm	Tack up and ride out.
5.40 pm	Return. Untack and throw rug over if cold. Offer drink. Give hay and, while pony is eating, remove droppings.
5.50 pm	Groom, working quickly but thoroughly, with body brush, ten minutes each side roughly, but don't forget mane and tail. Sponge face and dock.
6.10 pm	Bed down, give two buckets of fresh water plus very full haynet. Rug up. Feed. Before leaving, fill next morning's haynet and mix dry feed.
6.40 pm	Arrive home for evening meal with family.
7.15 pm	Start homework.

Although tough, this is the worst routine you'll ever have to do. I am assuming you have to do more or less everything for the pony yourself. You could save valuable minutes if you kept him on deep litter bedding during the week and just mucked out properly at weekends. Your tack will probably be cleaned properly only at weekends, too, unless someone else will do it for you. You can save time by getting a lift in a car to the stables where you might normally walk or go on your bike, but you can't really cut down on exercising or miss too much grooming. In fact, the exercise in this schedule isn't enough, so anything you can do to save time on other jobs and increase the exercise will help.

Combined system pony

7.00 am	Get up, cup of tea, dress.
7.20 am	Leave for stables.
7.35 am	Check pony, give water and hay. While he is eating, pick out feet, muck out and put on New

Zealand rug, if worn. Feed. While he eats, go and fill the evening's haynet and mix feed. Finally turn out for the day.

8.00 am	Leave for home.
8.15 am	Arrive home to wash, change and have breakfast.
8.40 am	Leave home for school.
4.00 pm	Leave school.
4.15 pm	Arrive home, cup of tea and biscuits. Change.
4.30 pm	Leave for stables.
4.45 pm	Arrive at stables. Bed down stable. Hang up haynet and put two buckets of water ready.
5.00 pm	Bring in pony. Check over thoroughly and groom while eating hay. If wet, thatch; unfortunately, you or someone else will have to return to check him and rug him up for the night later.
5.30 pm	Feed pony and refill hay and water, if necessary. Fill next morning's haynet and mix dry feed.
5.45 pm	Leave for home after putting New Zealand rug somewhere to dry off.
6.00 pm	Arrive home for evening meal with family.
6.30 pm	Start homework.

This is a much easier programme for both of you. You save exercise time and your pony is spared the dreadful boredom of standing in all day. If you want your pony fairly fit you will have to ride him at least two days a week for about an hour. Remember, though, he may be too wet and muddy to ride in the evening, so it would be best to make the effort in the morning when he'll be dry.

The grass-kept pony
This is the least time-consuming routine of all but also the least satisfactory if you want a fairly fit, clean pony. He will always be filthy

in winter. If you use a New Zealand rug he will stay cleaner, but these rugs can bring problems of their own when worn all the time. Even the best fitting rug may pull or rub when worn constantly and you'll need to keep a sharp eye out for rubbed hair or bare patches. You will need two rugs so they can be alternated daily and given a chance to dry out. Also, if one is damaged you are not left without a rug.

The following routine is for a hardy, native type who lives out happily with a field shed but no rug. He needs looking at and feeding twice a day and cannot be left for twenty-four hours without checking.

7.00 am	Get up, cup of tea, dress.
7.20 am	Leave for field.
7.35 am	Check pony thoroughly for injuries. Feel legs for heat through muddy wetness which could

indicate mud-fever caused by constant wet. This is less likely to occur in native-type ponies. Check his back if very wet, for signs of rain rash, soreness, tufted hair or scabs. Pick out feet, check for rotting horn, loose shoes. Clean discharge from eyes. Remove droppings from shelter, fill up haynets or rack and check water supply. If there is time, walk round the fencing to ensure it is intact. Finally, feed if necessary. If your pony is the only one in the field to be fed, he should be brought outside to avoid a possible fight.

8.00 am	Leave for home.
8.15 am	Arrive home to wash, change and have breakfast.
8.40 am	Leave home for school.

Tips on time

• One of the most time-wasting occupations is to sit worrying how you're ever going to get everything done. The only way to get anything done is to do it – so get on with it.

• Everyone has twenty-four hours in a day. It's how you organise them that matters, not how many you have.

• Learn to work quickly and briskly without chivvying your pony or rushing jobs so that you end up making mistakes and having to do them again – 'more haste, less speed'. Learn not to dawdle.

• Keeping your pony on the combined system means you need spend less time on exercising, so do try to organise some turn-out facilities for when you cannot ride, at least.

• Time can be saved on cleaning tack by using washable webbing tack which can simply be swished in soapy water, rinsed and hung up to dry. To save cleaning your saddle every time you use it, use a numnah underneath it; the numnah can be washed at the same time as the webbing tack.

• Modern man-made fibre rugs and blankets save time in laundering. They can be washed and dried in an ordinary washing machine at home and, in a warm place, are dry in a very few hours, unlike thick, heavy natural fabrics such as jute.

• Put the most important jobs at the top of your list, in other words those jobs which directly affect your pony such as exercising, mucking out, feeding and watering. Other jobs such as sweeping the yard and tidying the tack room can wait till you have more time. The pony's welfare is more important.

4.00 pm	Leave school.
4.15 pm	Arrive home, cup of tea and biscuits. Change.
4.45 pm	Arrive at field and check pony. Remove droppings from shelter and put in more bedding, if needed. Fill up haynets, check water supply and fencing. Feed if necessary.
5.00 pm	Leave for home.

Although this is the least troublesome routine, you will see that even a pony at grass will take up quite a bit of time. You will also have a wet, muddy pony to deal with much of the year, which is not very pleasant. You won't save much on feed or bedding because the pony has to be fed to keep out the cold and should have a properly bedded down shelter. Remember, ponies living wild don't restrict themselves to one small field and the ground is bound to get churned up and muddy in winter. A dry, comfortable place to lie down will be welcomed by most ponies.

I hope this chapter has helped you (and your parents) to realise that it certainly is possible to get everything done, provided you are really organised. Once you get into a routine it becomes easy. The trick is to teach yourself to work briskly and fairly fast without rushing or skimping on things. Develop the habit of getting on with the job and not dawdling and you'll become more and more efficient. Even grooming can be done quickly if you put your weight behind it and chivvy yourself along, and you will find you get fitter, stronger and able to work more quickly and thoroughly. And just think how glorious it will be to relax and have all day to do your jobs during the school holidays.

10. Health and sickness

Looking after your pony properly helps keep him healthy and happy, but there are times when accidents and illnesses will occur through no fault of your own, and you must know how to treat the pony and/or whether to call in the veterinary surgeon.

It is a good idea to buy a veterinary book and read through it to learn about the various disorders your pony can suffer, then keep it somewhere handy at the stables so you can look things up when you need to. Your instructor, Pony Club or riding club official or other expert adviser should be able to recommend a good, *up to date* book, or perhaps your vet would do so.

Whilst you cannot learn to be your own vet from such a book, nor should you want to, it will offer guidance on first aid for minor injuries and ailments and help you recognise more serious problems which need the attention of the vet.

Learning to recognise good and bad condition

When people say a horse or pony is in good condition or bad condition, they do not mean he is healthy and fit or otherwise, they mean he is either fat, just right or too thin. A pony's weight, like a human's, can affect his health. A very fat pony, for instance, can suffer heart and lung problems, as well as strained joints and tendons, because he is working harder than necessary carrying excess weight around. A very thin pony could be telling us that he is not getting enough food, that his teeth are hurting him so he can't eat properly, that he is infested with worms or has some serious disease that causes weight loss.

You can become a good judge of condition by studying as many horses and ponies as possible *in work*. Do not go to dressage or showing classes with the object of learning what a horse or pony in correct condition looks like because, unfortunately, many of the animals are simply too fat. This is a silly fashion which has gone on for years and should not be used as a guide for a working pony.

Instead, learn by studying horses at official BHS horse trials, long-distance rides, racing on television and affiliated showjumping classes. Such animals are usually owned by people who really understand how to get an animal in good working condition, which means lean but with plenty of muscle. You should be aware of the horse's shape – his withers, ribs, hips – without actually being able to say his bones stick out. His back, loins and quarters should be padded with muscle, not disguised by cushions of fat. If a pony looks like a barrel on legs, with a heavy, podgy neck, an appley bottom and a big belly, he is much too fat; if you can count nearly all his ribs, if his backbone sticks up and you can see the individual bones which make it up and you could, as they say, hang your hat

This poor pony is altogether too thin. Her ribs, backbone and hips tell you that she is grossly underweight.

on his hip bones, he is much too thin. The object is to have your pony somewhere in between.

Your pony's build will also dictate how he looks when in good working condition, and also what kind of work he is doing. He needs to be leaner and more muscled up for things like hunter trials and long-distance riding than for showjumping or active hacking. Gymkhanas are very strenuous, don't forget, but don't go on for long, so your pony should be as fit as for showjumping. If all you do is potter gently about or do a bit of showing, great fitness is not needed, but actual fatness must still be avoided, for the sake of the pony's health.

Signs of health and sickness

It is most important that you know how your pony looks and behaves when well and healthy. Study your pony carefully and get to know him really well so you can sense trouble at once. He can't tell you in words when he doesn't feel well – you have to spot it yourself.

A healthy pony, even one kept at grass and who, therefore, looks rather shabby, will have a bright, smooth coat, and if you place the flat of your hand on his ribs you should be able to move the skin over them quite easily. His eyes will be bright and he will have an alert, interested look, ears pricking to and fro paying attention to his surroundings. The mucous membranes (the sensitive skin inside his eyelids, mouth and nostrils) will be moist and a salmon-pink colour, slightly deeper after exercise maybe. His appetite should be normal for his size and build, neither poor nor ravenous.

Signs of poor health or sickness, either present or on the way, are a general dullness and lack of energy, loss of interest in humans or other ponies, or standing apart from his friends looking miserable, perhaps with his head held low. His coat might be dull or staring (the hairs standing away from the skin); the hair might feel stiff and rough and the skin may be tight and dry, known as hidebound. If you pinch the skin on his neck and it doesn't fall back flat straight away he is dehydrated, which means he is short of water. Maybe he isn't drinking enough (this is easy to tell in a stabled pony drinking from buckets or an automatic waterer with a meter) or maybe his body is not using the water properly.

His eyes might be dull and his mucous membranes could be yellowish, very pale, deep red or bluish. There could be a discharge from his eyes, or especially his nostrils, or the membranes could be too dry. The pony might look tucked up, that is look pinched and thin round his loins and hips. He might also be off his food, or more rarely, eating enough for two ponies.

A pony's droppings are a good guide to his general health. In a normal pony the dung is in large balls which crumble on hitting the ground. They are slightly shiny, moist and a

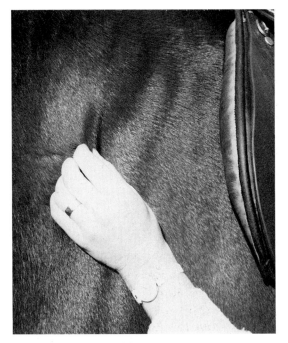

To check for dehydration, pinch up a fold of skin on the pony's neck like this, then let it go. It should fall back down almost immediately in a healthy pony who is *not* dehydrated.

khaki colour, like soldiers' uniforms. In a grass-kept pony they will be slightly looser and darker green.

Unhealthy droppings might be small and hard (constipation) or very loose (diarrhoea, although they are often slightly loose in grass-kept ponies). They might be a sickly yellow colour or very dark, and could be either slimy or dry. Also, they might give off a strong, offensive odour, whereas normal droppings have no bad smell. There might be undigested grain in them, which can be a sign of indigestion or teeth trouble.

The pony's urine can vary from being almost colourless, to creamy or yellowish, either clear or slightly cloudy but without a horrible smell. Signs of something wrong are very frequent attempts to stale, perhaps without success; coloured, dark or very thick urine; or a bad smell. A gelding should let down his penis to stale. If he does not, his sheath is probably blocked with discharge

and needs washing out; failure to do this could lead to an infection.

If you notice something unusual about your pony, keep a close watch on him all day. If you have to go to school, tell someone else – one of your family, the stable owner or some other experienced person who is going to be around – and ask them to contact your family if the pony seems ill. Make a careful note of what seems to be wrong and then ring your vet.

Your veterinary surgeon

A veterinary surgeon is an animal doctor, just as highly trained and qualified as your own doctor. Vets are normally the best people to ask about health matters, although a good instructor will have a fair knowledge about general health and sickness.

Although all vets receive the same basic training, some prefer to specialise in one kind of animal, such as horses. The best way to find a vet who is up to date on treating horses is to ask other owners who they have. Many riding schools and livery stables have one vet for all their horses so your pony would probably have theirs.

It's a good idea to have a vet reasonably near your stables because vets charge for travelling and the further he or she has to come the more it will cost, unless your pony is included with others in the area. Also, your pony will get treatment quicker in an emergency from a nearby vet.

The vet will give you instructions on what to do to help the pony get better. Injections will be given by the vet but other medications may have to be given by you or someone else.

Never be afraid to question the vet about what is wrong with the pony and what you have to do. If there is the smallest thing you don't understand, *never* hesitate to ask or worry about looking stupid for asking. The vet would much rather you made sure of your facts, otherwise you could make the pony worse rather than better. Of course, you must carry out his instructions exactly. Your pony won't get better if you don't.

Remember that vets are very busy people. They haven't time (and it's not their job) to chase ponies round fields, to tramp around looking for them and their owners, or to catch them up and bring them into a stable to examine them. You, or someone else, must have the pony waiting for the vet in a stable. Someone responsible must be there to take instructions, preferably writing them down so there is no misunderstanding. The floor should be reasonably clean, and so should the pony. And make sure you can offer the vet hot water, soap and a towel when he or she has finished dealing with your pony. This may be difficult with a grass-kept pony or a yard with poor facilities, but try anyway.

Be prepared to answer the vet's questions about your pony's feed, work, normal routine, when you first noticed the illness or injury and, particularly, about his normal appearance and behaviour. You know your pony much better than the vet and he or she will appreciate as much information as you can give.

Have a bridle ready for leading or holding the pony, as this gives better control than a headcollar. If lameness is the problem you will probably have to trot the pony up a few times for the vet to check his action, so practise this. Bring the reins over the pony's head and hold them about 30 cm (1 ft) down from the bit. Leave the head free so his natural action shows. Walk the pony on hard, level ground away from the vet, turn him round and trot him back. He or she might ask for other movements, too.

Make a careful note of when (and if) the vet is calling again and make sure you or someone else is there. If you have any questions between visits or have forgotten what the vet said, ring the surgery and ask. Again, this is much better than doing things wrong or not at all, and the vet won't mind.

Finally, when the vet's bill arrives, ask your parents to be sure to pay it promptly – nothing infuriates people (vets, farriers, feed merchants etc) more than having to wait for their money. They have been fair with you; be fair with them and pay up quickly. In extreme cases, you may find that you can't get them to come to you if you are known as a bad payer.

Some common disorders

There are an awful lot of things that can go wrong with your pony but a well-cared-for pony should rarely be ill. Here are the most common disorders to watch out for.

Laminitis

This is one of the most common disorders to affect ponies, especially those who are under-exercised and over-fed. Once a pony has had an attack he is quite likely to have another, so you should do all you can to keep your pony well exercised and properly fed.

It is caused by poor blood supply to the feet and generally poor circulation. When the pony digests his food, waste products are formed which can be poisonous. These poisons are normally passed out in the sweat, urine and droppings, but if the pony is given too much food, especially rich grass or concentrates (coarse mix, nuts, flaked maize, barley and oats in particular), there will obviously be more poisons as a result. If lack of exercise means the blood is not circulating efficiently and there is too much energy going into the pony for the work he is doing, laminitis can often be the result.

It is an extremely painful condition. In Chapter 5 the hoof was described as having a horny insensitive outside and a fleshy, sensitive inside. In laminitis, the sensitive parts begin to separate from the insensitive parts and in bad cases the pedal bone presses downwards on the sole and can actually push through it. The whole structure of the foot is foot is damaged and it can be very difficult to cure the pony.

The signs of laminitis are (often but not always) warm or hot feet (feet and legs should be cool), pottery, short steps with the pony either lame or reluctant to move, especially on hard ground. He may stand leaning backwards to put his weight on to his heels and off the most painful parts of his feet at the toes. He may sweat in patches and even wave a hoof in the air, which is a sign of great pain.

The pony must be taken where he cannot eat anything but has plenty of water – either a covered yard or stable bedded on anything but straw, which he may eat – and the vet must be called immediately.

Coughing

This can be just a tickle in the throat or a full blown chest infection such as influenza or an allergy. Some ponies will have a little cough when brought out of a stable and started on exercise, just to clear their wind, but if the cough does not stop after five or ten minutes, stop work and call your vet. Working a pony with an infection or chest allergy can permanently damage his breathing, so you must not take any chances.

Influenza

Equine influenza is a very serious disease which can put paid to a pony's active career because it can permanently damage or weaken his lungs and heart. An infected pony will look dull and sorry, probably with a watery discharge from one or both nostrils. He may or may not cough. Keep him warm by rugging him up, and in a well-ventilated but not draughty loose box, and call the vet.

Strangles

This is another very serious chest disease which can strike ponies on its own or, quite commonly, after influenza or some other chest problem. Again, the pony will look and feel ill and the glands under his throat may be hard and lumpy. Again, keep him warm and call the vet at once.

Lameness

Lameness is something we hear a lot about but it isn't as common as you may think. It is a sign of pain in the leg and can be due to many causes from a strained tendon, a bruised sole from the pony treading on a stone, to something very serious like navicular disease.

If your pony is lame in one leg, he will try to shift his weight off that leg by throwing it on to the sound (healthy) leg. If he is lame in a front leg, he will take a shorter step with the painful leg than with the sound one, and will drop his head lower when the sound one comes to the ground. If lame behind, again he will try to put more weight on the sound leg, and the hock and hip of the lame leg will seem to be carried higher than those of the sound leg.

Lameness can be very difficult to spot, especially if the pony is lame in two legs. The experienced eye of your instructor or adviser will help you here. In any case of lameness be sure you know what is causing the trouble and how to put it right; you should always ask your vet to look at the pony.

Heat and swelling

These are signs that a foot or leg is causing a problem so make a habit of checking for them every day. Feel with your bare hand around the hoof and up the lower leg (where most problems occur); they should feel cold and hard. If you notice any difference or if one or both feel warm and/or puffy, call the vet or someone experienced to help you.

Filled legs

This condition is caused by over-feeding and lack of exercise and some ponies are more prone to it than others. Usually the hind legs are affected, looking puffy and enlarged. If

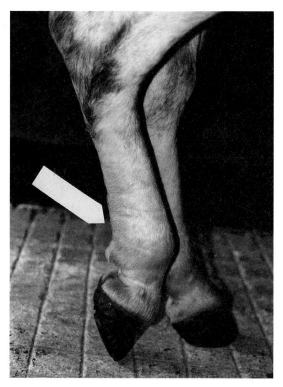

This leg is swollen and puffy due to a ligament strain to a hind fetlock (arrowed). The pony is resting the leg on its toe to relieve the pain. This type of injury can be brought about by galloping in soft, deep ground such as heavy mud or plough or soft sand.

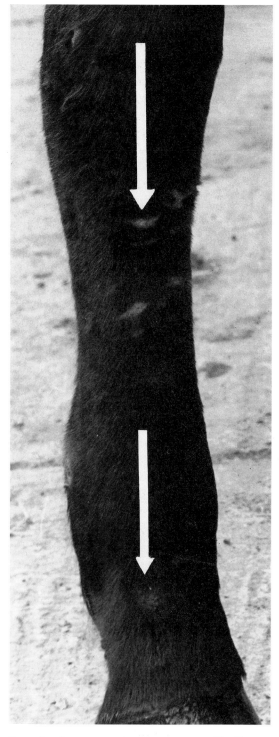

they are actually hard and warm the condition is a more serious one called *lymphangitis* which needs veterinary attention.

Colic

This is a painful disorder, frightening for pony and owner alike. The word 'colic' does not indicate a disease but a tummy ache, and it can be caused by several things. It means the pony has indigestion, and as ponies have such sensitive digestive systems, much more so than humans, it can be serious for them. If ever a pony feels sick he cannot vomit – his throat and stomach are just not made that way.

A pony with colic may become a danger to himself and those around him if he starts

Over-feeding concentrates can cause filled legs or 'big leg') and this can lead to ulcers (arrowed) and a more advanced stage of filled leg called lymphangitis.

thrashing around in pain (and some do), but even a mild colic can become serious if immediate veterinary attention is not given.

The pony may look listless and miserable; he may show patchy sweating (which means pain); he may paw the ground; he may look round at his sides and try to bite where the pain is; he may get down and lie flat out or try to roll, maybe kicking out and trying to plunge about.

Sometimes the colic may come and go in bouts, and in between painful spasms the pony may look quite normal and even tuck into his hay. At other times it will be continuous. In any case, as soon as colic is suspected call the vet at once. Ask for instructions over the phone about what to do in the meantime. If the pony is violent, it is safest for you to keep out of the way. Let the vet handle the situation but make sure you and an adult stay around to tell him what he needs to know, and to receive instructions for treatment and management.

Wounds

Wounds can range from a little scratch to a deep injury down to the bone. Obviously, the deeper, the more serious. There are various types of wound such as a plain cut, a tear wound (as on barbed wire) or a bruised wound (as from a kick). Kicks can also fracture the bone underneath. If more than the top layer of skin is damaged, the wound will need stitching – a job for your vet. Always bathe any wound as soon as possible according to the instructions in your veterinary book. A common cleanser is slightly salty water applied with *clean* lint, not a sponge or cotton wool which can stick to the wound. Running the salt water solution down the wound from the top should wash out the dirt. In any case, be sure you don't wash dirt further *into* the wound. Dirty wounds soon become infected and, in a bad case, blood poisoning can occur, so clean the wound promptly, and gently. If the pony won't let you, don't take 'no' for an answer; ask someone experienced to help you.

Nursing a sick pony

If a pony is sick or hurt he will be feeling very poorly, so treat him considerately. Be gentle in your care of him. Do not groom him vigorously, just enough to freshen him up; the sponging part of grooming will help greatly to refresh him. Do not disturb him too much when mucking out. Remove the droppings and the worst of the dirty bedding and see he has a good, thick bed as he will almost certainly want to lie down.

He should be kept warm and comfortable with enough rugs, which you should regularly adjust and straighten so he feels comfortable. He should not be kept in a stuffy atmosphere. He will need ventilation to provide plenty of fresh air with no draughts.

In some diseases the pony should be isolated (kept away from others) to prevent his neighbours becoming infected; in others, this is unnecessary. However, a sick or badly injured pony often does not want to bother with other ponies or people. He will feel happier if left in peace in his own familiar stable, but don't make him feel deserted. Visit him often to see he has everything he needs. You could perhaps keep him company by sitting quietly in a corner of his box reading a book, when he may come and stand by you. Do not fuss over him needlessly, though; if he seems to want attention give it to him, but do not pester him.

Your vet will give you any particular nursing details, depending on what is wrong with him. Once he is getting better don't be tempted to return him to work too soon as not only would this be cruel, for he will still be weak, but also he might have a relapse of some kind and be out of work much longer. Always be guided by your vet on this.

Help your pony to health

DO learn to recognise the signs of health and sickness so that you know when your pony is, or is not, healthy or ill.

DO keep an emergency savings fund so you need never be afraid to call the vet in an emergency because you can't afford it.

DO take your vet's advice regarding vaccinations, worming and other health matters. It's cheaper, and only fair to your pony, to prevent illnesses happening than to cure them.

DO remember that some serious illnesses cannot be cured. If you pony is incurably ill, don't hesitate to have him put to sleep by your vet at home. Never send him away alive as then you cannot be certain what has happened to him.

DO remember that, like you, your pony will need time to recover after an illness. He may be easily tired or bored till he has built up his strength again. Follow your vet's instructions regarding medicine, feeding and exercise until the pony has fully recovered.

DON'T be too quick to put the pony back to work, or he could become ill again quickly.

DON'T try to save money by **not** having vaccinations done, by **not** worming the pony often enough or by **not** calling in the vet when you should. This puts your pony's health at risk, is more expensive in the long run, and not fair to the pony.

DON'T have your pony too fat. It's worse than having him a little too lean, if anything.

DON'T be impatient with your pony if he is ill. Like sick people, you should make allowances for him because he feels unwell.

Parasites

Worms

Worms can kill your pony. Despite this, many people don't seem to want to give their ponies worming medicines often enough – maybe because they cost money. However, a badly infested pony can cost you more in extra feed to keep weight on him that the worming medicines would have cost in the first place. Also, 'wormy' ponies are usually weak and anaemic (with poor blood quality) and tend to become sick more often than others; so, again, you end up spending money on vets' bills which shouldn't have been necessary.

Apart from money, no sensible person would deliberately want their pony to be unhealthy when it is so easy to keep him practically worm-free.

There are several different types of worm and they enter the body as worm larvae (the young form of the worms), being picked up on grass and swallowed. The larvae travel around inside the pony, damaging tissues such as blood vessels and intestines and sucking the pony's blood. They block arteries and interfere with the blood circulation which can cause heart and digestive troubles. Many colics are caused by worms blocking the blood supply to the intestine, preventing food from passing through the system and ultimately poisoning the pony.

When the worms leave the arteries and return, as adults, to the intestines to mate and lay eggs, they attach themselves by their mouthparts to the wall of the intestine, damaging or even piercing it. Their eggs are passed out with the droppings on to the grass or bedding, and the whole cycle starts again.

Just because you can't see worms in the droppings doesn't mean there aren't any. You should ask your vet about worm infestations and he or she will advise how to find out how many your pony has and what kind of worms they are, how to get rid of them and, just as important, how to *keep* them away. This will probably mean you have to give your pony a worming medicine every six weeks or so. This is easily done with a plastic syringe containing the medicine in paste form. You insert the syringe in the corner of the pony's mouth, point it back towards his throat, press the plunger in and the wormer will land on the back of his tongue, when most ponies swallow it without trouble. If you do have problems, you can give worming pellets or powders in a normal feed with plenty of black treacle to disguise the taste.

Lice and ticks

There are other parasites (creatures which live off other creatures and harm them as a result) which can attack your pony, such as lice and ticks. These are little insects which bite or suck blood and live in your pony's coat, sometimes attached to his skin, especially along the neck, back and quarters. There are various treatments, powders and shampoos you can use to remove them, but, again, your vet is the person to advise you on this.

Vaccinations and annual check-up

The two main diseases your pony will be vaccinated against in Great Britain are influenza and tetanus. Influenza is very common and there are often waves of the disease (called epidemics) every few years. Tetanus is not so common (and so has not been listed earlier with the other diseases) but it is extremely painful and can kill your

pony by paralysing him. The germ which causes it enters the pony's body via dirt (usually the soil) by means of a wound, in particular small puncture wounds caused by pointed objects such as nails or thorns. In this type of wound there is little air, unlike in a gaping cut or torn wound, and this is what the tetanus germ likes.

Often the wounds are so small you don't even notice them, and therefore don't take the precaution of having the pony injected against tetanus. Then, when the pony goes down with the disease a few weeks later, it's a terrible shock.

Early symptoms of tetanus are general stiffness and slight difficulty in moving. The pony may breathe quicker and more shallowly and have trouble eating. If you put your hand under the pony's lower jaw and push his head up, a small membrane will come across the eye from the inner corner. This is the main test for early signs of tetanus, and is a signal to call the vet without delay. Don't wait to see if the pony gets better. He won't – not without veterinary help.

Fortunately it is quite easy to protect the pony against tetanus and flu by giving vaccinations. Your vet will explain exactly what is involved in providing protection for a pony who has never been vaccinated and one who simply needs 'booster' doses to step up earlier vaccinations. When you buy a pony, always ask his former owner for his vaccination certificates. If there are none, don't take their word that the pony's vaccinations are up to date, ring your vet and take his or her advice.

Your vet can work out for you a proper yearly programme for giving worming medicines, vaccinations and other routine health checks. Every pony needs his teeth checked once a year so that sharp edges can be rasped (filed) down, and an annual general check-up from your vet is also a good idea. This is best done a few months before your pony starts his busiest season, which will probably be during the summer. Therefore, early spring is a sensible time. To save on visits (and bills) the vet can do the check-up, see to the teeth and give vaccinations, all at the same time. He or she might take a small sample of your pony's blood to monitor his general health and condition, and also update you on your worming programme. New drugs are coming on to the market all the time, and veterinary knowledge is developing fast, so this annual check is a good time for a discussion about your pony, his work and his management.

Humane destruction

If any pony is so ill he will not live, is in great pain or very seriously injured, it may be necessary for the vet to destroy him rather than prolong his suffering or condemn him to a miserable life. It may be heartbreaking to lose him, but it would be very wrong to keep him alive and suffering purely to satisfy your own selfishness. If you love him, anyway, you will not be able to bear to see him in pain or misery.

This is equally true of an old pony. There comes a time in every pony's life when he is just too old or unsound to work any more, or maybe even live happily in retirement. He cannot do anything for you any more, but you still have to do just as much, if not more, for him in the way of looking after him and he will cost just as much to keep.

Some people retire their old ponies to grass, permanently exposed to the weather, with inadequate shelter and often insufficient food. They imagine he is enjoying life in green pastures, lazing away the days, whereas he may well be suffering considerably, especially if he has always been used to being partly stabled and cossetted. Old ponies feel the weather much more than young ones, and a retired pony can also feel very unwanted, left out of things and lonely,

apart from suffering from flies in summer and the cold, wet and wind in winter. Such treatment is cruel.

Old ponies are sometimes sold or loaned to 'good homes' in the belief they will be used as companions or quiet first ponies. The ponies get older and older and past their usefulness and often change hands again.

Once you have sold a pony you have no control over where he ends up. Even if you include certain conditions in the sale you might have to fund an expensive court case to get the pony back, and you are not bound to win. Ponies lent or leased to other homes are often no better off. They often 'disappear' – stolen or lent to yet another family – till all trace is lost. Sometimes these ponies end up at sales and once sold in this way the rightful owner cannot retrieve them, except by buying them again.

In fact, sending an unwanted pony to a sale is a pretty despicable way of disposing of him. Most sale animals are sold for meat, very few find private homes and even fewer find good ones. Many are hauled round from sale to sale, going from one buyer to the next with a view to making a few more pounds' profit for each transaction. Their travelling conditions are overcrowded and dangerous, with ponies falling on each other, getting crushed and having legs broken in the lorry. They are roughly handled and often crammed into pens at the sale premises with little if any shelter, food or water. Many die during the process. What a reward for a faithful old friend!

I strongly feel that the only right and fair way to dispose of an old pony no longer able to be of use to anyone who will give him a good home, is to have him humanely put to sleep by your vet *at home*, with someone he knows and trusts holding his lead rope.

Never send him away alive to a knacker's yard, believing that he will be put down on arrival. Not only might he be sold on by the knacker 'by mistake' and unbeknown to you, to suffer a fate similar to the one described above, but also even if he is destroyed on arrival, the strange surroundings and people, the smell of blood, plus the sounds and atmosphere of other frightened animals will terrify him. Once again, no end for a good old pony.

If the decision has been made to have your pony destroyed, ask your vet to come to your home or wherever you keep the pony, so he has no idea what is going to happen. The vet will take charge and the pony won't know a thing about it. The vet will also arrange for the disposal of his body.

Whatever else you do, never let anyone, whoever they may be, take the pony away alive because you can never be quite certain that the pony will be given the humane end he deserves.

11. Improving your pony's fitness

Getting a pony fit means conditioning every part of his body to undertake harder and faster work than he would have to do in the wild. Every part of him – his muscles, tendons and ligaments, his skin, lungs, digestive system, liver, kidneys – must be gradually attuned to working harder. His body has to adjust to processing more food, providing more energy and replacing more used-up body tissues, all because of his extra work load.

When a pony is fit his frame actually feels harder than when unfit; this is why people say unfit horses are in 'soft condition'. A fit pony's neck should feel like warm marble, not like foam rubber or jelly. If he is fat from too much or too rich grass during spring or summer he will probably feel soft and blubbery with it, and this fat has to be used up by gradually and gently increasing work. As the work progresses the muscles become harder and increase in size.

A fit pony is stronger and more agile than an unfit one. If you try to rush your fitness programme, or to work the pony fairly hard before he is fit, you will be asking for trouble. He could easily trip or fall, especially as the work continues and he gets tired, which will happen quite quickly. If he falls, so do you; if he trips, you may come off over his head. Therefore, you must get him fit in the safest possible way, for both your sakes. In any case, it is extremely bad horsemanship to work an unfit pony, as opposed to exercising

him to get him fit. The pony will become severely distressed and you will probably acquire a bad reputation.

Overworking an unfit pony can strain his legs and heart, stress his lungs and other body systems and make him sour in his work. If he comes to associate work with feeling distressed and exhausted, he may well become difficult and start refusing jumps, napping or rearing, depending on his temperament.

All this is quite unnecessary because anyone can get a pony fit with a bit of willpower and commonsense, plus a rough fitness programme as a guideline (such as the one given later in this chapter). It simply involves increasing the amounts of exercise and food, and maybe changing the type of food from mainly grass to less grass and more hay and, with care, concentrates.

Different kinds of fitness

As mentioned earlier in this book, there are different kinds of fitness. A pony doesn't really need to be fit if all you want to do is ride gently around the lanes, fields and bridleways. You can ride him at walk for half an hour or so with a little trot now and then without any risk at all. If you want to hack (ride out) more actively for an hour or more, walking, trotting, cantering and taking the odd little jump, the pony needs to be what is called half fit. If a pony starts off completely soft, having been out of work for some months, it will take about six weeks to get him half fit. This sort of fitness is adequate for showing classes.

Next up the scale come more active, longer hacks, dressage, light hunting (no more than half a day), schooling and instruction classes. You may be surprised to know that during an average riding lesson a pony can cover 6.5 to 8km (4-5 miles), most of it at trot, with turns and adjustments of pace, which is very strenuous.

After this, more fitness is needed for showjumping, hunter trials and harder hunting, with the hardest fitness being needed for eventing and long-distance riding.

Fitness in grass-kept ponies

Many people think that if a pony lives out at grass he cannot be made fit, but this is not true. Provided the pony is kept on poor quality grazing so he doesn't fill himself with bulky, watery grass, getting fat and soft, he can certainly be made very fit. The grass *must* be poor, though, then you can feed him concentrates, and maybe hay if the paddock is really bare, which, with his work, will be little different from the diet of a stabled pony. Combined-system ponies can be made just as fit as stabled ponies, again provided they have poorish grazing. Indeed, stabled ponies would be better off and certainly happier, which is important, if they were allowed out for an hour or two every day to enjoy a little of their natural food, grass.

Grooming and fitness

Some people say that thorough grooming is essential to get a pony fit because the skin needs to be clean and in perfect working order so that it can sweat freely to rid the body of waste products from feeding and exercise.

Facts on fitness

- It will take about six weeks to get a completely unfit pony half fit.
- It will take about twelve weeks to get a completely unfit pony fully fit, maybe longer for long-distance riding or eventing.
- Slow work is nearly always good for your pony. Fast work rarely is. Most of your exercise should be at a smart walk and steady trot, not a relentless canter for most of the ride.
- Spend the first two weeks of a fitness programme in walk. It may be boring but it will pay dividends later and forms the groundwork of your faster work.
- A fitness programme rushed is a fitness programme not done. You can't skimp on the fitness work without risking your pony's well-being later on during work.

He will be more likely to develop lameness and other problems if you fail to carry out the fitness work properly from the start.
- Once your pony is fit, it is fairly easy to keep him so, and you can ease off the work and give him more days off (but not stuck in the stable) without losing fitness.
- A fit pony does not necessarily fool around and buck you off, although an occasional frolic from feeling good may well occur. It is fresh ponies who go berserk and are a danger to themselves and their riders. Don't confuse fitness with freshness. Fresh ponies are those who are not having enough exercise and, probably, are having too much food for the work they are doing.

This is true to some degree, but as explained in Chapter 6, grooming was invented for stabled animals not exposed to rain. The skin of a pony living out some or all of the time should be in very healthy condition anyway, and the kinds of grooming described in that chapter are quite adequate during a fitness programme. In practice, grooming is not as important in a fitness programme as gradually increasing work and feeding – but of course, this doesn't mean you don't have to do it.

A sample fitness programme

The fitness programme described in this section can only be a rough guide because all ponies will react differently. You are advised to seek your instructor's help in devising a programme to suit your particular pony. However, the plan given here should provide a starting point from which to work.

It's a good idea to draw out your programme in an exercise book, using a page to a week and dividing it into seven sections with Monday running across the top part of the page, Tuesday underneath Monday and so on. Write down the amount of exercise you propose, the amounts by weight of the pony's different foodstuffs (hay, coarse mix etc) and leave a space for comments on how the pony is reacting. This is a useful record and if the pony isn't getting fit as quickly as you hoped you can always change the programme.

Most family ponies are in some sort of work all year round so will probably be half fit all the time. However, because you need to know how to start from scratch if necessary, the programme assumes a completely unfit pony, native type, about 14 hh high.

Bringing a pony up from grass
Suddenly changing a pony's lifestyle from being completely out to being completely in is a very sudden and drastic shock to him, and many ponies are quite upset for several days at their loss of freedom and change of food. The new diet can make them feel quite poorly, so if you *have* to make this sudden change for any reason try to make it as gentle as you can.

While the pony is still out, give him one small feed a day of dried grassmeal, say no more than .25 kg (½ lb), well damped and mixed with soaked sugar-beet pulp and/or diluted black treacle with a handful of chop in it. You may have heard that bran mashes are the thing in situations like this, but grassmeal is much nearer to the pony's natural food and is also more likely to be eaten. Do this for about a week, then when the pony comes in, give him as much sweet meadow hay as he wants, plus his small feed of grassmeal every night. Hayage can, of course, be used instead of hay.

This will make for a very similar diet for the pony and digestive upsets should be very few, although the pony might have loose droppings for some days.

While he is still in the field and without shoes, tack him up and ride him at walk round the field for half an hour a day. Keep this up for a week or a fortnight, and the first part of your fitness programme will have been done.

When he comes in altogether increase the exercise to threequarters of an hour daily, still walking, but don't increase the feed as he really doesn't need any more.

Now, before work really starts, is the time to call in the farrier to get the pony's feet trimmed and shaped, and a pair of lightweight shoes put on so that he becomes used to having weight on his feet again. This may also be a good time to arrange the pony's annual medical and check-up.

If you have both stabling and grazing you won't need to make a sudden change. If the pony is to be on the combined system reduce his grazing by keeping him in for part of the twenty-four hours, depending on the season. (It's usual in summer for ponies to be in by day away from heat and flies, and in at night in winter.) You already know that grazing for ponies should be poor quality and this is especially important for ponies who are to be made fit whilst living out all the time.

The next stage of the programme, probably week three, is to increase the exercise to about one hour a day, bringing in short spells (about a minute long to begin with) of steady trotting, on grass verges or in the field to begin with then on harder surfaces such as tracks and roads. Add to the grassmeal feed a single handful of coarse mix, nuts or whatever his usual concentrate is when in work. Keep the hay/hayage ration as before.

By week four the pony should be walking and trotting up to his bridle but relaxed and beginning to go actively and with more interest. He should now be on one and a quarter hours a day walking and trotting – sixty minutes walking and fifteen minutes trotting in, say, three spells. You do not have to be to the minute but you should wear a watch. Always walk for the first twenty minutes to warm the pony up and settle him, and for the last twenty to relax him and cool him down.

His concentrate feed should be the same weight as before but made up of half grassmeal and half coarse mix/nuts. Give his usual hay/hayage ration.

Week five should see a noticeable improvement in his fitness. Up to now you probably felt you were wasting your time but now he should be looking sleeker and feeling more active and responsive to you. Introduce schooling sessions now, if you wish; if you don't have anywhere special to school, just do it out hacking. Start paying particular attention to correct turns and bends, upward and downward transitions, lengthening and shortening of pace without changing the rhythm, and half-halts to prepare the pony

for a request and attract his attention.

This week you can also introduce canter work. Begin with short spells, as with trotting, cantering steadily and up to the bridle. He may give a joyful buck, and one is permissible provided it is not too big – two aren't and you should speak sharply to him and press him forward. Don't pull him up if he bucks but tell him off and ride him through it and don't sit *too* far forward – use a schooling canter seat rather than your jumping position.

His exercise could now be up to one and a half hours a day and his feed, say, the same weight (.25 kg or ½ lb) but all coarse mix/nuts, cutting out the grassmeal. By the end of the week this could be increased gradually to about .3 kg or ¾ lb. You'll have to keep a close eye on his condition and feeding and ask your adviser, if in doubt, about his diet. It is impossible to give precise instructions for your pony.

By week six, his exercise should be approaching two hours a day and his concentrates could be about .4 kg/1 lb per day. Some ponies will need more to provide the required energy but others may remain too podgy on this amount, even with the increased exercise. Your pony should be walking for at least an hour and preferably more, with the rest spent mostly trotting and with two five-minute spells of cantering. As always, his hay/hayage remains at however much he wants.

The pony can now be described as half fit. You can start including higher and wider jumps in your schooling now, if you want. The pony should be capable of a full hour's instruction class, a little easy showjumping, showing classes and rallies, provided the hack there and back is not too long. He could do half a day's hunting, go once round an easy hunter trial course and compete in one or two gymkhana classes, but no more as these can be rather strenuous.

To proceed further with the programme,

increase the exercise to two hours and the concentrates to roughly 1 kg/2 lbs, depending on how he seems. Always devote more time to walking, but introduce longer trotting and cantering spells, and find somewhere suitable for fast canter stints, say, two or three times a week. Take up a jumping position but stay well down in the saddle and with your stirrups only a hole or two shorter than normal riding length so you have proper control and a little more than just balance to keep you on board. The pony should never be asked or allowed to gallop flat out. Only racehorses or those equally fit should be asked to do this.

By the end of the eighth week you should be able to stroke your pony's neck and find it quite hard to the touch. He should now be ready for some fairly strenuous work – a day's hunting, showjumping, a couple of hunter trial classes, long picnic rides, a one-day event, in fact, almost anything you would normally ask of a hard, fit pony, within reason.

Long exercise periods are better split into two stints a day; one session might be a bit of a strain. Those going in for long-distance riding, of course, have to accustom their ponies to carrying weight for long periods, and often dismount during outings and walk beside their pony (whose stirrups must be run up and the girth loosened two holes) to rest his back. Read a specialist book on this sport if you want to have a go.

You don't have to ride your pony *every* day, but if you can't ride five days a week he will take much longer to get fit. On his days off, of course, never leave him standing in the stable but do everything possible to have him turned out. If he is on the combined system, you will have no problems. If he is at grass all the time, watch the quality of grass in spring and if it *does* get too rich and he starts putting on weight, stable him part of the time.

Riding up hills is a good way to make your

pony work without over-stressing his legs, and so is walking in knee-deep water (provided the bottom is firm and not stony). Deeper water will spoil his way of going, but at this depth he will simply have to make those muscles work. Keep hold of his head if he is the type to roll in water; if he starts to buckle at the knees as if to go down, kick on hard at once or you'll both be in for a ducking.

Keeping him fit
Once the pony is fit you can slacken off the work and concentrates a little. Give him a shorter ride one day with a little less corn, and always before a day off make the night feed grassmeal and soaked sugar-beet pulp, chop and sliced carrot or apple – with no concentrates at all – to avoid over-feeding. Over-training will sicken him and is just as bad as under-work. He can certainly have three days off a week, if necessary, once he is fit. Fitness is maintained quite easily once achieved, so don't worry about slackening off a bit. You can always build up the work again if your pony starts to lose fitness. Remember to reduce the concentrates slightly if you reduce the work; this is most important.

Letting him down again and roughing off
A pony cannot be kept very fit for more than about twelve weeks; after this he will begin to need a break. Preparing for a break is known as 'letting down'.

Just as you made him fit gradually, so you must let him down gradually, although the latter process doesn't take as long. It would be a big shock to his system if he were suddenly subjected to a completely new routine. The most extreme case is a stabled pony being let down to go out to grass.

Preparing a pony to go out to grass after being stabled is called 'roughing off'. If a stabled pony is to be let down and roughed off after a winter's work, it will obviously take place in the spring, when it can still be quite

It's true that . . .

● It is hard to overwork a healthy, fit pony provided his work and exercise are sensibly balanced. If he has been made properly fit, a day's work should not tire him unreasonably.
● Ponies can, nevertheless, become tired, just as we can! Be prepared to finish work if your pony is tired, or at least give him a rest.
● Working a pony on a full stomach is dangerous. It can cause colic and breathing problems. Don't feed for an hour at least before work, maybe two. Don't water later than half an hour before work.

It's not true that . . .

● You can't get a grass-kept pony fit. You can. The secret is to keep him on poor quality grazing and feed him more or less like a combined system pony. He may well be easier to make fit as he will be exercising himself gently all day, leaving you less actual exercising to do.
● You can turn a hot, sweaty pony out into a cold field after a day's work. If you do, you could well have a sick pony on your hands. Cool him off properly before turning him back into his field.
● Your pony shouldn't eat at all during a long day. He will feel very uncomfortable if you keep him without food all day. A few mouthfuls of grass or a small feed during a break in proceedings will do no harm provided you don't do fast work immediately afterwards. The same goes for water.
● Your pony **must** have a day off after a hard day. A short hack is fine provided he is not injured or exhausted. If he is, you overdid it the day before and you should certainly rest the pony.

cold. In addition, the pony will have been clipped and rugged up so the change will be considerable. Depending on the weather, it could take three weeks or even more.

You should always leave your pony's top door open unless wind and rain are blowing right in, but if this has not been done for any reason, your first step now is to leave the door open all the time. After about three nights, remove one of the pony's underblankets. During this time, his concentrate ration should be cut down by about one quarter. Keep the exercise time the same but stop fast work (cantering, galloping and jumping). Stop body brushing and wisping to allow the grease to build up in his coat for protection but carry on as usual with the dandy brush, hoof pick and sponges.

If he is already used to grass, leave him out longer than usual but if not re-introduce him to it gradually, giving him no more than thirty minutes' grazing a day, increasing to two hours by the end of the first week.

He will almost certainly need a New Zealand rug on during these spells in the field at this time of year.

Next, cut out another quarter of the original concentrate ration, remove another blanket, if worn, at least during the day, cut the exercise down to half the usual time and only walk. Groom as for the previous week and gradually increase the grazing until, by the end of this second week, he is out nearly all day.

For the third week, the pony should wear just a top rug at night, have only a quarter of his original corn ration and be out walking for only about thirty minutes a day. Leave him at grass until well into the evening if possible. Groom as usual.

In theory the pony should be ready to be turned out all the time by the end of the third week. However, it is essential you use your common sense during this process. If the weather is still cold, wet and windy keep bringing him in, and putting on one rug, at night, and keep the New Zealand rug on during the day. He should always have as much hay/hayage as he wants and his concentrates should be the same as for the third week. Ridden exercise is unnecessary, however. Groom as usual. You'll be able to leave him out at grass all the time – sooner if you have a field shelter with a decent bed in it.

During his first week out all the time, give him the remaining quarter of the concentrate ration, after which, depending on the growth of grass, he may be able to do without corn altogether. If the grass is very poor, however, you must continue to feed him as much hay/hayage as he will eat, otherwise he will lose weight and could become ill.

How long a rest you give him is entirely up to you. Family ponies in work more or less all year do well with a fortnight off in spring and again in autumn. A break may also be given when you yourself go away on holiday, provided someone else is there to look after him.

A pony will not lose much fitness at all in two weeks or even three, so when you start working him again use a shortened version of the programme given earlier, i.e. walk for a few days at first and gradually increase the exercise, feeding and grooming until in three or four weeks he is fit again.

12. A hard day's work

Whatever kind of work your pony does, the way you look after him before, during and after a hard day's work is basically the same. It also does not matter whether he has been working fast or slow. A long day at slow paces with maybe a lot of hanging around is as wearying as a short, sharp morning's hunting.

About a week before a big day make a special check on his shoes so there is time to have him reshod if necessary. If his feet are not up to scratch you will not be able to go at all.

The day before

Check your tack and see it is clean and in good repair. Put ready everything you will take with you. Make a list and tick off each item as it is put out. Use the same list the next morning when everything is loaded into the box or trailer, if you are using transport. If you are hacking to your show, rally or whatever, and your family are meeting you there, they can take your things in the car.

The pony should be thoroughly groomed, maybe shampooed and checked over, especially his legs and feet, for heat. Examine the feet and shoes as usual. He should receive some exercise, for about an hour.

With a grass-kept pony, it will be an advantage if you can bring him into a well-ventilated box for the night so he is handy and dry in the morning. If you are going to groom him the day before, it's no use turning him out again, obviously, as you will just have wasted your time.

On the day

Before you leave

Bring the pony in if necessary and tie him up under cover with his haynet, if you have no stable available. If he is wet, thatch him and leave grooming till last. You should give a concentrate feed, if he normally has one, two hours before setting off. He cannot work on a full stomach so give only about 2 kg (4 lb) of hay.

Check the pony carefully, as usual, and while he is eating load everything into the box or trailer, ticking it off as you do. Don't forget the first-aid kit and a camping container of water in case there is no supply at the place you are going to.

If the pony is to be stabled that night, muck out and bed down the stable so you do not have to do it when you return. Leave a full haynet tied up ready for the night but don't leave water standing in the stable all day or it will be thoroughly stale by the time he gets back and may have collected debris during the day. Leave a feed ready in the feed room, covered by a stable rubber. Do not damp it, of course.

If you groomed the pony the day before he should only need quartering now, otherwise

It's wise to wear a modern, properly fastened hard hat or skull cap whenever you ride, not just because competition rules say you must. A body protector is also a good idea.

groom him and plait his mane and tail if you wish. Try to make the pony stale before leaving.

Tack up or put on travelling clothes – and off you go.

On the way

If hacking, take the quickest and easiest route and go steadily. Walk and trot mainly but if the pony is well schooled and will canter without hotting up, short canters will speed up the journey. If the weather is hot, or the pony unclipped in winter, keep to walk and trot.

Travelling is dealt with in the next chapter. Just remember to keep checking the pony at reasonable intervals if it is a longish journey. He can have a haynet to munch on, but take it away about two hours before he is due to work. Many people withhold hay for many hours before work but this is, in fact, wrong. Not only will the pony feel extremely hungry and uncomfortable, and therefore in no condition or mood to work well, but also this can cause digestive troubles rather than prevent them.

On arrival

Be there in plenty of time to give the pony a rest on arrival. Dismount, loosen the girth and run up the stirrups, or unload from the box to allow the pony to stretch his legs, have a look around and stale. Inspect him quickly, especially legs and shoes. If it is cold, lead him round to keep him warm or throw a rug over him if you have one handy. If it is raining, try to find somewhere to shelter him or put him back in the box. If it is hot, however, he will feel better standing in shade.

Don't tie the pony to a tree and leave him alone. Apart from the fact that someone might come along and steal him (honestly – it *has* happened) he might become restless or something might frighten him, especially as he is in strange surroundings. He could panic, pull back on the rope and either break it and get loose or lose his footing and have an accident. Always stay with him.

Mount at the last possible minute before your class, lesson or whatever if you have hacked there; after a box journey, though, tack up in enough time to ride in and check the girth.

During work

The pony is, of course, there to work, but he must still be treated considerately otherwise you will find that he is tired out long before you meant to finish.

Do not sit on the pony more than you have to. Do not use him as a grandstand for seeing over other people's heads at the ringside or as a means of transport to and from the refreshment tent. Do not canter up and down with your friends for the fun of it or, worst of all, to show off. If you do so out hunting you will probably get told off by the hunt staff or Field Master.

Dismount at every reasonable opportunity, such as between classes or during a check out hunting; if there is time, loosen his girth a hole and let him have a few mouthfuls of grass and perhaps a couple of gulps of water, if convenient. Also, encourage him to stale if he will.

If he is hot and blowing, turn his head to the wind to freshen him up before leading round to prevent chilling. Otherwise, stand him tail to the wind as this is how ponies naturally shelter. Throw a rug over him if you have one. In summer, stand him in the shade.

Always use the easiest going when you have a choice. Avoid deep mud, ride in the furrow on plough and, if jump take-offs become poached, look for a firmer place. Do not jump or gallop your pony if the ground is very hard, even if that's what you went for – you will almost certainly jar his legs and feet and probably lame him.

Above all, *stop* when he is tired and go home, even if you have not done all you wanted. Otherwise you could sicken the pony for future occasions and he will come to dislike his work and may grow difficult about it. And remember, long-coated ponies in winter and grass-kept ones in summer both tire quickly.

Looking smart does help win cups. This rider is beautifully turned out in dark jacket and matching cap, and her pony looks superb, with patterned browband, plaited mane and tail and quarter marks.

Going home

When the work is done, bring the pony home in as cool and dry a state as possible as soon as you can. If you take him home hot and sweating and either turn him out or leave him standing in, rug or no rug, he will probably catch a chill in cold weather, which could lead to something more serious. In hot weather, ponies sometimes suffer from heat exhaustion. The signs are extreme lack of energy, staggering and stumbling, very high temperature, sweating and panting. If your pony gets like this, take him to a cool place and call a vet at once.

If you are going home by box, cool off the pony before loading. Lead him round and let him have a little grass every few minutes to calm him down. Frequent short drinks of about three or four swallows will also be welcome to help counteract dehydration. (You can count the swallows by watching the underneath of his neck where his food-pipe or gullet is, and you can see food and water going down.) If it is cold, a rug worn over an anti-sweat rug, if possible, will help avoid chilling and too-quick cooling down. If you have a sponge, damp it with cold water and wipe his face, behind his ears, neck, saddle patch, between his hind legs and under his tail to refresh him.

If it is raining, load him up, rugged as described, but if he is hot fold the rug back at the breast and keep it on temporarily with a separate surcingle if it is the modern, cross-surcingle type, otherwise it will slide back and off and he could get his legs tangled up in it. Fasten the breast-strap on top of the withers to hold the front up. If he is cool, rug up normally. He should have a haynet to eat in the box as this helps his digestion.

If the pony lames himself during work, obviously you will have to arrange transport home rather than hacking.

If hacking home or to your horsebox, first dismount and give the pony a chance to stale. Then hack gently, mainly walking. Loosen your girth a hole and let your stirrups down if you have been jumping. This puts you in a slightly different place on his back, which is a change for his back muscles. Ride on a long (not loose) rein and let him have a bit of grass occasionally. He can also be permitted a drink, if convenient, but keep walking on afterwards.

If it is raining, trot and walk alternatively as a pony who is slightly warm will dry sooner than a cold one on your return. Dismount, let the girth out another hole, run up the stirrups and lead him the last kilometre or mile or so to calm him down and relax him, provided you can control him properly when led. Try to choose the quickest, easiest and safest route. Riding on the road is less tiring than on grass or mud, but busy roads should be avoided whenever possible.

On arrival at the horsebox treat him as described above.

Back home again – the stabled or combined-system pony

With a stabled or combined-system pony, take him straight into the stable and untack him, rubbing the saddle patch with your hands to restore circulation. If he has come by box, remove his travelling gear. Encourage him to stale and let him roll if that is his habit. Then rug him up.

Bring the pony half a bucket of water and leave him to drink and nibble his haynet while you unload the box or car.

Now check the pony very carefully for injuries, under his belly and legs and feet especially. All injuries must be treated at once and anything serious must have veterinary attention.

In cold weather, if the pony is cool and dry, rug him normally. If he is still warm or damp with sweat or rain, thatch him or put on a rug over an anti-sweat sheet, fastening it back at the breast as described earlier, and lead him about till cooler. If it is raining leave him indoors and rub him briskly with straw

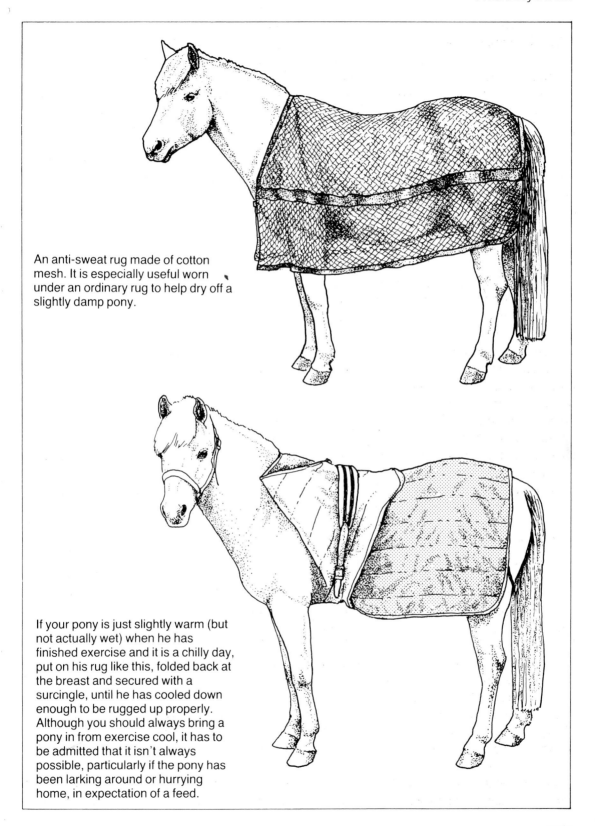

An anti-sweat rug made of cotton mesh. It is especially useful worn under an ordinary rug to help dry off a slightly damp pony.

If your pony is just slightly warm (but not actually wet) when he has finished exercise and it is a chilly day, put on his rug like this, folded back at the breast and secured with a surcingle, until he has cooled down enough to be rugged up properly. Although you should always bring a pony in from exercise cool, it has to be admitted that it isn't always possible, particularly if the pony has been larking around or hurrying home, in expectation of a feed.

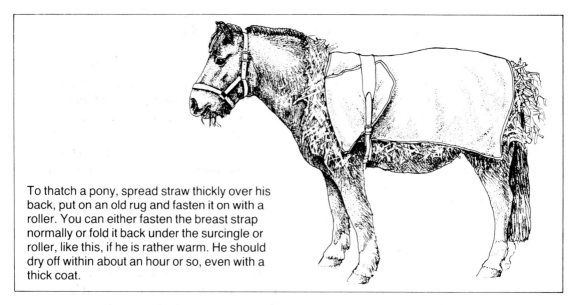

To thatch a pony, spread straw thickly over his back, put on an old rug and fasten it on with a roller. You can either fasten the breast strap normally or fold it back under the surcingle or roller, like this, if he is rather warm. He should dry off within about an hour or so, even with a thick coat.

or old towels, then thatch him. The most important parts to rub dry are the ears, throat, chest, loins and legs.

If he is muddy, deal with him as described in Chapter 6.

This sounds like an awful lot of work but it will probably take you only about forty-five minutes, less if you have help. You can now give the pony half his normal feed so as not to overface him as he will be tired, his haynet should be full and he should have another half bucket of water. Depending on the weather, he should be rugged up, maybe with stable bandages on, too – and at last you can go for your own meal.

Later that night

Go back and check the pony, remove the thatch if necessary, and feel him all over to see that he's dry, especially his neck, breast, loins, tops of legs, ears and heels. Then rug him up normally. If he is still damp, rub him down more and rug him up with an anti-sweat sheet under his rug.

If he is actually sweating, this is a sign that he has become very tired (sweating of this sort is called breaking out) and should be rubbed down and relaxed. Some ponies like having their ears gently pulled from base to tips but others don't. If the pony seems really

exhausted, and has an anxious expression and is not eating at all, you could have overdone things and should ring the vet. He or she will decide whether a visit seems necessary. Sometimes, exhausted ponies get colic which, of course, is a job for your vet.

If everything seems all right, however, give him the other half of his feed, fill up his haynet and water buckets and leave him for the night.

In warm weather, rugs of any kind should not be needed.

Back home again – the grass-kept or combined-system pony

With a pony who is to spend the night in his field, the object is still to get him home as soon as possible in a calm, dry, cool state.

Winter

In winter, especially if hacking home, it is unlikely that his long, thick coat will be dry on arrival. If he is clipped slightly he will sweat less and dry more quickly than an unclipped pony. Even if his coat is still wet or damp, it is quite possible that he is actually cool underneath it. He *must* be cool, even if damp or actually wet, before being turned out for the night otherwise he could certainly catch a chill.

The procedure for hacking or boxing home is the same as for a stabled pony. Once home, put him in a cool, airy box for a short while or tie him up under cover, rugged as described earlier. Encourage him to stale then offer him half a bucket of water. Tie up a haynet and examine him for injuries, treating anything you find. If he has any nasty wounds it may be necessary for him to spend the night indoors to await the vet next morning. A serious injury should receive veterinary attention that night, of course.

The pony must be rubbed down and led about until he is cool and dry enough to be turned out, with or without his New Zealand rug on. If he is soaking wet and is to wear a New Zealand rug, he'll have to be thatched for about half an hour first, perhaps while you have something to eat.

As soon as he is cool and dry enough to go out, give him half a feed and put him in the field. Give his normal hay ration in the field, preferably in the shelter, and check the water supply. Later, he should have the other half of his feed, if at all possible, plus another check.

Summer

In summer there is no need to worry too much about drying off. The pony will not catch a chill in warm weather and will not be wearing a New Zealand rug. If he is actually hot, lead him round for a while and rub him down, then turn him out. Grass will probably be what he wants now, but if he normally has a feed, give him half his usual amount and the rest later.

The day after

Next day, trot the pony out on a loose rope on level, hard ground to test for lameness, bearing in mind that the stabled pony will probably be rather stiff, having spent the night in his stable. All injuries must be treated again and the vet called if anything serious has developed or the pony is looking very tired or dejected. Ponies can go into shock from exhaustion and the vet will certainly be needed then.

Groom the pony according to how he is kept, paying special attention to the head, saddle and girth areas, legs and feet.

If he was very tired the night before, he must not be ridden today but allowed to recover. Otherwise a short, slow hack (walking, plus maybe a short trot) would be all right. A stabled pony should, in any case, either be turned into a paddock for a couple of hours to loosen up or be led in hand if this is not possible for at least thirty minutes. Let him eat grass, too.

If the pony is to spend most of the day in his stable, give him as much good hay or hayage as he wants and, as always, plenty of water. Leave him two buckets rather than one. If he normally has feeds as well as hay, give grassmeal and soaked sugar-beet pulp, chop, sliced carrots and just one small handful of his usual concentrates to keep his digestion used to them. If the pony is out normally, he should have whatever feeds he usually has. If the pony does not seem to want food it is a bad sign and could mean the previous day's efforts have overtired him. He could take several days to recover. If the pony refuses more than one feed, ring your vet and offer small tempting feeds of whatever he likes best.

In winter, keep a special eye on thick-coated ponies that sweat a lot in work. They can lose condition amazingly quickly and you may not notice it under all that hair; so poke through it with your fingers to check.

Give the pony a really good bed in his stable or shelter so he can lie down and rest.

And the day after that

The pony should have a more or less normal day unless there has been something wrong. After being very tired, this should still be an easy day, even if the pony seems normal; the usual routine can be started again tomorrow.

13. Travelling

Very few ponies go through their lives without having to travel at some time. Some do not mind it, others dislike it and some are frightened of it. They show fear or dislike by not wanting to go in the box or trailer or by playing up once inside. Very few refuse to come out.

Bad travellers often do better if there is someone in the back of the horsebox with them. (It is unlawful to travel in the back of a trailer with a pony as these are more dangerous due to the possibility of swaying, jack-knifing and turning over.) The person can calm the pony and if he starts to panic can alert the driver.

Travelling *is* tiring to a pony, especially long journeys. Some people think nothing of setting off very early in the morning, travelling several hours, competing hard and then making the same journey back in the evening. The pony is often very tired and stressed by the time he arrives, so goodness knows how he must be feeling by the end of the day.

After a long trip ponies should have a few hours to relax before being asked to work. This might mean travelling to the destination the day before and staying overnight. If this is not possible it is only fair not to expect too much from the pony on arrival – he will not be able to work at his best anyway. Some ponies lose condition after a gruelling day, some suffer from shock and others get colic or laminitis soon after the trip.

Suitable vehicles and conditions

The best vehicle is a proper horsebox, provided it is in good condition. They are steadier than trailers and usually have more room. Trailers are cheaper and, therefore, popular; again, they must obviously be in good, safe condition. I personally dislike single-axle trailers, that is, those with only one bar underneath supporting the wheels. Even with four wheels, this type of trailer rocks and sways more than the twin-axle type (with two bars), no matter how carefully driven.

Cattle waggons are no good for transporting horses and ponies (or cattle, in my opinion). There are no proper partitions to separate the animals, only single poles, which is dangerous. Animals can fall and be trodden on by neighbours. Tying up a pony does not stop him falling; he can hang suspended by his lead rope, possibly unable to get to his feet again. It does not take much imagination to realise the horrible injuries that can result from this.

Also, cattle waggons usually have ventilation gaps half-way down the sides, which cause most uncomfortable draughts.

The width and length of a pony's travelling compartment must be adequate so that he is not cramped, otherwise he will be even stiffer than usual on arrival. He should have at least 30 cm (1 ft) at each side and in front of and behind his breast and quarters.

Also, his head must have at least twice that distance in front of it if he is to feel reasonably comfortable. A pony of 13 hh to 14.2 hh needs at least 1 m (3 ft 3 ins) of room above his head when he is standing normally, although many trailers do not provide this.

The ideal way for a pony to travel is facing backwards, that is, with his tail to the engine. Ponies carry two thirds of their weight on their forehand, but when travelling facing forwards, the momentum of acceleration throws their weight back on to their quarters, which are not really meant to bear so much weight. This is why ponies travel with their back and quarter muscles braced and their legs splayed outwards against this unnatural force, trying to keep their balance. This can be extremely tiring to the pony and can cause serious muscle cramps over a long journey. In addition, ponies do not feel safe like this and it causes many of them to become frightened of travelling.

Although it is possible for ponies to travel tail-to-the-engine in many horseboxes, there is no trailer allowing this in Britain at present, although some manufacturers will make or convert one for you. If you would like more information on rear-face travel, write to Dr Sharon Cregier, University of Prince Edward Island, Charlottetown, Prince Edward Island, Canada, C1A 4P3, who has, along with others, carried out much of the research proving that rear-face travel is best.

In any box or trailer, there should be some way of preventing the pony moving backwards and forwards. This is usually provided by a wooden or metal bar across the breast and a breeching strap or chain behind the pony.

There should not be a large gap between the ramp and the floor of the vehicle, no more than 6 or 7 cm (2 or 3 ins), otherwise ponies can easily get their hooves and legs down this gap with disastrous consequences. There should also not be a large step

between the ramp and the ground as ponies dislike this. They can hurt their legs and feet if they misjudge it or if it has become worn and rough. They can even trip and fall – and *any* unpleasant or painful experience connected with travelling can put them off.

The flooring of the ramp and inside the vehicle is important. The pony must feel able to keep his feet. The ideal is 15 cm (6 ins) of slightly damp sawdust as this really pads the floor; straw is a good second choice. Bare wood is not suitable as droppings and urine can wet and rot the floor, making it slippery and susceptible to wear from the ponies' hooves. Proper travelling mats can be bought for floors and ramps, and bedding can be laid on top.

All matting (whether coconut, rubber or synthetic) should be guaranteed non-slip when wet. Do not buy any which is strengthened by metal threads or links as these are dangerous when they begin to wear.

Some vehicles have room for your equipment, others have living quarters for humans as well and are quite luxurious.

Whatever type you have, it must be properly maintained by a garage and tyres, brakes, hitch, lights and general structure checked before each trip. Fortunately, you should be able to leave all this to your parents, which is one less job for you.

Preparing for the journey

Prepare and load the vehicle with your equipment before the pony is to go in. After the previous trip it should have been cleaned out and the mats and/or floor hosed down and allowed to dry out. Put down bedding for this trip and place the vehicle so the sun, or other light if it is dark, shines inside (put on the interior light if there is one) so the pony can see where he is going.

Face the vehicle downhill, if possible, so when the ramp is lowered it will be less steep for the pony to clamber up. Boxes and some trailers usually have wooden gates which go down the sides of the ramp when loading or unloading to keep the pony straight, and which close behind him once he is in; these should be in place before the pony arrives.

The pony

Ponies should wear protective clothing when travelling to help reduce knocks and injuries. Stable bandages, over-reach boots, knee pads and hock boots should be worn (or all-in-one travelling boots), plus a tail bandage and a poll guard (a padded 'hat' with holes for the ears, in case he throws up his head). A rug in winter or summer sheet in summer, over an anti-sweat rug, will protect him from rubbing and should help keep him dry if he starts to sweat. His headcollar should fit properly and be in good

condition; it should have a strong lead rope. Do not tie the pony too short as he needs to be able to move his head to keep his balance. He should not, however, be able to reach across to interfere with travelling companions.

Loading the pony

Of all the problems people have with ponies, this is one of the most troublesome. Ponies have very long memories and once something unpleasant or frightening has happened to them they never forget it. If they are given a rough ride during travelling, become tired, suffer from cramp, are beaten up when loading or have a small accident, a fall or whatever, they may associate it with transport and travelling for the rest of their lives.

It is obvious, therefore, that every care must be taken to avoid accident and injury and to make the whole procedure as pleasant, or at

All-in-one travelling boots, fore and hind legs.

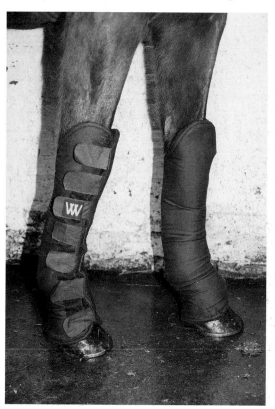
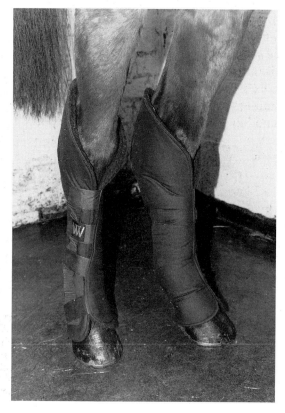

least as uneventful, as possible.

Your own attitude can have a great effect on the pony. If you are nervous, uncertain, in a hurry or a bad temper, the pony may sense it and refuse to load. But if you are calm, unhurried and confident that the pony will go in without fuss, he probably will.

With a pony who is a good loader and traveller you have little to worry about. Take his lead rope and, standing by his shoulder, walk him towards the ramp in a straight line, up it and nip in before him. Someone should immediately fasten the breeching strap, in case he decides to back out again, while you tie him up. Don't pull on the rope at all, don't interfere with him or get in his way – and don't trip up or you'll cause an accident.

If he hesitates wait with him and he may continue after a minute. If not, take him back, turn him round in a small circle two or three times near the foot of the ramp and then go straight up it. If he still doesn't go in, ask someone to put one of the pony's forefeet on the ramp, which often works. Coaxing with titbits or a bucket of food, particularly those special titbits you use for catching him or his favourite treats, sometimes works, as does loading his friend first.

Putting plenty of familiar bedding on the ground, up the ramp and inside the trailer or horsebox can reassure an uncertain pony.

If you park the vehicle so that one side of the ramp (whether it has a gate or not) is against a wall, will prevent the pony from moving away to that side and helps keep him straight while loading. Whoever is loading him should walk on his 'open' side so he feels less able to go anywhere but forward.

If there are partitions inside the vehicle and your pony dislikes narrow spaces, load him with the partitions swung to one side to widen his entrance point. This makes it easier for you to avoid bumping into him during loading, too.

The final method which usually works for a quite difficult pony is to fasten two lunge reins, lengths of rope or clothes line, one to each back edge of the trailer or box about half way up, usually to the pins which hold up a trailer ramp or to the hinges which hold the gates on a horsebox. You will need two assistants, each to hold the end of a lunge rein straight out behind the trailer, making a sort of corridor. Lead the pony to the foot of the ramp. The assistants then take the lunge reins behind the pony, so they cross and tighten behind him, just over his hocks. Usually as soon as a pony feels them he jumps forward, so be ready. If he still refuses to budge, the assistants keep on walking, tightening the ropes so the pony really is forced to go in as there is nowhere else to go.

If none of these things work, you either

A two-horse trailer, ready for its first passenger. The central partition has been pushed to one side to widen the entrance and the side ramp is down to make the inside light and airy.

have a pony who has become very upset or is an unusually bad loader and it is best to leave the task to someone more experienced. However, under no circumstances whatsoever must you allow your pony to be thrashed or ill-treated in any way, which may well put him off travelling for life.

Very often, loading problems are all in the mind and someone who has been around horses and ponies all their life or who is a professional transporter can just take hold of the lead rope, have a word with the pony and lead him up the ramp with no fuss.

Long-term cure for difficult loaders

Start by leaving the trailer or box ramp down, facing south, in the paddock or stable yard to let the pony sniff round it in his own time. After this start feeding him near it at normal feed times. After a few days put the bucket on the foot of the ramp and gradually work your way up and inside over several days. At first the pony might stretch his neck over the ramp to get to the bucket, so put the gates down the sides. Soon, however, he'll be forced to enter the trailer to get his food.

If he decides he can do without feeds rather than enter the dreaded cave, try the same thing with his water using the same idea mentioned in Chapter 7 for catching a difficult pony. Proceed gradually, taking weeks if necessary. Make sure he is quite at ease and drinking freely at each stage before moving the bucket on. Don't water him anywhere else. Offer water before each feed and after exercise and last thing at night. Remember, a pony can drink up to 45 litres (10 gals) a day in hot weather and not much less in cold so it might be necessary to put out two buckets each time. It might be a nuisance, and you might have to pick school holidays to try it, but I have known it cure several ponies.

Don't forget, when the pony makes a little

progress, praise him. Every time he walks up the ramp, even if he's a good loader, praise him. In fact, every time he does something to please you, praise him – at once, not seconds afterwards as he must associate the praise with what he's doing then.

When the pony will load without fuss take him for pretend short journeys, dressing him up properly so he won't get the idea that there's always an event of some kind at the other end, and will not always get excited. Eventually, take him to another district, go for a hack and then box back. This can make a nice day out, especially if you take a friend, and makes a good change for you and your ponies.

With patience and perseverance your pony should gradually get used to travelling, even if he does not actually like it. Always see you do nothing to frighten him, leave plenty of time for loading and travelling and have a steady driver, and your pony should stay trouble-free.

How your driver should drive

As you aren't old enough to drive yourself, you have to depend on an adult – and some of them are terrible drivers. They become very over-confident, swinging the box or trailer around, accelerating quickly, braking suddenly and cornering too quickly and sharply. It seems to be a case of: 'To blazes with the ponies in the back, let's get going!' They forget that if it weren't for the ponies in the back they wouldn't be going at all. The whole point of going is to arrive with ponies in a fit condition to work, otherwise you might as well not bother, and they won't be in a fit condition to work if they've been given a shake-up in the back, especially if they have been travelling facing forwards rather than backwards.

Ideal travelling conditions, whether the pony is facing forward or backward, are for the vehicle to be going along a smooth road at a constant speed in a straight line, with no accelerating, braking or turning. Of course, this is impossible apart from when you're on a motorway or main road, and even then, adjustments of speed and lane changes are unavoidable.

Therefore, the driver has to make your journey as close to that ideal as possible. He or she should accelerate as gradually as possible, change gear very smoothly, brake very gently and smoothly and take bends in the road, roundabouts and corners *slowly*, especially sharp turns. The driver should keep plenty of distance between your vehicle and the one in front to avoid sudden braking, much more than when driving an ordinary car, wait until there is plenty of space before pulling out into another lane to avoid sudden speeding up, and drive really slowly on bumpy roads, avoiding as many pot holes and lumps as possible.

It is an excellent idea to have a large notice fixed to the back of the lorry or trailer to warn drivers behind that ponies are on board. Red lettering on a white or yellow background will be easily seen and will attract attention. The wording should say something like: 'Live cargo – Please keep clear and pass slowly.'

Driving high-sided vehicles such as horseboxes, or vehicles with separate towed containers such as trailers or caravans, can be very risky in windy weather and it is really best not to go on a journey in such conditions. If it is essential (such as a sick pony being taken to a veterinary hospital, not something like travelling to a competition), avoid open main roads and motorways if at all possible and use as many sheltered roads as you can. Large trucks passing at speed, especially in windy conditions, on open roads which encourage fast travel, can give your

---

Travel topics

- All the latest research shows that ponies travel more comfortably facing backwards, or with their tails to the engine, as this better suits their natural balance. Always choose a compartment in a horsebox where your pony can travel backwards, if possible. With trailers, however, at least in Britain, the pony will probably have to face forwards as rear-facing trailers are rare. It is not safe to try to convert an ordinary trailer without special instructions, as the balance of the trailer is not designed for rear-facing travel.

- Try to persuade your driver to carry out all manoeuvres very gently indeed, especially cornering. Speed must be built up and slowed down gradually. This way you will not unbalance your pony or frighten him. Tell the driver to imagine there is a glass of expensive wine on the bonnet or dashboard and that he or she must not spill any!

- Learn the proper procedures for loading and unloading your pony. Doing things the wrong way can be dangerous and may result in the pony becoming difficult about travelling.

- If your pony is hard to load, beating him up and thrashing him will not get him inside, but will make him associate travelling with pain and fear. A gradual retraining programme could help, but a badly frightened pony can become a bad traveller for life.

- Long journeys are as tiring for your pony as they are for you, probably more so. Arrive at your destination early enough to give him a leg-stretch and a rest before starting work, and, particularly, to let him stale.

vehicle a real buffeting from the draught as they pass, especially if they won't slow down – and most don't.

During the journey

Take account of the weather and adjust the ventilation in your vehicle accordingly. If the pony dislikes closed-in spaces, try to leave open a flap so he can see out and, in a horsebox, stay with a nervous pony to calm him. If, with box or trailer, you feel the vehicle sway or pull on your car, or hear banging from the back, stop and go and see what has happened, in case a pony has fallen or had some other accident.

On long journeys (say, over two hours), try to find somewhere suitable to stop and unload the ponies so they can stretch their legs, stale and have a nibble of grass, if at all possible. Many ponies do not stale whilst travelling and may appreciate an opportunity to do so.

Unloading the pony

To unload a pony, untie him before you undo the breeching strap and open the gates (if fitted) or he might pull back, thinking he is going out, and panic.

When someone has cleared the way behind, making sure there is plenty of room, gently encourage the pony to back out if there is not enough room to turn him round or you do not have a front ramp. Push gently on his breast and give the command 'back'. Let him take his time and feel his way with his feet, also tilt his head so he can see behind him where he is going. If he is hesitant, get someone to put a hind hoof on the ramp. Do not restrict his head.

It is important that someone is on the ground to help the pony back out straight. A gentle but firm guiding hand should be placed on his quarters on whichever side is nearer to the edge of the ramp, otherwise he could easily step off the edge, go through the gate, hurt his leg or fall. It takes only one such accident to put him off travelling, and even if he gets over it he will never forget.

If the pony is going out forwards, such as down a front unload ramp, untie him first and stand with him while someone takes away the breast bar. A person should stand outside by the ramp but on the opposite side from you (that is, if you are on the pony's right he or she should stand on the left of the ramp) so the pony has someone on each side to keep him straight. He might leap down suddenly so be ready to go with him. It is best to let a pony unload at his own pace, but if he makes a habit of rushing down or trying to jump down, he should be corrected as this can be dangerous. Talk to him and restrain him with the lead rope; if you still have problems ask an expert to teach him to slow down.

Left: This pony is backing out of his trailer, something many ponies find difficult and frightening. These handlers are letting the pony take his time, and one of them is on the ground to guide him down, if necessary.

14. Ponies on the highway

Riding horses and ponies on the roads, or leading or driving them, can be very dangerous. From the figures available at the time of writing, it seems that eight accidents involving horses and ponies occur on Britain's roads *every day*.

Ideally, no one would take ponies on public roads at all, but many people have nowhere else to ride. You can't ride round and round the same field, outdoor school or, even worse, indoor school all the time, but until there are many more bridleways and horse tracks and other riding areas available, the roads *will* be used.

Your rights

Although many motorists feel otherwise, people with horses have as much right to be on the roads as cyclists, motor cars, lorries and everything else. A common cry from motorists is that horse riders don't pay road tax or have to take a test and so should not be allowed on the roads, but neither do cyclists and an irresponsible cyclist can be as much of a hazard to other road users as someone on a horse or pony.

So whatever anyone else tells you, the law allows you to ride on the roads. If ever you learn to drive a car or other vehicle with a motor engine, such as a motor bike, you will have to know the *Highway Code* before you can take your test. On the subject of horses and ponies, the *Highway Code* says you must make sure you can control your animal in traffic before riding it on the roads. When riding, you must keep to the left of the road. If leading a horse or pony you should also keep to the left and keep the led animal on your left (placing yourself between the pony and the traffic). In one-way streets, you must go only in the direction of the traffic and keep to the left. You must not ride, lead or drive a horse on a footpath or pavement by the side of the road. You should wear a hard hat and if riding after sunset (and before sun-up) you should wear light-coloured or reflective clothing and carry lights which show white to the front and red to the rear.

If you obey these rules and ride sensibly, in a controlled manner and without causing danger to other people, no one can complain about your being on the roads.

Useful leaflets to read

It is well worth buying a copy of the *Highway Code* from your local Post Office. Read through it to get an idea of how motorists should behave and what the various road signs mean. You will also learn how other road users should act in given situations, such as at junctions, traffic lights, roundabouts and so on.

The most important leaflets for riders are the BHS and Pony Club ones which are all excellent. These are regularly brought up to date and the titles sometimes changed. The current one is called *Riding and Roadcraft*.

The leaflets are never more than a few pence and should be regarded as essential reading – and learning – for anyone taking a pony or horse on the roads.

If your parents are members of the AA (Automobile Association), that organisation also produces a useful leaflet, aimed at motorists mainly, telling them about horses on the road and how to act when they meet them, so perhaps they would get you a copy.

The Riding and Road Safety Test

The BHS and Pony Club run the Riding and Road Safety Test with the help of the police, and *Riding and Roadcraft* is a must for anyone taking the test. You are strongly advised to take this test – it could save you and your pony from an accident. It is not difficult but will make you learn the correct procedures on the road and teach you what to expect from other road users. Once you have passed the test, you are well equipped, provided you have a traffic-proof pony, to go out on the roads. Don't forget about the test once you have passed; put it into practice every day because your life depends on it.

Correct procedures

At present, the whole situation regarding horses and other road users is unsatisfactory because the correct way for horse riders to proceed is not the same as for motorists, and this causes the motorists to get angry and think the riders don't know what they're doing. In fact, it is the motorist who is at fault for not understanding how riders are advised to behave. Unfortunately the 'horse' way of doing things is not, as yet, described in the *Highway Code*, and therein lies the problem.

This situation will, it is hoped, change when a new edition of the *Highway Code* is published, but until then, we have to do our best to behave properly, otherwise motorists will never learn.

One instance of how riders do things differently on horses is in turning right. We must signal clearly by putting our right hand out (you'll have to learn to ride with one hand) but keep to the *left* of the road up to and just past the centre of the junction. When we are sure the traffic has given way to us we then turn sharp right across the road on to the left side of the road we want to take. However, when cars or other vehicles want to turn right, they go into the middle of the road, rather than keep left, and *then* turn. When motorists see us doing things our way, many of them get impatient or even abusive.

Another case is at roundabouts, when we, on horses, must keep to the outside (left) even when turning right, whereas cars etc should be in the right-hand lane.

Some of our hand signals are confusing to motorists. For example, the one we use to ask vehicles to stop, perhaps when they are coming up behind us too quickly, is right hand out, palm down, moving up and down. Unfortunately, to a motorist this means that *you* are slowing down, so the car will probably actually overtake you instead of stopping.

However, everything will be sorted out for you when you go to the classes for the Riding and Road Safety Test. You'll have full opportunity to discuss everything not only with instructors and Pony Club representatives but also the police, which will reassure you.

Be noticed
Obviously, no matter how careful and conscientious you are, this will have no effect if you cannot be seen properly. Even during daylight, it is sensible to wear a reflective tabard over your riding jacket, bearing a standard caution sign (an exclamation sign inside a red triangle) or the horse and rider sign. One sign which other road users nearly always give way to is the large red letter L used to signify a learner. You may feel

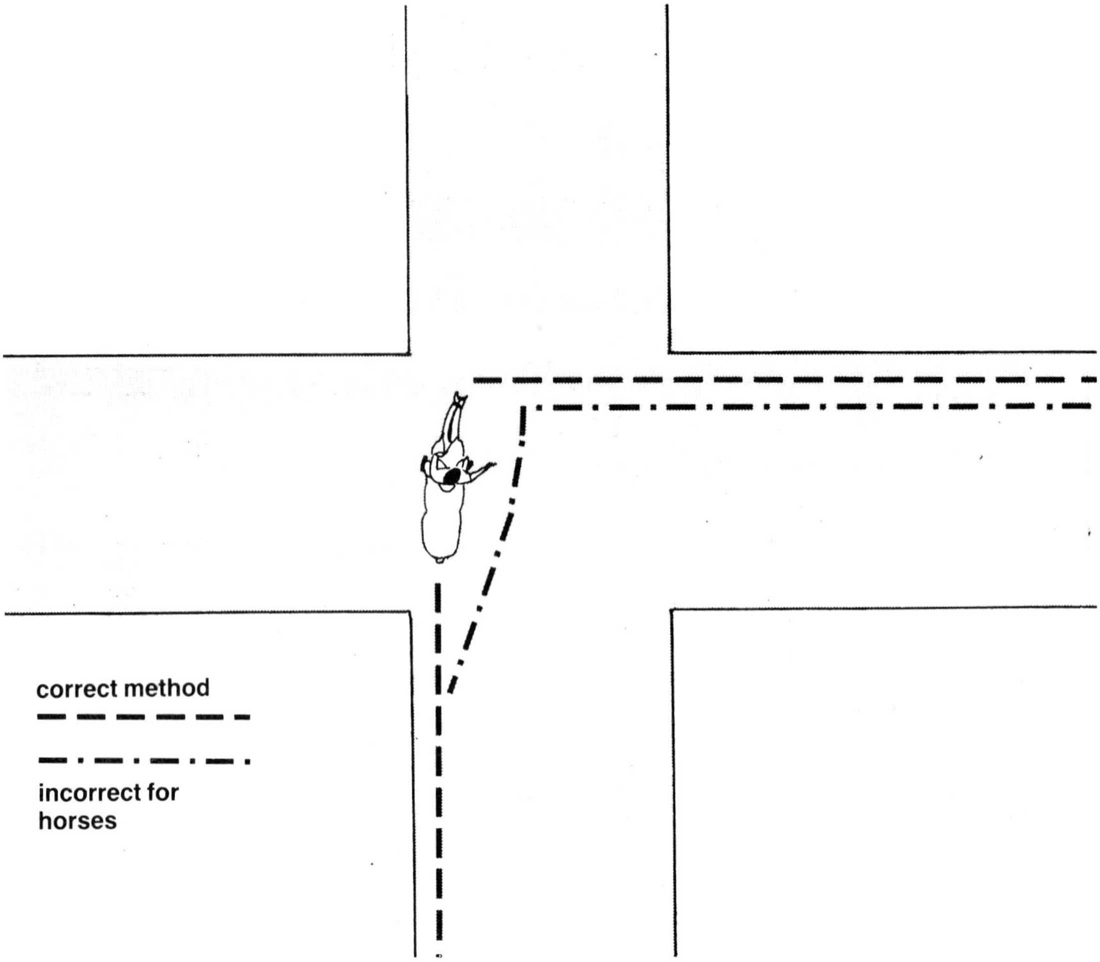

correct method

incorrect for horses

Turning right. Horse riders must turn right by following the dashed line and keeping well to the left all the time. The other method shown, indicated by the dash-dot line, is correct if you are riding a bicycle or in a car, **but would be dangerous on a pony or horse**.

embarrassed wearing this, especially when you don't have to, but it really does put them on their guard and encourage them to give you a wide berth or stop if you are having problems.

You can stitch two L-plates on to a reflective tabard over the ordinary sign, and this will work quite well.

The British Horse Society and many saddlers sell a wide range of tabards, reflective hat covers, wrist and leg bands and, sometimes, reflective exercise sheets for your pony. Reflective bandages are available (for both right legs) and strips for his bridle noseband. These will all make you easily seen, especially in dusk and dark conditions (if you absolutely have to ride then) as the light from the cars' headlights pick out the reflective areas.

A sturdy stirrup light with a strong battery is essential for riding at such times. It must show white to the front and red to the back. Good saddlers sell various sorts (the kind which clip to your leg are not as good but are better than nothing). Also, cycling shops sell wrist lights (so your signals can be clearly

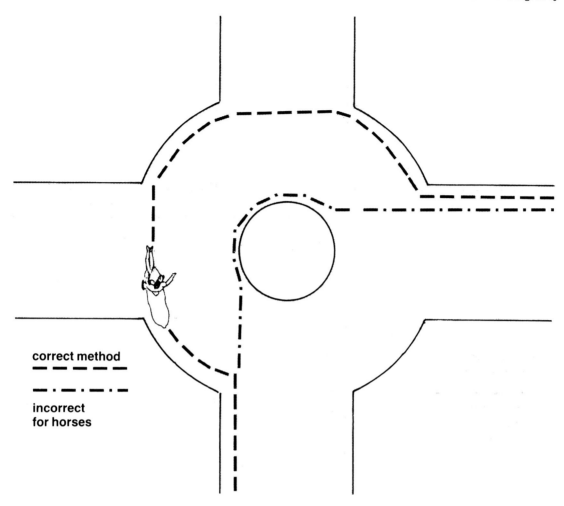

correct method

- - - - -

incorrect
for horses

seen – and do wear white gloves as well) and cross-belts with lights on. If cyclists can wear them so can you.

All these lights, however, do not make it safe for you to ride in fog. This is one instance when you really are advised *not* to take the pony on the roads at all as it simply is not safe. Most motorists drive far too fast in fog and, lights or no lights, may come on you too late to stop.

Driving ponies

Horse-drawn vehicles must by law be fitted with lights after sunset and before dawn, white to the front and red to the rear. It is also required that the vehicle has reflectors (like those on bicycle mudguards) and advisable that the usual red triangular

Turning right at a roundabout. As for the ordinary right turn, follow the dashed line and keep well to the left all the time. Again, the dash-dot line is correct if you are on a bicycle or in a car, but would be risky for horses and ponies.

caution sign to be fixed to the back. A sign saying something like 'Please keep clear and pass slowly' is also a good idea, as are those L-plates again.

The pony can wear reflective strips or bandages on his right legs and on his bridle. The signals and procedures for horse-drawn vehicles are like those for motorised traffic, *not* ridden horses and ponies.

Life-saving tips

- Be sure to learn the correct procedures on the road for riders, preferably by taking the Riding and Road Safety Test through the Pony Club or British Horse Society. It could save your own life and your pony's.
- Send off for, read and learn the Pony Club/British Horse Society road safety booklets. Carry out the recommendations.
- Make sure you can be seen by other road users. Even when it is not dusk or dark, wear a reflective tabard over your jumper or jacket. If you **have** to ride in dusk or dark conditions, **always** wear a stirrup light on your right stirrup.
- Never take a pony out in mist or fog, even with a light.
- Always be considerate to other road users and thank them if they help you by slowing down or giving you a wide berth, so that they won't be impatient or ill-tempered in future and possibly cause an accident.
- Get expert help to traffic-train your pony. If he is habitually bad in traffic, don't take him on the roads.
- Never, ever ride on the roads without a properly fastened hard hat.

Common sense and good manners

Apart from knowing what is required of you by law, you can help yourself a good deal on the road simply by using your common sense and being polite to other road users. You, too, are a road user, and others have responsibilities towards you. If the driver of a motorised vehicle of any kind does not behave carefully and considerately, does not pay attention to his driving or is reckless, he can be fined, disqualified from driving or imprisoned, depending on the offence. He

This rider is wearing correct clothing for riding at dusk or in dark conditions. She is wearing a reflective tabard with a light on her right boot. The pony wears reflective boots on his right legs. You must keep well to the left on public roads.

also commits an offence if, after an accident, he does not stop and give his name and address, and other information such as insurance details. The problem is, if your pony has been badly frightened or injured, you may be in no condition to notice his registration number as he speeds away if you are fighting to control the pony.

Generally, you will command more respect, and therefore correct treatment, from other road users if you look efficient and behave responsibly. Make sure you read and know the recommended road safety leaflets, and take your Riding and Road Safety Test. Wear reflective clothing and a stirrup light when necessary. Wear a hard hat to the standard currently approved by the British Standards Institution and secure it with a proper harness. It's a good idea to wear a special body protector, too (like a neat padded bodice) available from many good saddlers or by mail order through adverts in horse magazines. Also wear proper riding boots, jodhpur boots or stout shoes with hard soles, not wellingtons or trainers, which can be dangerous.

Keep to the left, ride on a comfortable contact and stay alert. Don't slop along as if you hadn't a care in the world in the middle of the road, as this is dangerous and infuriates other road users. Give your signals properly, wait till it is safe, and above all, thank vehicles which slow down for you, not necessarily by taking your hand off the rein to raise your hand in thanks, but at least by a nod of your head, a nice smile and you could also mouth the words 'thank you'. Good manners cost nothing, but the next time that driver meets up with a pony on the road, he or she will probably behave considerately whereas if he has received sullen, ignorant treatment from you he may well think all 'toffee-nosed horse-riders' are the same and not bother to be careful in future.

If riding with a friend or friends, there is nothing wrong in riding two abreast – you could check what your local branch of mounted police recommends on this by ringing them up and asking. However, on narrow roads and round bends it is better to go in single file. If one pony is a little nervous in traffic, it should be on the inside (left) with a more confident pony on his right, but keep close together and to the left.

Always look around and behind you before carrying out any movement such as turning. Signal clearly and be sure all is safe before making your move. Then proceed at a *steady, controlled* trot unless the road is slippery. Motorists may think you are dawdling if you walk.

Keep an eye out for anything that may make your pony shy, such as paper blowing about, a farm dog dashing out or someone with an umbrella. Keep the pony under good control and if trouble seems to be on the way try to take the pony into a convenient gateway till it has passed, or on to a grass verge provided it is not ornamental. If there is a suitable verge for riding on, always use it rather than the road if at all possible; unfortunately those with long grass can hide litter, such as broken bottles or tins, and also drainage channels. Get to know your area and where it is safe to ride.

Always carry a whip in your right hand to help control your pony and keep him in to the left. Ask your instructor if he or she thinks blunt spurs might also be a good idea to reinforce your leg aids on a reluctant pony.

If your pony is not traffic proof, do not take him on the roads unless accompanied by a bomb-proof pony and competent rider when gradually training him to accept traffic. If an older pony is frightened of traffic, you are unlikely to improve his behaviour and he must not be ridden on roads.

Do carry a piece of paper in your pocket with your name, address and telephone number and the telephone number of the stable yard, so that if you should be unfortunate enough to have an accident while riding alone and end up unconscious, people will know who to contact. Also, attach to one of the front dees of your saddle a dog-collar disc giving your stable yard address and telephone number, so if your pony gets loose in an accident and gallops off whoever finds him will know where to ring.

If you are leading a pony on the road, say from field to stable or vice versa, keep well to the left and place yourself between him and the traffic, on his right. Lead him in a bridle and a cavesson as well if he is a little difficult – a headcollar doesn't give enough control. Wear your tabard and, if dusk or dark, carry a lantern in your right hand showing white to the front and red to the back. If possible, have someone else carry the light for you and give help if you need it.

Bridleways and the countryside

All problems we have with ponies on the roads would be avoided if we had more bridleways.

There are other routes riders may use apart from official bridleways, although the way they are classified can be confusing. The BHS publishes useful leaflets on riding in the countryside and it's a good plan to ask the Society for the name and address of the secretary of your local bridleways group so you can discover where you can and cannot ride in your district.

Apart from helping you learn how to map read and recognise permissible tracks, these local groups can obtain help from the British Horse Society whenever problems arise over matters such as obstructed bridleways, landowners refusing rightful access, mad bulls in fields through which you are allowed, and so on. These problems can be almost impossible to cope with alone, but with the group and Society working together for you, most can be solved.

If we are not vigilant over rights of way they will be taken away from us on the grounds of disuse – then we'll *have* to use roads nearly all the time, and nobody wants that.

The rules about consideration for others and good manners, plus common sense and respect for farm property and livestock, are

Be country-wise

- You are entitled in law to ride on bridleways. Join your local bridleways group and help them all you can – it's in your own interest, after all. If you find a bridleway blocked, report it to them so that something can be done about it.
- Be considerate of farm stock. Walk, or trot **slowly**, through fields containing animals, even though you **are** on the bridleway.
- If someone stops you while out riding and bars your way, do not argue with them, but do tell them you believed this was your right of way. Do not ask permission as you could lose your future rights. It's usually better to return the way you came if the person will not let you pass. Report the matter to your bridleways group and ask an adult to accompany you next time, if you find out definitely that you do have a right of way. If you do, persist in riding it, accompanied, preferably by bridleways group members and officials, as this is your right. If we do not use our bridleways, or allow others wrongly to put us off them, they will be closed.
- Try to go out of your way to help farmers over whose land you ride. For instance, if you see a cow on the road or a sheep on its back (sheep cannot turn themselves over and could die there), report it to the farm at once.
- Don't leave gates open if you've undone them, and don't ride over crops growing over rights of way. Wait until they have been harvested before using that track again.

just as important on bridleways etc as on the roads. We have both a right to enjoy the countryside and a responsibility to look after it and be considerate.

Appendix

Useful Addresses

Association of British Riding Schools
Old Brewery Yard,
Penzance
Cornwall
TR18 2SL

Automobile Association
Fanum House
Basingstoke
Hampshire

British Equine Veterinary Association
Hartham Park
Corsham
Wiltshire
SN13 0QB

British Hay and Straw Merchants Association
Hoval House
Orchard Parade
Mutton Lane
Potters Bar
Hertfordshire
EN6 3AR

British Horse Society
British Equestrian Centre
Stoneleigh
Kenilworth
Warwickshire
CV8 2LR

British Show Jumping Association
British Equestrian Centre
Stoneleigh
Kenilworth
CV8 2LR

British Show Pony Society
Mrs J Toynton
124 Green End Road
Sawtry
Huntingdon
Cambridgeshire

British Vaulting Association
Gwanas Fawr
Dolgellau
Gwynedd

Commons, Open Spaces and Footpaths Preservation Society
25a Bell Street
Henley-on-Thames
Oxfordshire
RG9 2BA

Endurance Horse and Pony Society of Great Britain
15 Newport Drive
Alcester
Warwickshire

Equine Behaviour Study Circle
Mrs O. Way
Grove Cottage
Brinkley
Newmarket
Suffolk

An international group of amateur and professional horse enthusiasts interested in all aspects of how horses and ponies behave. Runs visits to places of interest in the horse world, sends its journal, *Equine Behaviour*, twice a year to members, holds informal discussion groups and runs special projects (including youth projects) for members to carry out at home with their own ponies.

Equine Management Consultancy Service
20 Victoria Road
Bulwark
Chepstow
Gwent
NP6 5QN

Independent advice at moderate fees on all points of horse and pony management.

Farriers Registration Council
PO Box 49
East of England Showground
Peterborough
PE2 0GU

Horse Rangers Association
Royal Mews
Hampton Court Palace
East Molesey
Surrey

Particularly good if you do *not* have your own pony. Branches around the country.

Horses and Ponies Protection Association
64 Station Road
Padiham
Burnley
Lancashire
BB12 8EF

International League for the Protection of Horses
Overa House Farm
East Harling
Norwich
Norfolk

Ponies Association UK
Chesham House
56 Green End Road
Sawtry
Peterborough
Cambs
PE17 5UY

Pony Club
British Equestrian Centre
Stoneleigh
Kenilworth
Warwickshire
CV8 2LR

Equestrian Security Services
(Freeze-marking)
17 St Johns Road
Farnham
Surrey
GU9 8NU

The Side Saddle Association
Highbury House
Welford
Northants
NN6 7HT

Society of Master Saddlers
The Cottage
4 Chapel Place
Mary Street
Bovey Tracey
Devon
TQ13 9JA

Western Horseman's Association of Great Britain
36 Old Fold View
Barnet
Hertfordshire
EN5 4EB

Worshipful Company of Loriners
The Old Granary
High Street
Barcombe Cross
Nr Lewes
East Sussex
BN8 5DH

(Loriners make bits, stirrups and spurs.)

Index